EVERYTHING

YOU LOVE

WILL BURN

_____

Inside the Rebirth
of White Nationalism
in America

VEGAS TENOLD

NATION
BOOKS

Nation Books
116 East 16th Street, 8th Floor, New York, NY 10003
http://www.publicaffairsbooks.com/nation-books
@NationBooks

Printed in the United States of America
First Edition: February 2018

Published by Nation Books, an imprint of Perseus Books, LLC,
a subsidiary of Hachette Book Group, Inc.
Nation Books is a co-publishing venture of the Nation Institute and Perseus Books.

The Hachette Speakers Bureau provides a wide range of authors for speaking events. To find out more, go to www.hachettespeakersbureau.com or call (866) 376-6591.

The publisher is not responsible for websites (or their content) that are not owned by the publisher.

Editorial production by Christine Marra, *Marra*thon Production Services. www.marrathoneditorial.org

Book design by Jane Raese
Set in 10.25-point LinoLetter

Library of Congress Cataloging-in-Publication Data has been applied for.
ISBN 978-1-56858-994-7 (hardcover)
ISBN 978-1-56858-995-4 (e-book)

LSC-C
10 9 8 7 6 5 4 3 2 1

For H & L

CONTENTS

AUTHOR'S NOTE

As I write this, nineteen people are being treated at University of Virginia Medical Center for injuries sustained when a white supremacist drove his car into a crowd on the streets of Charlottesville, Virginia. One woman is dead. The victims were struck as they protested one of the largest gatherings of right-wing radicals in America in recent history. Last night I watched hundreds of predominantly young, white men march in a torchlight parade, paying tribute to a history that produced slavery, Jim Crow, and a society that still discriminates against its minorities in a million ways, large and small. They were not only paying tribute to white hegemony but also protesting the cracks in that hegemony, airing grievances that seemed both petty and fabricated. As they marched en masse to chants of "Jews will not replace us!" I had to wonder exactly how Jews were replacing them and how these young, white men—by any statistical measure perched at the top of the societal food chain—had come to feel so deeply aggrieved as to see the world's progress as an attack on them.

I've tried to write a book that explains the resurgence of right-wing radical groups that, as of this moment, seem only to be growing more confident and exuberant by the day. This is a book about the people who, for various reasons, have come to hold opinions and beliefs that most of us find abhorrent. It is not primarily about what is known as the *alt-right*, the anonymous, internet-dwelling trolls who rose to fame during the 2016 presidential campaign; instead, it's about those who march in the streets, whose beliefs are rooted in the flotsam of decades of American racism, anti-Semitism, and white supremacy. In writing this book I have attempted to step aside and present as unvarnished a look into the lives of those on the radical right as I can.

It should be stated that I'm not a neutral observer. In many ways I represent what my subjects believe to be the enemy. As long as I've been able to vote I've voted socialist (in my native Norway that is still, thankfully, a viable option), and I've made no secret about that in my reporting. Still, I've tried to approach the subjects of this book without bias, and I'm grateful for the way they have, in large part, returned the favor.

The main characters in this book, including Matthew Heimbach of the Traditionalist Workers Party, Jeff Schoep of the National Socialist Movement, and Dan Elmquist of the KKK, represent three contemporary yet disparate approaches to American white nationalism. Respectively, they represent a modern, more pragmatic strain, a European National Socialist strain, and a profoundly American strain. Taken together they are a cross-section of white nationalism in America today, but there are others—some who are mentioned in this book and some who are not—who are also part of the tapestry. This book was never meant to be an exhaustive account of everything that stirs on the far right. There are others—the writer Leonard Zeskind, for one—who have already done that admirably.

There were many parts of this book I found difficult write, and there are parts that may be difficult to read. It's safe to say that this book contains slurs, racial and otherwise, and I debated at some length whether to include them. In the end I decided to keep any offensive quotes untouched because the words people choose matter. It is not my place to take offense on behalf of others, nor would I want to make the opinions and statements presented by the subjects any more or less offensive than they are.

This book also contains scenes of violence. Some of these events were reported to the police; others weren't. There were instances during the reporting for this book when I witnessed extreme violence and did nothing to stop it. I believe that for my own safety and for the safety of those with me at the time I had no other choice.

For that reason some names in this book have been altered. The social cost of being active in white nationalist or supremacist groups can be considerable, and for those who weren't prepared to participate with their full names, I made allowances. I pushed back against most requests for anonymity and afforded it only to those whose jobs and personal safety would be affected. Most names remain intact.

The reporting for this book always took place with the full knowledge and consent of my subjects. I never concealed who I was or presented myself as anything but a journalist. For the very few scenes in the book where I wasn't present, I have relied on firsthand witness accounts, which I have corroborated as far as possible. Descriptions of inner monologues are based on extensive interviews. Descriptions of events that took place before my time are based on the reporting and research of others.

For terminology I have tried to keep things as orderly as I could. The white nationalist movement is awash with different terms for seemingly similar beliefs, and figuring out what to call the different factions and ideologies is a daunting affair. There are those who believe that everyone on the radical right, from the so-called alt-right to the skinheads, should be called "Nazis," and it is a point well taken. They all show an affinity for the words and teachings of Adolf Hitler, so calling them all neo-Nazis makes sense. However, the terms *Nazi* or *neo-Nazi* refer, specifically, to National Socialists, and because there is a distinct faction within the far right that identifies as National Socialist, using the terms *Nazi, neo-Nazi,* or *National Socialist* as a catch-all term becomes problematic because it makes it impossible to describe the actual Nazis in the movement.

"White supremacist" is similarly problematic because it assumes that everyone in the movement believes the white race is superior to others. Although there certainly is a large contingent of those who believe in the inferiority of any race that isn't white, there are also those who don't, so labeling everyone "white supremacists" becomes an oversimplification.

I have chosen, then, to use the terms *white nationalist movement*, the *far right*, or the *radical right*. These terms aren't perfect. Some might argue—and rightly so—that these terms are either too facile or too generous, but I've tried to be as specific as possible when the situation requires.

If I set out to write this book with the goal of understanding the far right or, perhaps more broadly, racism and bigotry, then what I have learned is perhaps unsatisfactory. As much as I would like to have found one single, underlying reason for racism and bigotry, I cannot say that I have. There are many contributing factors, and even identifying those is not enough to provide a satisfactory explanation for far-right ideology. Social status, income, education, location—these are all elements that contribute to a person's worldview, but they cannot paint a complete picture. It is often said that the KKK is generational: you join the Klan because your father was in the Klan and his father before him. This is also patently untrue—I met many men and women in the Klan who were first generation. But even if it weren't, it wouldn't sufficiently explain why its members believe the white race is superior. In our current world information is ubiquitous, and simply being raised with certain beliefs isn't an excuse for maintaining those beliefs. Even Klansmen know that their worldview isn't considered appropriate. Poverty also isn't enough to explain the rise of racist nationalism; it is quite possible to be poor and tolerant.

Perhaps the answer to why some people believe in the inferiority of other races lies in how we see ourselves. Richard Spencer, the person who first came up with the term *alt-right*, told me he was an "identitarian" and that his identity was first and foremost a white man. By defining who we are, we are also defining who we are not, and if we are not "them," then our interests are not theirs. This is the only way to rationalize the construct of white pride, on which the members of the far right base their lives.

But white pride is itself problematic because it presupposes that all whites share common cultural bonds in which to take pride. This is a fallacy. There is no such thing as white culture—or

European culture, for that matter. There is German culture, Irish culture, and Norwegian culture, but in the absence of a homogenous European culture, it becomes easier to define white culture not by what it is but by what it is not. In the eyes of the people I've covered in this book, that tends to mean not African American, not Hispanic, not South Asian, not East Asian, not Indigenous, not gay, lesbian, queer, and so on. The list contracts or expands depending on who you talk to. If six years spent with the radical right taught me anything about the underlying reason for white nationalism, it is this: "We are not them, and they are not us."

August 13, 2017

Election Day 2016

To do evil a human being must first of all believe that what he's doing is good, or else that it's a well-considered act in conformity with natural law.

—Aleksandr Solzhenitsyn, *The Gulag Archipelago*

On the morning of the 2016 presidential election Matthew Heimbach's beat-up, silver Toyota Corolla slowly made its way through the town of Paoli in southern Indiana. Both the car and the town had seen better days. The car's chassis slumped over the wheels as it lurched through the damp morning, passing boarded-up storefronts and dark windows. "This used to be all stores and restaurants," Matthew said. The man who had been called "the affable, youthful face of hate in America" was wearing a heavy, olive-green parka and Angry Birds pajama pants. Despite it being almost noon, his jet-black, bristly hair stood out in awkward angles, and his beard was tussled. It was a slow day. He'd only just gotten out of bed and had decided, perhaps in a show of solidarity with Donald Trump on the day of his presumed electoral loss, that the act of voting didn't require pants.

Matthew had a large head, made larger by the thick foliage growing from it, and a face that gathered around his nose, giving him a jovial if slightly cartoonish look. That face, along with a self-deprecating laugh, was his livelihood and somehow smoothed over the often wildly racist things coming out of his mouth. Discarded hamburger wrappers and soda cups lay on the floor of the car, left over from Matthew's endless crisscrossing of the country to spread his nationalist gospel. The car was a mess, but rentals were expensive, and Matthew was far from wealthy. Like his face, he had worked this into a plus, spending years perfecting an aw-shucks, folksy persona who one moment talked about the simple pleasures of bagging groceries at a local store and the next warned of the terrible danger the international Jewry presented. Matthew had no doubt that the elites were bought and paid for by the Jews, and if there was one thing no one could accuse Matthew Heimbach of, it was being part of the elite.

NPR was battling to rise above the static on the car's stereo, and presently a voice broke through enough to make out that things were looking good for Hillary Clinton. "If the blue wall holds," a reporter on *Morning Edition* predicted, "then Clinton would win."

"Goddammit," Matthew muttered and turned the radio off. "Well, shit. It's not like we didn't see this coming." Everyone had seen it coming. Perhaps with the exception of Donald J. Trump, nobody doubted that Hillary Clinton would cruise to victory that night. As if he was on the ballot himself, Matthew had been working on a concession speech that he would read to his podcast listeners the morning after the election. In fact, it was less a concession speech than a secession speech, with Matthew arguing that the election of Hillary Clinton was not only proof that nobody cared about the white working class but that life under President Clinton would be so deeply ruinous and authoritarian in nature that it would all but guarantee that God-fearing white folks in the heartland would need to withdraw from the Union and build their own country. In that way, a Clinton win would even be a good thing for the cause: it would usher in the destruction of the Union and the birth of a white homeland.

In the back, latched into a worn child safety seat, sat a small boy of just over a year. The boy gargled happily as he attempted to eat a large, plastic toy. Matthew had decided to take his son along to vote because he felt his wife, Brooke, could use a break. "She's probably at home playing Skyrim on the computer right now," he said. "It's funny—she's the greatest wife I could ask for. In the game you can do whatever you want. You can slay dragons! But all she does is rummage around in the forest surrounding her virtual house, collecting herbs for potions. She really is the perfect woman." We passed a squat house where a father had stabbed his wife and killed two of his children before taking his own life. The house was run down and battered, but no more so than its neighbors'. "This kind of stuff happens all the time around here," Matthew said. "It's depressing as hell." He pointed to a large industrial building perched on a bare hilltop above town. "That's the Paoli Furniture Factory. It's closing down, and three hundred and fifty people will lose their jobs. Can you imagine what that does to a town of thirty-five hundred people? They are killing us, literally killing us." Matthew made a fist and pounded the steering wheel with each "killing." He had a flair for the dramatic.

"They" were the Washington elites in general and the Democrats in particular. According to Matthew, through indifference, incompetence, and downright malevolence, they had allowed things to deteriorate in the rural part of southern Indiana, along with everywhere else in the Rustbelt and abutting Appalachia. Things here were miserable and had been for a long time. Jobs were leaving, coal mines were closing, and factories were shuttering. All over Ohio, mines were laying off their workers by the hundreds, and it was the same story in coal towns elsewhere in America. In the 1920s, when the coal boom was at its peak, the industry provided some eight hundred thousand jobs. At the time of the 2016 election the number of people working in the mines wasn't even a tenth of that. The steel towns around Pittsburgh were deserted and quiet. West Virginia was twice broke, with coal disappearing and an epidemic of opioid dependency ravaging the state like a plague, far outpacing other states in terms of opioid drug overdoses; for the sixth year in a row 2017 saw the state's indigent burial fund run out of money because of rampant drug overdoses. The debasement of Appalachia had been going on for decades—ever since the early 1980s the demand for both coal and US-made steel had been in decline—but somehow it felt to Matthew and his supporters like things had gotten worse under Obama. Say what you will about George W. Bush, but at least he wasn't actively gunning for you, which is what Matthew believed Obama was doing. To him it was as clear as day that the elites in Washington hated his kind, by which he meant hard-working, Christian, and—most importantly—white Americans.

"I don't know how anyone can look at what's going on and not see that it is a clear and orchestrated war on whites," Matthew said. "Take immigration for one thing: Who are the Democrats' core voters? Because it sure as hell isn't the white working class anymore. It's the black and the brown people. Of course the Democrats want to flood the country with immigrants—because it will ensure that they stay in power forever. Meanwhile we have no jobs, we have no education, and our communities are flooded with heroin and OxyContin. We are dying, and nobody gives a shit because the people in power either don't need us or actively hate us. Either way, white people are screwed."

He pulled into a KFC drive-thru and got an order of chicken tenders that he passed to the backseat. "Here you go, Nicholas," he said as his son enthusiastically began inserting the strips of meat into his mouth. He was named after Tsar Nicholas II, the hapless ruler of Russia at the time of the Russian Revolution. Matthew hoped that his son, like his namesake, would be a great man, but he worried that he, again like his namesake, was destined to be among the last of his kind.

"I mean, I kind of feel like our future is doomed," he said. "We'll be a minority-majority country by 2040, but the white working class will have been ignored and decimated for years before that. Nobody cares."

The rain was getting worse, and the gloom outside matched Matthew's mood. He was trying to put a combative spin on things, and it could be argued that Trump getting this far was an enormous victory for nationalism in America, but that wasn't enough to cheer him up. He had said many times that Trump wasn't his guy, that he just happened to share a lot of Matthew's views, but Matthew had gone to many of his rallies and screamed louder than most when Black Lives Matter activists had interrupted them. Once he'd been caught on camera pushing a female activist who was tearing down Trump banners. In a weird legal twist, this led to Matthew and Donald Trump being named as codefendants in a lawsuit brought by three of the protestors. He was still waiting to find out if the suit would be allowed to proceed, but the whole thing was another reason to hope for a Trump victory. Either a judge would rule that, as president, Trump was immune against such a suit and the whole thing would go away or Matthew would get the dubious claim of being codefendant with a sitting president.

He switched on the wipers and watched as the threadbare rubber strip redistributed the rain across the windshield. He needed to get new ones. In fact, he needed to get a new car, but he had no money since losing his job at Child Protective Services in Indiana when they found out about his other life as one of the most notorious nationalists in the country. It wasn't the first time he'd been fired for his politics: he had been excommunicated from his church, cut off by his family, and suffered daily death threats since he was a teenager. Losing a job was nothing new, but it did make it harder to do political work when he had to hustle to find new employment. Also, Brooke was pregnant with their second kid—Matthew wanted a large brood—so there was that to pay for. Recently he'd found a new job as a picker in one of Amazon's giant warehouses, but it was lonely, miserable work. The warehouse was vast, and to save money on electricity Amazon had installed motion detectors that made sure the light was only on where the picker was, meaning Matthew spent close to twelve hours per day walking around in a small cone of light, barely ten feet in diameter, surrounded by endless darkness.

Three people had huddled together under umbrellas in the drizzle outside Matthew's polling station. A couple of them had set up lawn chairs and posted a few Trump/Pence signs in the soggy grass. "And there's the Trump patrol," Matthew scoffed. "As if you need to steal an election when you can just let in enough brown people to win it legally." Throughout the campaign Trump had been actively trying to sow doubts about the integrity of the election, and lately he had been deputizing his followers to stand guard outside their local polling places to make sure no Hillary supporters voted, switched coats, and then voted again. The people outside Matthew's polling place, however, looked much less sinister. He rolled down the window as he parked alongside them. "Just another day in paradise, huh?" he said amiably.

He left me in the car with Nicholas, who was still chewing on chicken strips, and went out into the rain, holding a hand over his head for protection. He made small talk with the folks outside the polling station for a while, explaining how Indiana's local politicians had stabbed them all in the back and that he would probably be voting Democrat down ballot under Donald Trump because the only thing worse than a Democrat was a cucked Republican who was so enamored by multiculturalism and globalism that he had forgotten where his bread was buttered. "Yeah, the GOP are really the worst," he said. "They're the ones who claim to be speaking for us, but they are the ones selling us out. At least the Democrats are open about hating us. Anyway, none of this will matter when Hillary wins and the country goes to hell." With that he gave a wave and went in to cast his vote for Donald Trump.

By November 2016 I had known Matthew for a few years, having met him in the early days of what would be a six-year field trip into the underbelly of the American white nationalist scene. It had been a journey littered with skinheads, Klansmen, fights, bad barbeque, rallies, threats, and endless highway miles. Matthew was an unexpected encounter, a seemingly earnest and in some ways sensible outlier in a sea of virulent racists—which isn't to say that Matthew wasn't racist, merely that he wasn't so unambiguous about it. Also, you didn't need to wince your way through a conversation littered with racial slurs when talking to him, which set him apart from many of his fellow white nationalists. One could argue that this made him all the more dangerous—an ostensible voice of reason covering up an insidious form of white supremacy—but it also made him easier to talk to.

What had initially motivated my excursion into the world of white supremacy was curiosity about a brand of politics that seemed almost too outdated to be real—and one that I was surprised to find thriving throughout the country. At the time my impetus was little more than a fascination with the strange and offensive. But then, in the summer of 2011, only a few short months after my initial reporting had begun, Anders Behring Breivik massacred seventy-seven people in Norway. It was a confounding act of hatred and bigotry, aimed at the youngest members of Norway's governing party and perpetrated by a man who believed that the white race was at war. The act exposed a world of far-right radicalism that I had scarcely known existed until then and certainly had not believed capable of such a level of carnage.

I became convinced that the path to defeating extremism was through understanding it. I began reaching out to more white supremacists and nationalists in the United States, eventually leading me into a world of racism, vitriol, staggering ineptitude, and quixotic ambition. Only toward the end of my foray did I realize that the far-right radicals in America were in the forefront of a nationalistic zeitgeist that would upend the entire 2016 presidential election as well as the political landscape of America in the months following it. In 2011, when I first began reporting on neo-Nazis, skinheads, and the Ku Klux Klan, they weren't even a blip on the media's radar; rather, pundits were preoccupied by what we then thought was about as extreme as US politics could get: the ascendancy of the Tea Party and, on the other end of the spectrum, the Occupy movement.

My interest in the groups of the extreme far right and its members was purely sociological. I was fascinated that there are still those in America—a country whose history is steeped in government-sanctioned white supremacy—who believe that the white race is under siege and in danger of extinction. And they don't stop there: they believe that the steps taken by the nation, often reluctantly and always overdue, to rectify its shameful treatment of minorities are in fact targeted attacks against whites, devised and directed by Jews and communists. They see progress as a zero-sum game in which someone has to lose if others are to win, and they believe that all the gains made by blacks, Latinos, LGBTQs, Muslims, Jews, immigrants, and others over the decades have come at the expense of whites. The march toward equality in America, in their minds, was really a crusade against white people.

In truth I was also curious to explore what drew people to these groups. Who were the neo-Nazis and white nationalists in America, and why would they be willing to shoulder the considerable cost, both monetary and social, that came with being an out-and-out white supremacist? Were their political views merely fronts for plain, humdrum racism, or was there any truth to their claims that they weren't racist but merely concerned for their race? Also, even if these people thought they had a good argument for the direction America should be taking, did they really believe that marching under the swastika, arguably the single-most hated symbol in the world, would garner them anything but derision and loathing?

What I found often confirmed but sometimes confounded expectation. There were plenty who had no more profound an ideology than hating other races, but there were also those who defied stereotypes. I found movements whose members all had varying motives for joining but shared a similar confusion and anger about where the world was heading as well as a deep sense of being left behind. This feeling of loss was at times understandable—it is difficult to travel through the hollows of West Virginia without a palpable feeling of being in a part of the world whose time has come and gone—but in the minds of those who joined the ranks of the far right, it had festered into a warped ideology of white entitlement and hatred. Of course, white nationalism exists on a spectrum, and although there are certainly those who will happily expound on their hatred for anything black, brown, and Jewish, there are also those who claim that the white race is not inherently better than others, merely that it is their race and that they should be allowed to take pride in it.

Matthew fell squarely in the latter camp. He saw himself as a scholar and historian, and his disdain for those who believed in the white übermensch was fervent. Still, he took a somewhat paternal attitude toward them and preferred bringing them into the fold, believing he could make them see the errors of white supremacy in favor of a more pragmatic nationalist approach. To this end his patience with skinheads and Klansmen—whose politics rarely went beyond doing something about black people and compulsive whoops of "white power!"—seemed almost endless. That's why I began tagging along with him in the spring of 2014. I figured the best way to navigate the backwaters of white supremacy was with a nationalist who wanted to recruit them all to his team.

Through Matthew I experienced a movement in crisis and disarray, consisting of groups and factions whose beliefs were often not only wildly disparate but also seemingly completely incompatible. Matthew, however, believed differently and worked enthusiastically to corral them all to his cause. He didn't mind mixing his own brand of nationalism with the white supremacy of Jeff Schoep and the National Socialist Movement (NSM). Nor did he have a problem reaching out to his friend Dan and his comrades in the Ku Klux Klan or the brutish skinheads of the Hammerskin Nation.

At first I couldn't quite understand how this meshed with his ostensible postsupremacist form of nationalism, but I soon saw that Matthew had a profound belief in his own ability to bend groups to his will. He was happy to accept any group into his fold so long as they acquiesced to his vision of white nationalism. Matthew knew that the scattershot far right could be corralled under the right leader, and despite his humble front, Matthew, I suspected, very much intended to become that leader.

WE'D STOPPED BY a liquor store to stock up on beers in preparation for a night that would be miserable for at least one of us. As depressed as Matthew was about Trump's prospects for the evening, I was feeling nervous, having watched Donald Trump defy every expectation since the primaries began. His rise had taken everyone by surprise except Matthew, who would patiently explain that you could only kick the white working man for so long before he would get up and kick back. As unlikely a champion for the working man as he was, Donald Trump was that kick. I'd watched how Donald Trump's particularly egocentric brand of nationalism, which had fed on the same fears and resentments that drove Matthew's movement, had validated Matthew's efforts to bring the far right together. I saw how deep the anger ran and how willing Trump had been to embrace it in his campaign.

By nine o'clock I was miserably watching the apotheosis of white fear and anger in America, and my worry had shifted from Hillary losing, which by then was an almost certainty, to whether there was enough beer on hand to drown out the gloating from Matthew and his friend Miles. We were on a threadbare sofa in one of the two trailers that made up his home and the headquarters for his political party, the Traditionalist Workers Party. His buddy Miles was leaning against the wall, furiously vaping. Another party member, Jason, was sitting on the floor, and Matthew Parrot, Matthew's friend and father-in-law, was walking in and out, endlessly checking the odds on the betting sites.

Matthew was standing up more often than he was sitting down—shouting at the TV, jeering if Hillary was on the screen, cheering if Trump was, and intermittently reminding Gary Johnson, who was siphoning votes from Trump in Florida, to go fuck himself. Hillary needed Pennsylvania and North Carolina to win, but they were looking shaky. If they went to Trump, the game was over.

The consensus in the trailer was that the Democrat-shilling traitors at CNN were too deep in their Jewish taskmasters' pocket to call the election for Donald Trump. It didn't surprise them—they expected very little from the media—but it was still annoying as hell. "Goddammit, just fucking call it!" Matthew shouted.

He blew an angry puff of vapor from pursed lips, repeating it a couple of times, impatiently huffing on the conical mouthpiece of his vape. The plume expanded under the low ceiling, enveloping him and clouding Wolf Blitzer's face on the screen. A sweet, sweaty smell filled the trailer. Pizza boxes littered the floor. Empty beer bottles crowded the underside of the sofa, spilling their remaining drops of dead beer on the thick carpet. Then Trump took North Carolina, and it looked like the election might be over. "Fucking Trump!" Matthew shouted to Parrot, who just then came back into the room. "Fucking Trump is going to win this for us!" Parrot had his laptop in his hands and was refreshing a website every few seconds, watching the odds slowly tilt in Trump's favor.

"Still too early to say," he cautioned. "But it's not looking bad." He refreshed the website again. "Not bad at all."

"Fuck you, it's not looking bad," Matthew said. "We got this. Hillary is fucking done." Matthew didn't normally swear, but he seemed to have made an allowance for tonight. He smacked me hard on the back. "You liberal pieces of shit are going down!" he said, and Miles asked me if I was going to cry. Wolf Blitzer came on the screen again, saying that although it was still too early to call Florida, the Trump campaign must be feeling good right now. "You're fucking cowards!" Matthew screamed at the screen. "It's so clear that they're working for Hillary."

Not that he could blame them for dragging it out. Their world was collapsing. The elites, the media, the liberals—every single traitor was about to wake up in a country where the white working man had finally struck back and taken power. Every swing state that tumbled into Donald Trump's column was a validation of what Matthew had been working for all this time: A nationalist in the White House. A wall on the Mexican border. No more Muslims coming in. And, most importantly, white men and women in this country had a voice again. "Fucking finally!"

The whole thing disgusted me. Perhaps not so much Matthew's gloating but the miserable idea that the majority of Americans might agree with Trump's politics was almost too much to bear. I'd watched as the far right in America had gone from a bickering, dysfunctional group of racist malcontents to what it was now: still bickering and dysfunctional but, as far as they were concerned, about to put their guy in the White House.

We were out of beer. Matthew was in my face shouting. Miles was jeering from behind a cloud of smoke. Jason's brother Zach loomed next to me at his desk, where he kept a gun that he sometimes pointed at imagined enemies on the wall. Wisconsin was still out, but I couldn't take it anymore and got up on unsteady legs. I needed fresh air, but more than that, I needed to get out of there. All the time I had been reporting on the far right, my one big comfort had been that these people would probably never get to power, that their worldview would never be validated. But now here we were. On the precipice of God knows what—but certainly nothing good. "You're not going to watch us win?" asked Matthew. I mumbled something about stealing his car as I grabbed the keys from the counter and stumbled into the dark. I drove at a snail's pace back to the hotel, trying to will my vision not to blur and the road to stop moving around. The TV was on in the lobby of the Best Western, but I covered my ears and closed my eyes as I rushed past, thinking for a second about Schrödinger's Cat and how, at that moment Clinton had both lost and won the election. I jumped into bed and fell into a black sleep. My phone woke me up at three in the morning with a text message from Matthew:

Wisconsin goes to Trump! Everything you love will burn! LOL ☺

The far right had their president, and all I had was a splitting hangover and five years' worth of notes that I hoped would help me figure out how they'd managed to pull it off.

CHAPTER 1
_____

The Battle of Trenton

This time we'll hate, alright—but we'll hate the ENEMY—
the vicious gang of colored scum attackers and Jewish-
Communist traitors—rather than one part of our own people
hating another part for the benefit of the Jews and their army
of SCUM!

—George Lincoln Rockwell,
"White Self-Hate: Masterstroke of the Enemy"

It was late November of 2010 when an email landed in my inbox
from someone calling himself Lieutenant Duke Schneider of the
SS. He explained that he was writing to me in response to an interview request I had filed with the National Socialist Movement—

the largest neo-Nazi group in the country—several months back and that he would be happy to provide me with any information I wanted, short of personal details, member numbers, chapter locations, and strategies. For a while, since I first heard rumors of skinheads roaming the Greenpoint neighborhood in Brooklyn, I had wanted to do a story on neo-Nazis in America and had spent a week or so emailing various groups I found online. None had responded, either because they didn't want to talk to me or because they were defunct. Some of the websites looked like they were made sometime in the mid-nineties, so I assumed the latter. Eventually I learned that most of the Greenpoint skinheads had long ago aged out of the movement and that the scene itself had decayed into almost nothing. Apparently all that was left was the NSM and Lieutenant Schneider.

He invited me to meet at a deli in downtown Manhattan not far from Ground Zero. We had coffee and pastries, and he told me about his old job as a corrections officer at Rikers Island and his collection of turtles that he rescued from shelters. For a neo-Nazi he didn't seem like a monster, and I was having trouble picturing him cheering the extermination of several million Jews before heading to his local ASPCA to look for turtles to adopt. More than anything he came across as an otherwise relatively normal guy who claimed an officer rank of the SS, an organization that, as far as I knew, hadn't existed for over sixty years. He was a large bulldog of a man in his early sixties, with a thick neck and a powerful torso wrapped in a black tank top with a picture of a wolf on it. His face was red and splotchy, making him look like he came directly from lifting weights.

We met several more times after that until he finally invited me to come to one of the NSM's gatherings. "You'll see how we're just a bunch of normal folks getting together," he said.

So a few weeks later I found myself in Sheepshead Bay in Brooklyn, together with Schneider, his daughter Kate, and a guy I had never met before named John. It was a hot Friday morning.

Unseasonably warm for April. We were waiting for a couple of guys who were late, and Schneider was sweating and annoyed in a thick wool shirt.

"Lot of Jews here," John said, squinting and looking down the street.

"Yep," Schneider answered as he checked his phone again. "Passover."

"That'll give them something to crow over," John chortled. "Fucking pieces of shit."

Schneider flipped open his cell and tried calling them again, with no luck. Schneider put the flip phone back in the holster on his belt and frowned toward the station exit. "There's just no excuse," he muttered to himself. "If they were in the SS, they'd be right out on their keisters. We're leaving at exactly 11:05! If they're not here, they can take the Jersey Transit."

Six minutes later we were headed for New Jersey without them. We were on our way to the annual convention for the NSM. It was to be held somewhere in New Jersey, and there would be a march in Trenton, New Jersey, on Saturday. This was all I had been told, and to the best of my knowledge this was about as much as most people in the NSM knew. The location of the hotel and the venue for tonight's banquet were closely guarded secrets to which only the members of the leadership were privy.

John and Kate were in the backseat. John had only been a member of the NSM for a short time, and this was his first convention. Kate, who worked as a claims adjuster, was telling him about a black woman who had tried to claim children she wasn't caring for on her insurance. Her round face became distorted and her voice became broad and exaggerated: "What you mean I can't claim fo' them children jus' 'cause they livin' wi' they baby-daddy?!"

John laughed. "Baby-daddy!"

In the front Schneider was telling me about the Holocaust. "None of us were there, so how can we know?" he reasoned as the Kia crossed the Verrazano-Narrows Bridge from Brooklyn to Staten Island. "I've heard accounts for and against, and I can't know. I met a woman who survived the Holocaust, and she never saw any atrocities. She was a cleaning lady, and she once saw Hitler, Hermann Göring, Adolf Eichmann, and Josef Mengele board a plane. Eichmann and Mengele both escaped to South America. I think Hitler did too." Elton John's "Tiny Dancer" came on the radio, and Schneider stopped talking and turned the volume up.

"Did you hear there's a cover of Elton John on Michael Jackson's new album of unreleased material?" Kate shouted from the backseat. "Don't Let Your Son Go Down on Me." John and Kate both laughed. Schneider frowned. He pulled out a CD and slid it into the stereo, handing me the cover: "Panzer Marches. From Original Third Reich Recordings." The car filled at once with the crackling of an old gramophone that was quickly replaced by the tinny sound of old marches recorded during the war. Schneider winked and hummed along.

> When before us an enemy army appears, we go full throttle against
>   them and rush at the foe!
> What difference does it make if we give our lives for the army of our
>   Reich?
> Yes, the army of our Reich?
> To die for Germany is for us the highest honor.

"Where are we going?" I asked. We had just crossed from Staten Island into New Jersey. Schneider winked again. He winked a lot.

"Confidential," he said, repeating what he had told me for the last two months about our destination for the weekend. I had been told that there would be no photography or recording that weekend, so I had to relinquish my phone before leaving New York. The rules seemed extremely paranoid, especially as Schneider kept insisting that the NSM was a regular political party and should be treated as such. The limitations had been eased since—presumably on order of NSM high command—and my camera, phone, and recorder were in a bag in the trunk of the Kia as it made its way deeper into New Jersey.

I had gotten used to the clandestine disposition of Schneider and the NSM. Every meeting with Duke for the past five months had been cloaked in secrecy. I was always told to meet at the Avenue U station in Brooklyn, where he would be waiting in his car. From there Schneider's Hyundai would crisscross around blocks, making U-turns, doubling back before always ending up outside the same diner in Sheepshead Bay, roughly half a mile from where we had started. He said it was because he was under constant surveillance by any number of organizations—"CIA, FBI, DHS, JDL, ADL, ARA," he listed—until I was convinced he was just naming various letters. "I don't mind. If the CIA is watching us, then they must be watching the Jews and the terrorists too. I'm not doing anything wrong." He would often and haphazardly change times and locations for meetings, citing various security threats, sometimes based on little more than a car he didn't recognize parked outside his house. I had no way of verifying whether he was right or simply paranoid, but from what I knew, it seemed unlikely that he would be surveilled in such a manner. The FBI were almost certainly keeping tabs on members of the NSM, but their usual way of doing things was to use informants rather than unmarked cars and stakeouts.

Schneider had told me that the NSM had chapters in almost every state, but it was impossible to verify and, as I soon would see, most likely wildly exaggerated. No one outside the movement really knew how many members they had, and no one in the movement would say. The party was run by Jeff Schoep, who, according to Schneider, was akin to the second coming of Adolf Hitler, and it had its roots in the American Nazi Party, founded in 1959 by George Lincoln Rockwell, known as the father of American National Socialism.

The NSM was notorious because of the replica Nazi uniforms its members wore during marches and the provocative nature of their public events. In 2005 members of the NSM insisted on marching through Toledo's North End, a poor and predominantly black neighborhood. In the riots that followed, dozens were arrested and the NSM members indignantly claimed they had been attacked while exercising their constitutional rights. The right of National Socialists to mount protests and demonstrations as part of their First Amendment rights was long established, ever since the American Civil Liberties Union (ACLU) in 1977 successfully argued in front of the Supreme Court that the National Socialist Party of America—only tangentially related to the NSM—had the right to march through Skokie, Illinois. The ACLU had taken on many similar cases in the name of free speech, but after Charlottesville they announced they would no longer defend groups that protest with firearms.

TWO HOURS AFTER we had set off, Schneider turned the Kia into the parking lot of the Comfort Inn in Bordentown, New Jersey. Bordentown is the kind of small town that seems to be made up entirely of diners, bars, and burger joints lining a six-lane highway for which it is hard to imagine there is any need. A motley group of people stood in the parking lot outside the squat, yellow building, waving as our car pulled up. Some were tattooed skinheads in combat trousers and bomber jackets. Others looked like ordinary tourists with sun visors and T-shirts from the Grand Canyon. Kate jumped out to hug a grandmother-like woman in a trucker hat whom she hadn't seen since they marched together in Phoenix during last year's convention. Schneider clambered out of the car slowly and shook hands with a short, older man with slicked-back gray hair and a swastika armband on his brown shirt. John hung back by the car and kicked a rock against the curb until Schneider introduced him jovially as "a new potential storm trooper." Everyone waved. John, who looked unsure of whether to wave back or give the Nazi straight-arm salute, settled for grinning sheepishly. The older woman who had hugged Kate introduced herself to me as Sandy. "Welcome to Jersey, kid," she said.

A young, smiling skinhead in a bomber jacket and with "SS" tattooed on his neck in bold, red letters came over to me and introduced himself as Juan, quickly adding that his dad was Spanish, not Mexican—a vital distinction. Spain is European and therefore good. Mexico is Mexican and, consequentially, very bad. He welcomed me and said he was happy to talk to me. He was from Albany, New York, and had been a member of the NSM for two years.

"The banquet will be good," he said. "These are nice people."

Everyone met two hours later in the lobby. The Pakistani receptionist looked terrified at the scene unfolding in his hotel. The Nazis had been told to wear their dress uniform, so the lobby and bar resembled a scene from a World War II movie. "Who are these people?" he whispered to me pleadingly, hoping against hope I wasn't one of them, as I was the only one not currently draped in swastikas.

In one of the chairs next to the reception a heavy-set SS soldier with angry red skin and a black cap that seemed to belong on a much smaller head was educating a young girl on race theory while a cleaning lady, also Pakistani, stared at him in poorly disguised disbelief.

"What you see in the black communities are that something like seventy percent of mothers are unmarried," he pontificated, while the thick, fleshy folds of his neck pressed against the collar of his shirt. "Now their kids are all half-sisters and half-brothers, and they don't know who their fathers and uncles are. So they start doing it, and soon you have a lot of inbreeding and a recessive gene pool. We need to put some chlorine in that gene pool. The kids grow up angry and with learning disabilities. And if they get upset, they go straight to the gun. They want to kill you. They're going down, and they're taking us with them." When he finished he looked around the room. The people around him, with the exception of the cleaning lady and me, were solemnly nodding their heads at this incontrovertible truth.

Schneider came up to me and asked, "Ready to go, champ?" Another wink. He had changed from his plain black fatigues into a heavy, black woolen gala uniform with riding trousers and black boots. Around his left shoulder were thick, silver tassels, and a leather strap ran across his chest. His right arm was wrapped in a bright red band with a white circle and a black, bold swastika sewn on. A long ceremonial dagger dangled menacingly from his belt. His chest was covered with medals and commendations that made the uniform seem almost believable, and a giant black hat, complete with the eagle of the Third Reich and the skull and bones of the SS, was perched on his head. Commander Schoep came out of the elevator, and Schneider jumped and ran to him. He had told me earlier that one of his main duties at events like this was to serve as the personal bodyguard to the commander. Once, while driving me around, he told me that it would be his honor to die for the commander.

Commander Jeff Schoep was the only one not wearing a uniform. He looked young and scrawny, almost thuggish, with a shaved head and a stern demeanor. He wore an ill-fitting, wrinkled pin-stripe suit, and he looked tired. His wife was on his arm, endlessly fussing over him and dismissing everyone who approached her husband as if he were a tender starlet surrounded by paparazzi. Walking briskly through the sliding doors of the hotel, he completely ignored his bodyguard. Schneider followed as fast as he could, struggling to keep up with his charge. It was hard to imagine him diving in front of a bullet.

The carpool convoy pulled up outside an AA hall in Pemberton, New Jersey. I'd caught a ride with SS Sergeant Wilson from Oklahoma, whose son had just been expelled from school for wearing a "White Power" T-shirt. "I bet you anything that wouldn't happen to someone wearing a Brown Power T-shirt," he said indignantly. "There are no rights left for whites in this country."

The interior walls of the hall were covered in large, blood-red banners with black swastikas and the flag of the NSM. "It's a mix of the American flag and a Nazi banner," an old woman with a swastika armband said helpfully. Tables filled the room in a horseshoe shape, and every place setting had a white paper plate and a red plastic cup, both adorned with little swastikas. In a corner someone had set up a couple of tables filled with merchandise for sale. There were badges, medals, books, epaulets, paintings, toy tanks, T-shirts, and CDs—all adorned in some form or another with swastikas. An older Nazi was browsing the table, trying to decide whether he should buy a large, painted portrait of Adolf Hitler or a copy of *The Eternal Jew* or maybe an action figure of a panzer tank operator. Sergeant Wilson came over to me and said, "You want to get a picture of this." He gave a straight-armed salute to one of the action figures on the table, giggled, and left.

We had meatballs, lasagna, and salad for dinner. A little girl of around ten and her mother, both in black skirts, white tops, and swastika armbands, fussed around the kitchen, making sure everyone had enough to eat and drink while NSM members, around twenty-five or so of them, milled around the room making small talk and laughing. It felt like a family reunion. The NSM is spread all over the United States, so most members only see each other during conventions. Schneider paraded around the room, patting backs and laughing, while the commander sat at the end of the table not talking to anyone, surveying his troops while his wife doted on him. He'd been the commander of the NSM for seventeen years, but if it wasn't for his suit, he could easily have been mistaken for a young recruit.

At seven that night, as the Nazis were having coffee, the doors to the hall burst open and Gunner, a young, portly SS soldier, crashed through, falling to the floor. His face was bright red and tears were streaming from his swollen eyes. "Attack!" he shouted. "Reds!" The room erupted in roars and screams as everyone got to their feet and stormed toward the exit. Grabbing my camera, I pushed my way through the front door and into the parking lot, where I was faced with roughly twenty masked men, dressed in black and carrying bats, bricks, and knives. Nazis pushed past me, carrying metal folding chairs over their heads while the masked group across the street stormed to meet them, weapons raised. They crashed violently, their mutual disgust and hatred for each other outweighing any concern for personal safety. There was a loud crack as Wilson

The Battle of Trenton. Members of the National Socialist Movement clash with Antifa in Trenton, New Jersey. Commander Jeff Schoep (far left, wearing suit) was pepper sprayed.

slammed his metal chair into the face of one of the attackers, who collapsed on the ground. His body was welcomed by kicks from heavy steel-tipped boots. Behind me someone screamed "Nazi scum!" and I turned just in time to dive out of the path of a flying brick aimed at my head. I ran for cover and saw Juan, the sweet kid from Albany, landing a blow with a heavy stick to the head of a skinny kid in a mask. Blood poured from an open gash on Juan's head, soaking his face in thick black and red. The masked kid slumped to the ground, and some of his friends grabbed him and pulled him away. Juan's feet faltered and he stumbled. Someone took him by the shoulder and pulled him inside. Commander Schoep was running for cover, yellow spots of pepper spray covering his face and tears streaming from his eyes. Schneider ran behind him, unscathed but out of breath. A flying brick shattered the windshield of the car behind me, and it seemed like every car alarm within fifty miles had been set off. Neighbors stared in disbelief from their windows as their street was turned into a pandemonium of crashing chairs, swinging bats, stomping boots, and falling bodies. There was blood on the ground in puddles, smears, and red boot prints. The battle was primal and hateful. There was no grappling or confused wrestling—only fists, boots, weapons, and the desire to damage skulls, jaws, teeth, and bone.

Eventually it became clear that the Nazis were winning. They had hit harder and cared less that they were bleeding. The masked attackers, disarmed and beaten, ran off down the street as wailing sirens drowned out the shouts. Some of the Nazis gave chase but turned back after only a few short yards. They had won the battle and they knew it. The police arrived in force. Then the state police came, and finally SWAT, armed with MP-5 submachine guns, running down the street, setting up perimeters, and shouting orders. Inside the hall was as chaotic as outside. "They got my husband! Those motherfuckers! Those motherfuckers got my husband!" the commander's wife was screaming as she dabbed a wet towel on her husband's swollen face. Next to her a giant SS officer called Mark sat calmly, enjoying his meatballs as thick blood poured from a gash in his head that left a part of his skull exposed. He seemed unconcerned and ate with gusto as the blood soaked his collar. "Fucking cowards!" a tall, skinny Nazi called Tony shouted. "We sent them packing! Cowards! Goddamn that was fun!"

"I took a chair and smacked that motherfucker!" a young skinhead said as he shook his head in happy disbelief. "Right in the face. Commie motherfucker!" Outside in the parking lot the police were taking statements.

"We were just having dinner and they attacked us, officer."

"I have no idea who they were, officer. Probably Jewish Defense League."

"All we did was defend ourselves, officer."

Juan was in the back of an ambulance getting examined by paramedics. He smiled and gave a thumbs-up. A few of his friends had already been driven off to the hospital. Commander Schoep was inside whispering with his lieutenants in the kitchen. "Someone told them where we were. Someone fucking told them." They stopped talking as I walked past, eyeing me suspiciously. Schneider looked at me. He was the guy who had brought a journalist into the room, and he was hoping he hadn't brought a snitch in too. A guy called Greg came over to me. "I just can't understand why some people just don't like Nazis," he said, his voice filled with genuine wonder as he shook his head in confusion.

"Are you kidding?" I said. "You're *Nazis*."

"I know," he said, shaking his head again. "I just can't understand it."

"Who were those guys?" I asked Tony.

"Jewish Defense League," he said. "Or Anti-Racist Association. Perhaps Black Panthers, although I doubt it. They don't usually wear masks. We just call them Commies." Local news later reported that a group calling itself Anti-Racist Action had attacked the NSM. It was the first time the NSM had been attacked while privately gathering, and the night soon went into NSM lore as the "Battle of Trenton."

The ambulances and most of the police left, leaving a handful of cars and about a dozen officers standing guard on the now quiet street outside. The Nazis were jubilant. Commander Schoep was pumping his fists in the air. "What we experienced today with the Commie scum was just a test of what we'll see tomorrow. I was honored to stand with each and every one of you today. Today and forever we and our revolutionary forefathers stand against the on-slaught of the masses."

"Sieg Heil! Sieg Heil! Sieg Heil!" erupted from the room. "We fought the Commie scum in the street and we sent them to Hell! We're fighting for the future of our children!"

THE NEXT MORNING was slow, wet, and gray. I woke to the sound of radio static. The parking lot outside the hotel was crowded with SWAT and National Guard. They had been there all night to make sure the Nazis weren't attacked in their beds. The lobby was crowded again, and the Pakistani owner looked exasperated. "I've asked them to not hang around the lobby," he complained. "They're scaring the hell out of all my customers."

Sandy, the older woman I had been introduced to the day before, came over. "Come here," she whispered conspiratorially. "I want you to know something the government doesn't want you to know." She introduced me to Heath and Deborah Campbell, a couple from New Jersey who had lost custody of their children over allegations of abuse. "They can't talk to you," Sandy said. "The court says they can't talk to anyone. But the court didn't say anything about their godmother talking." Three years earlier the state of New Jersey had taken their three children because of the names they had given them: Adolf Hitler Campbell, JoceLynn Aryan Nation Campbell, and Hozlyn Himmler Campbell. They were fighting to get them back.

"I named my kids the best names I knew," Heath said, momentarily forgetting his gag order.

Sandy interrupted him. "It all started with a birthday cake," she said. "You can start your story like that. Write 'It all started with a birthday cake.'" She pointed at my note pad, then at Heath. "Tell him." She too apparently forgot that the Campbells weren't allowed to speak.

"I went to the bakery," Heath continued. "I wanted to get a birthday cake for my son, and I wanted it to say, 'Happy Third Birthday, Adolf Hitler!'" Apparently the name had alarmed the bakery owner, who Heath said was Jewish, and he called the authorities.

"They call it abuse," Sandy spat in disgust. "Abuse! They're good names."

"Isn't it possible it can lead to them being teased?" I offered.

"Nonsense!" Sandy almost shouted, incredulous at the ridiculous question. "I was teased for my name in school all the time. People called me Sandy Koufax. I had a hell of a time. Kids are going to tease no matter what."

"Besides," Heath shot in, "who uses a middle name anyway? The schools don't even know the kids' middle names. Who cares if it's Hitler? It's a good name." I tried again to suggest that with names like that, teasing, bullying, and misery were downright guaranteed, but they didn't understand me, so I left them in the lobby with a promise to write something.

A few minutes later the Nazis piled into cars and drove with a police escort to a rendezvous spot outside Trenton, from where we would be ferried into town in prison buses. After the battle last night the authorities were taking no chances, and security was extensive. The plan was to march a few hundred yards to the capitol building, where Commander Schoep and others would speak on the steps about what was wrong with America. Before we got on the buses everyone was searched and told to leave brass knuckles, sticks, and clubs behind. Sergeant Wilson had to take off his flak jacket because he didn't have a permit for it. He took off his bracelet on the bus and wrapped it around his hand as a makeshift brass knuckle. "I got five bucks for every fist to the face!" he shouted to the back of the bus. "Last night was nothing!"

The entire route of the march was lined with National Guard and riot police. They had closed off every access point, and no one was around to watch the Nazis trudge along the wet streets while the rain soaked their black uniforms. They arrived at a wide square in front of the capitol building. A few modest steps led up to the entrance, and a small podium stood at the top. Police had cordoned off the entire square. In the distance the counter-protestors had gathered. The police, fearing another showdown, kept them two blocks away from the Nazis, just barely within shouting distance. So the rally was reduced to a couple dozen neo-Nazis screaming obscenities at fifty or so antiracists down the street, while the antiracists screamed right back. "We kicked your asses last night!" Wilson roared. "We'll do it again today!"

Juan, who had been released from the hospital the night before, stood in the pouring rain in front of the podium holding a NSM banner. His head was adorned with twelve bloody staples, and he now had red laces in his boots, meaning he had shed blood or drawn blood for the cause. "Hey," he said. "Great night last night."

At one point the NSM tried turning their speakers toward the antis in the distance. "This is my town," Lieutenant Hiecke, leader of the New Jersey chapter, shouted into the microphone. "I'm here because I care about Trenton and what's happening here. I'm here for you." The antis shouted, and the Nazis shouted back, and so it went for about two hours before they called it quits and marched back to the waiting prison buses.

"We're going to go shopping for our wives later," Wilson told me excitedly on the bus. "Shopping" is when the NSM go into a town in their uniforms to stir up trouble and get into fights. "We're going to go right back here after the police leave, and we're going to find something nice for our wives. I don't care if we have to go into every shop in Trenton."

"Fuck yeah!" someone shouted. "White power!" They never went, and I have the distinct sense that they never intended to.

Later that night everyone gathered in Lieutenant Hiecke's backyard for a final night of celebration. The weekend had gone better than expected, and the Nazis were jubilant. Lieutenant Hiecke had erected a large gazebo tent, draped swastikas along the plastic walls, and filled it with tables and chairs. In one corner was the guy with the merchandise from the night before and in another was a drum kit and amps.

"Have a beer," an older guy who had once been a Grand Dragon in the KKK told me. "We did something this weekend." Other than being attacked and shouting abuse for two hours, I wondered what they had achieved. "We got out and did something, that's what," he went on. "We used to do something in the Klan. Then everything changed, and now all the Klan does is sit around in the woods and barbecue. That's why I joined the NSM. We get out there and give the kids something to look up to."

A skinny guy with a manic look came over to me. His name was Josh Steever, and he had recently founded a group called the Aryan Terror Brigade. "Check it out," he giggled and pulled his T-shirt off. On his chest was a large tattoo of two plungers in a cross with a swastika in the center. "70th Precinct" was written in bold, gothic lettering. It was his homage to the officers of the 70th precinct in Brooklyn who sodomized Abner Louima with a broken plunger in 1997. He grinned and turned around. "Kill Niggers" was emblazoned on his back. On his forehead was a pale blue shadow of what had once been the word "Racist."

A couple of young skinheads were talking at a nearby table. "In ten to fifteen years, not even that," one of them said seriously, "the Muslims will have enough people here to elect the next president of the United States."

"Yeah, there's a state, Oklahoma or Kansas or something, where they've actually voted to institute Sharia law! In the Heartland. I mean, come on!"

"You know Muslim men are allowed to marry from when they are one, right?" said another. "They can get married when they're only one year old! A woman on the internet said it. One year old, swear to God."

Gunner, the heavy-set blond and baby-faced twentysomething who had sounded the alarm during the attack the night before, was playing with his mobile phone distractedly. "I can't download any white power music on my phone," he said. "Sprint is letting me down."

The rain was getting worse outside the tent. The rain and heavy boots had turned the lawn into deep mud, and every so often forks of lightning illuminated the swastikas on the walls. Commander Schoep sat alone in the corner. He was wearing his combat uniform: black boots, black cargo pants, and black shirt with a red armband. "How has your weekend been?" he asked when I sat down. I told him that it had been good, illuminating. "People don't get that we're just regular people and a regular party," he said. I looked over at Josh with the plunger tattoo. He was talking excitedly to a man dressed completely in white with the words "It's not illegal to be white . . . yet" written on his T-shirt.

"The reds attack us and want to get us, and we're a peaceful, nonviolent group. But we'll defend ourselves, and we always win. But we don't like violence. We are who we are, and if what we do provokes them, tough. But it's not about provoking. That's not why we do this." Schoep believed his movement was on the verge of gaining some kind of popular acceptance and that from there the road would be short to running candidates in elections, both on the local and national level. "We're a white civil rights organization," he said. "Like us or hate us, we're involved in a lot of good things, and I think many Americans are starting to agree with us. The Democrats and Republicans are basically the same group. There are no strong differences between them, and that's where we come in. National Socialism is neither left wing nor right wing. It takes the best of both wings and combines them."

Schoep didn't see his party as racist or hateful. He was concerned with establishing a white, secure homeland and really didn't care what other races thought about that. Ideally the other races would go when his party came to power. "They could go back to their own homelands," he suggested. "It's not like we'd rip them out and send them off. They'd be repatriated." He explained that if a black person owned a house here, he would of course be given a house in his new homeland. I assumed he meant various countries in Africa, but he didn't expand on how he would convince foreign governments to offer housing to American citizens. "We can do it if we stop immigration, bring the troops home, and stop giving out all this foreign aid," he said, repeating the NSM solution to pretty much everything. I had been told several times that weekend that the United States could easily be fixed if we brought the troops home and placed them on the border with Mexico, the origin of most of the problems in the United States. A sergeant I had spoken to earlier had seen a Mexican man in Connecticut and presented it as undisputable proof of a mass exodus of criminals, degenerates, and rapists from Mexico. "It's an America First policy, and it'll bring in tons of money," Schoep said confidently, unknowingly foreshadowing Trump's platform five years hence. "Immigration and the economy are the biggest problems facing the nation. And they're two sides of the same coin."

He disagreed with those who labeled the NSM a hate group. If they were, he argued, then Martin Luther King was a hater too. "There's a real double standard when it comes to whites," he said. "If you're white and proud, then you're called a racist, but if you're black and proud or any other race then that's okay. If you look out for white people, then all of a sudden you're a racist. I'm not a racist. I don't hate anyone because of his or her color, creed, or religion. That's ignorant. I prefer to be with my own people, but I don't hate anyone."

Schoep explained that whites would be the minority in the United States by 2020, big business was run by Jews, who he didn't consider to be white, and the white politicians in Congress were traitors who didn't care about their constituents. "Most people don't want immigrants here. Most people don't want the war. But the politicians don't listen. We're here to change that."

Lieutenant Hiecke came in from the rain, soaking wet. "We're about to light 'er. She needs about ten gallons of fuel, but she'll light." Everyone got up and went outside. The rain was coming down harder than ever. Hiecke's backyard was a quagmire lit up by forks of lightning. In the middle of the yard was a large swastika, six feet across and nailed to a wooden beam that had been driven into the soaking earth. Hiecke was crouched next to it. Tiny flickers of his lighter illuminated his face and hands as he struggled to set fire to the dripping wet structure. Eventually small flames appeared on the bottom right angle of the swastika, slowly making their way to where their four arms intersected. "White power!" someone screamed. The rain seemed to get worse, but no one went back inside the tent. Everyone stood around watching as the flames engulfed the swastika and grew stronger and brighter. "Sieg Heil!" people shouted, giving straight-armed salutes while water poured from their outstretched hands and arms.

"Sieg Heil! Sieg Heil! Sieg Heil!" The neighbors were in their windows watching the group of Nazis, soaking uniforms clinging to their bodies, illuminated by the flickering light of the burning swastika. Schneider stood next to me. He had his hat in his hand, and the heavy rain was pounding his bald, round head. His right arm was outstretched, and flames lit up his eyes. His lips were pursed and his back was straight. Water was dripping from his eyebrows into his eyes, but I never saw him blink.

I wondered what he had achieved that weekend. The Nazis had faced off their attackers, frightened hotel workers and their neighbors, and marched in their uniforms. They had cuts and bruises to boast about, and they had given each other medals and commendations for it. There had been much backslapping and agreement about what was wrong with America, but I had a feeling that that was pretty much it. The next day everyone would go back home. They would listen to white power music, talk on internet forums, and shake their heads at the number of Mexicans in their country. Then they would say that something needed to be done and that they should be in power, safely knowing that it would probably never happen and that their theories and ideas would never be tested. I said bye to Schneider, who didn't hear me, and walked to the parking lot where I would hitch a ride with a photographer going back to New York. I could still see Hiecke's house illuminated by the burning swastika, and as I got into the car I could still hear their Sieg Heils. It would be a year until I saw them again, and in the meantime some of the members would leave and others vanish.

CHAPTER 2

The Little Führer

You are kept apart that you may be separately fleeced of your
earnings. You are made to hate each other because upon
that hatred is rested the keystone of the arch of financial
despotism that enslaves you both. You are deceived and
blinded that you may not see how this race antagonism
perpetuates a monetary system which beggars both.

—Thomas E. Watson, leader of Reconstruction-era Populist Party

The first time I met Matthew was in 2011, shortly after my trip to
New Jersey with the NSM. Our meeting was completely coinci-
dental, and we would both forget about it for several years until
we met again. That summer I found myself in the woods of northern North Carolina at the invitation of the Loyal White Knights

of the Ku Klux Klan. My experience with the NSM had resulted in more questions than answers, and I figured that if I wanted to understand the white supremacist movement in America, I might as well start with the "Original Boys in the Hood," as one of their more popular T-shirts stated.

It took some driving around to find the location of the Loyal White Knights rally. That was another thing that had changed over the years. There was a time, only a few decades ago, when Klan rallies were, if not announced and attended by the public, certainly tolerated enough to be held in the open. In 2011, even in North Carolina, they had been relegated to the backwoods, as far from people as they were from relevance. At the turn-off to a narrow dirt road stood a decrepit old tractor that someone had taken the time to drape in a Confederate flag. It seemed like a clue, so I took a chance and turned left into the woods.

The Knights were a small group, and their leader, Chris Barker, was generally regarded as a joke in the movement. Short and rotund with a chubby face adorned with a donut beard, he had a reputation for drinking and accepting into his group pretty much anyone with a white face and the wherewithal to buy a robe. There were also rumors, which would later be confirmed, that he was a federal informant. (For more on Barker, see Chapter 8.) With a rap sheet littered with DUIs and arrests for violence, the FBI recruited Barker to provide evidence against an associate of his who was attempting to raise funds to build a homemade ray gun that he intended to use to kill Muslims and Barack Obama.

Barker's behavior was enough to get him kicked out of at least one Klan group and prompted Billy Snuffer, Grand Wizard of the Rebel Brigade, to say that Barker gave the Klan a black eye. Despite all this—or perhaps because of it—Barker seemed happy to invite me and promised there would be some interesting people there and that it would really give me a feel for the sanctity and fellowship that is the KKK. "You'll see that we're far from a hate group," he told me on the phone. "We're just good Christians who like the company of other Christians."

I had no idea what to expect from my first Klan rally but was nevertheless slightly disappointed as the thing seemed to be little more than a handful of guys drinking warm beer in a field. Some were bikers, others just regular folks nursing Bud Lites and making small talk in the drizzle. At one point Barker was struggling to thread his arms into a dark green robe, and for a few seconds he stumbled around the field looking like one of those inflatable advertising signs that flap their arms wildly outside car dealerships.

Some skinheads from Blood & Honor America, a semiofficial affiliate of the legendary British white power music label Blood & Honour, suddenly tore into the field in a pickup, and Matthew was among them. At the time he was running the White Student Union (WSU), a white-pride organization that patrolled the Towson University campus in Maryland to protect students from a perceived—and, in fact, entirely nonexistent—wave of black-on-white crime. He'd made some local headlines, but outside of the readership of the local student newspaper, few people had ever heard of the WSU, even within the white nationalist movement. With him were his friends Brian Scorch, of the midlevel white power band Empire Falls, and Jon Pressley, who claimed to be involved with Blood & Honor.

The Klan looked worried that their event was about to be commandeered by godless Nazis. Ever since the skinheads came on the scene in the early 1980s there has been little love lost between them and the KKK, so that night the Klan kept to themselves under a tarp they had erected between a clutch of trees and tut-tutted about the skinheads.

"Our relationship with the skins is not the best," Christian Petrie, a scrawny Klansman in his twenties, said to me. "I guess you could argue that we share the same goal, but we do things differently." In his own euphemistical way, Christian was telling me that the Klan regarded the skinheads as mindless thugs whose only redeeming quality was that they were pro-white. The skinheads mostly regarded the Klan as hopelessly outdated sticks-in-the-mud who dressed up in silly costumes and didn't drink.

Matthew, I would soon learn, didn't quite fit in either camp. He was a pragmatist and, if such a thing exists on the far right, a realist. He understood that the in-your-face violence of the skinheads was unlikely to win them any new friends and that the stigma of the Klan ensured that they would never reenter politics. Matthew wanted a modern movement, and over the next two years he worked tirelessly to grow the White Student Union to several campuses throughout the country, manned by students who worried that white people were being preyed upon by marauding blacks or nefarious Muslims. I was still chasing down various skinhead and Klan outfits around the country, but I would sometimes hear talk about Matthew and his WSU. By 2012 or 2013 he had become someone to watch on the American far right. Press stories made him out as some kind of sympathetic monster, an image he seemed to relish, guffawing as reporters confronted him with various hateful things he'd said in the past, as if it was all some kind of misunderstanding taken out of context. From what people in the movement were telling me, he wasn't a neo-Nazi, but he had secured a kind of grudging respect from white nationalists of all flavors as a smart kid on the rise and a new voice on the scene. The neo-Nazis liked him because he wasn't afraid of marching in the streets, the bloggers liked him because he had a good head on his shoulders and seemed to have a strategy to lift the movement out of the slump it had been in, and the media loved him because he was relatively charming yet unafraid to say wildly offensive things in a disturbingly casual and friendly manner.

I started emailing with him in the summer of 2014, and eventually he told me that he'd be speaking at the annual Stormfront conference in Knoxville that October and that I could meet him there.

Stormfront was the first real online forum for white supremacy, and its founder, Don Black, a former Klansman turned national socialist, was for a long time one of the most influential white nationalists in the country. However, since Stormfront's inception in 1995, the internet had become a busier place, including far-right forums and social media, which cannibalized Stormfront's monopoly on white nationalist chatter. According to a study done by George Washington University's Program on Extremism, the number of white nationalists on Twitter went up by 600 percent between 2012 and 2016. As a result Black had seen his influence as the gatekeeper to the far right's preeminent message board wane. I reached out to Black and asked if I could come to the conference, but citing extreme danger of infiltration and espionage—much like Duke Schneider and the NSM had three years earlier—I would have to make do with attending the reception at the hotel following the actual conference.

As it turned out, by "reception" Black had meant taking advantage of the Country Inn & Suites in Knoxville's policy on free cookies in the lobby, and by the time I showed up, the nationalists had devoured all of them. They were excited to see I had brought beers, because they themselves didn't have any.

Don Black, faded with age, was hunched over a cane in the corner, while David Duke, former Klan leader and former state representative for Louisiana's 81st district, looking resplendent and vital in a way that only plastic surgery can achieve, was milling around, shaking hands. Matthew was sharing a table with a retired merchant marine with white hair and a Karl Malden nose as well as a younger guy with stringy hair and a whiskery, rodent-like mustache.

"Imagine the scene from the *Star Wars* movie, where the Death Star is scanning the continent of Africa, telling the computer to kill everything but the animals," the merchant marine said, revealing a tenuous grasp of the plot of George Lucas's movie. "If you did that, you would instantly kill all the niggers on the continent and I guaran-fucking-tee you that it would become a pretty nice place to be."

He was big and powerfully built with a pock-marked face that glowed pink around the cheeks and a big paunch that peeked through the straining buttons of his shirt. He had been part of the national socialist movement in America since the 1960s and a close associate of George Lincoln Rockwell, the leader of the American Nazi Party. He had even been the driver of Rockwell's "Hate Bus," a Volkswagen bus that Rockwell had decorated with swastikas and slogans that they used to hound the freedom riders throughout the South.

"That's the only solution to this nigger problem," he continued with the air of a man who had tried many different solutions with no luck and now, almost reluctantly, found himself at the end of his rope. "Yep, we have to kill them all."

Matthew had been mostly ignoring him, talking with the rodent man who turned out to be a Slovakian called Remy who had a penchant for tying every problem in the world to the genetic inferiority of anyone not Aryan.

"Wait a minute—can you say that again?" Matthew said to the merchant marine, suddenly paying attention.

"All I was saying is that an inferior race such as the blacks doesn't deserve to live," he repeated. "They can't have nice things, and so they have got to go."

"What do you mean 'inferior race'?" Matthew asked. "There's no such thing as an inferior race. We're all the same, only different. No race has more of a right to live and prosper than another."

The man looked stricken. "Nonsense," he said. "Look at the things these niggers do. There's no way to help them."

"Even if you were right and they are an inferior race—which I don't believe they are—they would still have the right to be happy," Matthew continued. "They still have the right to exist."

"Bah," he said. "You don't know what the hell you're talking about."

Matthew wasn't invited back to Stormfront.

NINE MONTHS LATER, on a sweltering mid-July day in 2015, Matthew and I were driving east from his home in Cincinnati, toward Kentucky, where his friend Tom Pierce was hosting a flag rally in support of the Confederate flag. The floor of the passenger side of

Matthew's car had a puddle in it; water had been seeping in from a broken condenser that Matthew had neither the time nor the money to fix. The towel that Brooke, Matthew's wife, had placed there was soaked through, slowly sloshing from side to side as it relentlessly filled up. "Sorry about your shoes," Matthew said. "I've been meaning to get it fixed, but there hasn't been time lately with all the traveling."

Matthew's car, affectionately nicknamed Serenity after the spaceship in the TV show *Firefly*, made its way down a two-lane highway on the outskirts of Knoxville, Tennessee. In the last year Serenity had crisscrossed the country several times, taking Matthew from his home in Cincinnati to pretty much every state. "You got to take your message on the road if you want people to hear it," he said. He had disbanded the White Student Union and replaced it with his new party, the Traditionalist Workers Party, and was in the middle of a project of expansion, talking to as many groups and people as he could to invite them into the fold. He'd spoken to skinhead crews from Pennsylvania to California, representatives of the Greek party Golden Dawn in Queens, League of the South in Florida, and various unaffiliated nationalists across the country, all in an effort to convince them that his brand of nationalism would carry the movement into the future.

Matthew's star was rising on the far right. He'd even gotten his very own profile in the Southern Poverty Law Center's Intelligence Report, where they nicknamed him "The Little Führer," a moniker his fans had affectionately appropriated. "That 'Little Führer' stuff is just nonsense," Matthew said. "Funny though. I also enjoyed being called 'The new face of organized hate.' That was a good one. I mean, look at me—does this look like the face of organized hate? If they want to call me the new face of hate, then God bless them, but, I mean, it's clearly ridiculous. C'mon." Matthew saw himself as neither hateful nor racist, and he claimed he'd been trying to convince others on the far right that they would never get anywhere by walking around calling other races inferior. Their beef, according to Matthew, was not with a race of people but with a system that had marginalized and decimated white workers for years. Using racist epithets wasn't going to make anything better, and waving a Swastika around wasn't going to get you the kind of supporters you wanted. Even the merchant marine from Stormfront had recently been convinced by Matthew's logic and expressed interest in joining the TWP. Matthew felt he was picking up steam.

Serenity drove past endless strip malls, most of them shuttered and boarded up. Shopping trollies lingered on desolate parking lots, and graffiti covered much of the plywood that barricaded the empty storefronts. The only businesses that were open were pawn stores and payday loan peddlers that seemed to occupy every other storefront. "This is what I'm talking about," Matthew said as we rolled past a store offering quick cash, no credit needed. "This part of the country is mainly poor and white, and it's being crushed. The blacks have the NAACP and the browns have La Raza, but what does the poor, white man have? Nothing. These are towns with no internet, terrible phone connection, and the EPA has shut down all the mines. I don't care if people call me a racist or a bigot—I'm going to speak for these people. We have to help ourselves because no one else will. Nobody ever helped a hick but a hick himself."

The way Matthew saw it, diversity was the problem. It wasn't that there was anything inherently wrong with African Americans, Asians, Latinos, or even whites; it was just that they didn't get along. Multiculturalism and modernity were creating a society where no one felt at home, no one had each other's back, and no one thrived. And it wasn't just a race thing either. The way society was set up, it was pitting conflicting values against each other, forcing people to live in a culture of moral relativism and imposed principles. The United States was a country where millions of ethnicities, religions, cultures, and value systems had been thrown together and told to place nice, even though they had nothing in common.

To Matthew, one of the great American tragedies was that the South had lost the Civil War. Not because he was a fan of slavery—

he wasn't—but because it had forced the South to remain in a disastrous marriage with the North when an amicable divorce would be better for everyone. Recently he had joined the League of the South, a southern secessionist group who refused to refer to the Civil War as anything but the War of Northern Aggression. "Why shouldn't the South be allowed to secede?" he said. "It doesn't have to be antagonistic. We would be better off and so would the North. If San Francisco wants to have gay and transgender weddings, that's fine, just leave my family and my community out of it. All I'm talking about is self-determination. We have different views from the North, and I don't understand why that is a bad thing."

Matthew had given me his pitch about compassionate nationalism before. As he made clear, he wasn't advocating for sending African Americans back to Africa, interning Jews, or deporting Mexicans—which was common thinking among most groups I spoke to. He was fond of explaining how the white race wasn't smarter than other races—"Heck, it might even be dumber than most"—but that it was *his* race, and even if the whites were the dumbest people on the planet, they were still his people and he loved them.

"Why is Teach for America sending white, liberal teachers to educate kids in Detroit?" Matthew asked. "It's the White Savior complex. Black kids in Detroit should have strong, black role models from Detroit that understand them. Black communities should be policed by a black police force and have black judges. The black community doesn't need us to speak for them and stand up for them. They can stand up for themselves."

Unlike Klansmen, neo-Nazis, and white power militias, Matthew didn't envision an inevitable race war where the land would finally be purged of anyone deemed nonwhite; rather, he saw an amicable division of assets. He and his wife lived in a predominantly black neighborhood on the outskirts of Cincinnati, a city 45 percent black. If he had it his way, he and his fellow whites would cede Cincinnati to the city's black residents and go their merry way to build an enclave somewhere whiter. "Stop the hate, separate," Matthew would say, in his eyes solving a problem that had been bedeviling politicians and activists for decades simply by making it rhyme.

Yet plainly his vision created more questions than it answered. His utopia consisted of culturally homogenous enclaves of like-minded people of similar ethnic and cultural backgrounds. Who would create these enclaves, settle disputes during their creation—not all of Matthew's neighbors might be as enthusiastic about leaving Cincinnati as he was—and decide by which criteria people would get together? How would the country be divided? How do you reverse engineer a global society back into a tribal state? And perhaps the most pressing problem: not everyone wants to live in a society surrounded only by people exactly like them.

These were all questions for another day, however. For now Matthew was happy spreading the message of nationalism, setting up new chapters of his party throughout America, and nurturing awareness about pride in one's race. He would work with Nazis, Klansmen, skinheads—whatever it took to get the job done—and according to him, people were beginning to come around. "Membership is growing," he said. "Other groups want to get involved. Like Tom's guys, for instance. They're good people who want to help."

Tom Pierce and his guys were members of a white nationalist group called the 10 Milers, which meant that no member lived more than ten miles from another. Matthew liked this concept because it encouraged local activism and care for the community. Tom had invited Matthew down to speak at a protest his group was putting together against banning the Confederate flag. "You'll like Tom," Matthew had said as we drove up to his house. "He's a good ol' boy."

Tom and a friend were sitting in a white pickup truck parked in the driveway. As Serenity pulled up, Tom gave a whoop and waved a black cap out the window. He had the mannerisms of an actor who had been told to play the archetypical redneck, and he did so with relish, slapping his thigh, yipping, and hollering at even the slightest encouragement. His friend stayed behind in the car drinking a soda as Tom jumped out and bounced across the lawn to greet us. "Did you find us okay?" he asked. "If you got lost, you should have asked for White Power." He pointed toward the pickup truck. The words "White Power" were painted on the back. He had also fastened a couple of Confederate flags on the tailgate. "Yessir. Everybody around here knows White Power." He whooped again and did a little jump. "So do you know what you're going to say at this thing, Heimbach?"

"I figure I'll just do what I always do. Cross my heart, say a prayer, and wait for whatever comes out."

That amused Tom to no end. "Well, I'll tell ya. It'll be a good crowd tonight. We got good people here."

The plan was to meet at a rallying point on a Kroger's parking lot, then drive into Knoxville and wave some Confederate flags at everyone. It was pretty much a carbon copy of the last protest Matthew and Tom had staged, where they met at a Kroger's and drove through Knoxville protesting gay marriage. "Lot of gays in Knoxville," Tom said sadly. "Didn't use to be."

Soon Serenity was trailing White Power into town. To get us in the mood, Matthew put "Dixie" on the stereo and sang along. I told him that I liked Elvis's version on *An American Trilogy*, and Matthew responded that he hated that version because it included "The Battle Hymn of the Republic," which was a Civil War Northern song that disgusted him. Since the Civil War, he went on, it had been humiliation after humiliation for the South, and this recent move to ban the flag was the latest one. "It's a war on us," he said as "Dixie" was winding down. "It's a war on the South, a war on white working men and women, and a war on our values." He handed me a Red Vine and took one for himself.

I was having a hard time seeing the war he was talking about. "I think the whole notion of the white race being under siege has me a little confused," I said.

"Well, all one has to do is walk into Appalachia," Matthew said. "You'll see the poorest areas of the country where there are no relief programs, no advocates, and a cycle of poverty that is soul crushing. Whether it's teen pregnancy, drug abuse, or suicide, they are epidemics in majority white communities. These people need advocates."

In the parking lot Tom raced around handing out flyers that described the federal government's illegal and aggressive takeover of southern life. More a manifesto than a flyer, the full page of text explained how banning the flag was the latest in a long line of incursions designed to demolish southern pride, culture, and way of life. It blamed the government for economic policies that had crippled the South ever since the Civil War—a war, the flyer claimed, not fought over freeing the slaves but rather the crushing tariffs the North had supposedly leveled against the South.

"Why do the North hate you guys so much?" I asked, after reading the flyer.

"Well, shit," Tom said. "If you don't know that, you don't know much. Look at how the Feds are trying to blame our flag for this one jackass shooting everybody." A couple of days earlier avowed white supremacist Dylann Roof had walked into a black church in Charleston, South Carolina, and killed nine people. In several pictures Roof had posted online he posed with the Confederate flag. The massacre had prompted a national discussion about whether the Confederate flag was a symbol of hate. "They're using it as an excuse to attack our history. They call us racists so it becomes easier to hate us. Now, they want to force all this homosexual marrying and all this other nonsense on us, and we don't like it. The South was the last Christian nation to go to war over faith and principles, and that's what the flag means. Calling it racist is nonsense."

Tom hadn't been an activist for long but had started printing flyers and organizing rallies when he noticed that people in his community were becoming more vocal about the government telling them what to think and say. The level of anger he saw surprised even him. In the movement of pissed-off southerners, a guy driving a car called White Power discovered that he was a moderate.

"I always used to be the radical in any conversation. Now I'm a moderate, man. I got people around me talking about rising up, and I'm thinking 'Holy shit, these people are p'd off, man.' People around me are, like, 'Charge!' and there I am saying, 'Now wait a minute here, we can still do this without wrecking the Union.'"

The grievances voiced by Tom and others in the movement ranged from the petty to the downright paranoid. "Listen," said Tom, talking to a guy who was sitting in a folding chair next to his American flag–decorated F150. "I heard that the government puts some sort of chemical in our meat that makes men more feminine. Now I don't necessarily believe that, but you have to wonder sometimes."

"Yeah, I heard that too," his buddy said. "They put some kind of stuff in there. I think it's true."

"It's soy," said Matthew. "Soy increases your estrogen, and the packaged stuff you get at Walmart usually has high levels of soy in it, so no wonder men aren't acting like men anymore when we're pumping estrogen into ourselves. That's science."

"Now hold on there," said Tom. "I'm eating the same stuff everyone else does, and I ain't feminine. Maybe it's when you get saved or something it washes all that dadgum feminine soy out of your system."

"Amen," said Matthew.

Someone handed Matthew a bullhorn, and he climbed onto the back of a pickup and began his speech. If Matthew makes a weird sort of sense one on one, he uses a different tack when addressing a crowd, either because he realizes that a crowd won't get on its feet from pragmatism alone or because he feels freer to call it like he sees it in front of a friendly crowd.

"We the southerners are a people," he said. "No matter what Obama says or the federal government says, we are a people. And this flag is our symbol. We southerners are facing an attack, more than we've faced one since 1865. We need to stand against the federal government that hates everything about us. They hate our families, they hate our folk and our nation. They even hate our God."

The crowd cheered every time he mentioned the South and booed every time he mentioned the government or Obama. Matthew kept going, tossing them pounds and pounds of red meat. He spoke about how Planned Parenthood ("boo!") was gleefully chopping up and selling live fetuses with the blessing and protection of the government, and he talked about how the Civil War was fought because the South wanted a just and righteous government.

"And don't be fooled into thinking that the Republicans don't hate you too. I'd rather have an enemy that looks me square in the eye and tells me that he hates me instead of one that will smile in my face and then stab me in the back. We need to understand that both parties hate us."

He warned the crowd that the government would steal their children's futures, reducing them to aliens in a country their forefathers had built, where their culture wasn't respected and their language not even spoken.

"And when you go home to your families tonight, remember that we are under attack on every front. If the Republicans and Democrats won't represent us, then we have to stand up for ourselves as southerners. The system hates us and everything about us. If you think your children deserve better, brothers and sisters, then it is time to raise our battle flag. Not for tradition but for the future. We need a free, independent Southland. And remember: if at first you don't secede, try and try again."

"Hot damn, that guy can talk," someone said after his speech. Matthew was pretty pleased too. He'd touched on all his major issues: the government's hatred of the South, economic destruction of the homeland, and the importance of family and folk in a confusing and frightening world.

After the speech everyone piled into their cars and onto their motorcycles and rode the ten or so miles into Knoxville center, honking and hooting as they went. "This feels amazing," Matthew said as he drove. "Can you feel the change here? People are coming to. America is changing. They can call us racist, but the fact is that there are hundreds of people here celebrating their heritage. Who cares what they call us."

Matthew's friend Scott Hess was in the back, clutching a flag pole as he waved a Confederate flag out the window of the moving car. A sudden gust of wind tore it from his hands and sent it fluttering up in the hot July air before coming to rest on the shoulder of the highway.

Matthew was livid. "Gosh darnit, you dropped it, Scott? Seriously?"

"Well, I'm sorry," Scott protested. "We were going really fast, and it was hard to hold on. The pole was digging into my fingers."

"I can't believe we lost the Battle Flag out the window during a flag rally," Matthew said. "I'm going to pull over and you're going to run as fast as you can to get it."

He slammed the brakes and turned onto the grassy shoulder. Scott, short and rotund, with strawberry blond hair that framed a plump and red-cheeked face, jumped out of the car and waddled as fast as he could against traffic toward where the flag had alighted. Matthew watched as he ran in the rearview mirror. He put his hand on his face and groaned.

"Sometimes what we do is embarrassing."

Through the rear window we watched as Scott, dodging traffic as best he could, grabbed the flag from the ground and shook it off before waving happily at us. He shouted something inaudible before starting back for the car.

"I said I got it," he said as he fell into the backseat a few seconds later, out of breath and cherry red. "I think I twisted my ankle."

"Let's just hope nobody saw us drop the flag," Matthew said as he tore back onto the highway.

The parade ended outside a Walmart, where Matthew suggested they all take a group photo to show their displeasure at Walmart deciding to remove the Confederate flag from all their merchandise.

"Since there are so many people here and so many flags," Matthew said. "Why don't you join me in a couple of verses of 'Dixie'?"

Matthew was about the only one there who knew the words, but the crowd hummed enthusiastically.

"It's exactly like Matt said," Pierce told me as the crowd sang. "Our whole Western civilization is going down the shitter, and us white folks have to stand up for once. I've traveled the world and seen the destruction. Appalachia is the last bastion of Christian civilization, but unless we fight, we will lose it all."

Matthew, who by his own admission couldn't carry a tune in a bucket, veered in and out of the song. How it sounded wasn't important; being there as southerners, coming together as groups was. To him this event was proof that it wasn't a shared hatred toward other races that brought them together but rather a shared love of tribe. Everyone there was a brother or a sister, and Matthew realized that perhaps this was the key to bringing the far right together to celebrate what bound them as well as to fight those who would keep them down. If others wanted to call him a Nazi or the Little Führer, then that was on them. Matthew didn't have time to care. He was going to build something special.

CHAPTER 3

The Defender of Western Civilization

Every civilization sees itself as the center of the world and writes its history as the central drama of human history.

—Samuel P. Huntington, "The Clash of Civilizations and the Remaking of World Order"

One of Matthew's earliest memories is of his mother being worried. It was an evening in 1995, and like they always did, Matthew and his parents were watching the six o'clock news on their old wood-box TV. Matthew was sitting cross-legged on the white and brown carpet in the living room. His dad, Carl Heimbach, sat in his usual place in a recliner along the wall, and his mother, Margaret, was walking in and out from the kitchen, ostensibly checking on dinner, while she cast anxious glances at the screen. It was during the tail end of the O. J. Simpson trial, and the country was speculating not only about whether Simpson did it but also about what would happen if he was found guilty. Just three years earlier, in 1992, riots tore LA apart after the police who were filmed beating Rodney King were acquitted. These memories were fresh in everybody's minds, and as the newscaster discussed the pending Simpson verdict, the screen flashed to the riots' footage of truck driver Reginald Denny being pulled from the driver's seat of his truck and beaten mercilessly. One of the assailants pelted a mango-sized brick into the side of his head from point-blank range. The footage showed Denny slumping over onto his face as blood pooled around him.

"It'll be the same thing all over again if O. J. goes to jail," Matthew's dad said, and his mom left the living room again. She liked the news but only if they showed happy stories. Preferably something with animals.

Matthew was born in 1991, the oldest of three siblings, in Poolesville, a small town in Montgomery County, Maryland, on the outskirts of Washington, DC. Montgomery County is a peculiar mix of the bucolic and the suburban, where farmers and DC lobbyists share a tepid coexistence and the county's Confederate history and pride at times clash with the liberal values of the DC newcomers. The family lived on a quiet, leafy street, not far from the school where both parents worked, in a tidy, midcentury house with white siding and cherry-red shutters that Matthew's mother took care to paint every spring. In front of the house was a small yard with evergreen bushes that his mother tended meticulously and that each summer blossomed with hundreds of small red flowers.

His neighborhood was overwhelmingly white, and most of his friends grew up either Methodist or Baptist. Matthew's dad was a lapsed Lutheran, but because Matthew's mom was a devout Catholic, he had converted to make her happy. None of the adults in his life growing up were particularly political, although his grandfather would keep the conservative pundit Sean Hannity's show on in the background as Matthew and his brother and sister played on the rug.

His childhood was, for the most part, a happy one. Matthew's maternal grandparents lived close by and took care of him and his siblings whenever Margaret wasn't around. His grandfather, Roger Sears, was the head of the Izaak Walton League, a national organization that promotes outdoorsmanship and conservation. He would take Matthew and his siblings on long hikes, teaching his grandkids to shoot and recognize animals. As Matthew got older he would spend countless hours roaming his grandparents' forty acres of streams, hills, and woods, cataloguing the things he saw and asking his parents and grandparents about it later. His mom would say that she couldn't even take him for a walk down the block without him driving her to distraction with questions about every bug and leaf he found on the street.

Margaret Heimbach coached the Poolesville Indians, the women's basketball team at Poolesville High School, where Matthew's dad taught history and would eventually become the athletic director. His bookshelves at home were crowded with encyclopedias and history books that Matthew would leaf through. As a kid Matthew was close with his dad, and the two spent hours talking about history and, particularly, the Civil War, which fascinated and terrified him in equal measure. Poolesville had sided with the Confederacy during the war, and there were still those in town who took pride in their southern heritage. Matthew sided with his dad, who was a Yankee.

Because his family—his mother at least—was Catholic, Matthew was enrolled in Catholic school from first to fourth grade, when he transferred to Poolesville Elementary School. He was a smart kid and got good grades, and when he flunked out of chorus because he couldn't carry a tune, he convinced his teachers to allow him to make up the lost credits by teaching a thirty-minute class in history every Friday. He would spend hours preparing, taking his dad's notes from his high school history lessons and adapting them for an elementary school audience. He brought in clear sheets of overhead plastic on which he wrote names, dates, and battles, focusing on his two favorite wars: the Civil War and the Vietnam War, as those were also his dad's favorites.

In 2001 the Montgomery County school board decided that the name "Poolesville Indians" was offensive and needed to be changed. The school board, along with the Maryland Commission on Indian Affairs, had recently voted to ban all Native American–themed names and mascots from county schools and offered Poolesville High School $80,000 to remove the Indians' logo—the profile of a stern-looking Native American brave in a feather headdress—from all uniforms, signs, and buildings and replace it with something more fitting of modern times. Matthew, who had grown up with the Poolesville Indians and spent endless Fridays watching his mom's team play, was offended. And he wasn't alone. The town, in a show of defiance when offered the chance to vote on a new name for the team, overwhelmingly voted for the Poolesville Indians. Someone even painted the words "Go Indians" on the town water tower. As the local Poolesvillians were mocked in the national news as backward rednecks and racists, the board decided that the team would now be known as the Falcons—and that was that. Matthew had his first taste of being labeled a racist. It stuck with him.

BEING A PRECOCIOUS KID, Matthew got into politics when he started high school. As a teenager, mostly to piss off his parents, he fell into left-wing politics. Growing up, most of his friends were Baptists, and as he got older he began questioning what they believed. Some of the more outlandish dogma, such as creationism, offended his love of both history and science, and he began showing up for meetings of his high school's Christian Club full of questions. He would ask them how it was possible to believe that humans once rode dinosaurs, or how it made sense that the earth was really only six thousand years old and that all evidence to the contrary was just red herrings placed there by God to test us. He'd grown up reading the Bible and became adept at pointing out inconsistencies between the Old and New Testament and religious tenets that to him seemed bizarre or cruel. He had inherited a fierce anti-abortion stance from his Catholic mother, and the lack of action from Christians to stop the killing of millions of innocent babies disgusted him. He met with priests who told him about the importance of standing up for the lives of innocents and then watched how they never put their words into action. Once he asked a priest what reason, other than his own cowardice, there was not to kill a doctor who was planning on performing abortions—surely it was worth taking the life of one man to save many. As Matthew recalled, all he got in reply was a lot of hemming and hawing about not killing. Matthew never planned on killing any doctors, but the complete lack of spiritual conviction and convincing answers from religious leaders made them seem weak and pathetic. If they couldn't even fight for the lives of the unborn, then what good were they?

To strengthen his arguments he began reading books by atheist writers such as Richard Dawkins and Christopher Hitchens, which in turn introduced him to the leftist politics of Noam Chomsky. This was during the early days of the George W. Bush administration, and the more Matthew read, the more he thought he recognized the absurdities of the day. As he saw it, the United States was imposing its values on defenseless states, demanding that they let America play world police in exchange for Coca-Cola and whatever version of democracy the neocons in Washington, DC, saw fit to bestow upon them. At home his childhood version of the Christian faith was being distorted by Jerry Falwell Jr.–style evangelicals who preached that Jesus wanted you to make money and be rich. As far as he could tell, there was no longer such a thing as compassionate conservatism, and hucksters who put Christianity to work in support of the government's imperialism were co-opting whatever goodwill toward mankind American Christians once had. The whole thing disgusted him.

A friend of his had a sister at Towson University, and once a week she gave him a ride to campus to attend meetings of the Socialist Student Union, where he sat in awe listening to guest speakers and the older kids discussing the dangerous and profoundly unjust traditions of American imperialism. At one of these meetings one of the college students gave Matthew a CD by 1960s radical folk singer Phil Ochs, and as he slipped the disc into his CD player and heard Ochs sing about America being the cops of the world, Matthew's world was changed.

From then on, he devoured any piece of political folk music he could get his hands on. It wasn't so much the peacenik sentiment of the songs that grabbed him but rather the fundamental unfairness of the United States imposing its will on other people.

Once, after a concert at Towson, Matthew cornered the anarchist folk singer David Rovics and told him how important his music was to him and that it had given him a sense of purpose. Rovics smiled and told him to never give up. Matthew was impressed that a star like Rovics had taken the time to talk to a nobody like him, and he came away inspired.

In high school Matthew fell in with the theater crowd and started building sets and decorations for school plays. He never tried his hand at acting but did discover that he was good at building things. He also liked the people he met through the theater. Most of them were left leaning like him, and many of the girls were impressed by the fact that he regularly hung out with college kids at Towson and that he seemed to know his way around an argument.

Around the same time Matthew and his grandmother, mostly for fun, got into genealogy. Matthew discovered that one of his ancestors, a Joseph R. James from North Carolina, had fought for the Confederacy in the Civil War. He was still exceedingly fond of history, even then picturing himself following in his dad's footsteps and becoming a history teacher, and the revelation that his own blood had fought in the war prompted him to go to meetings at the local chapter of the Descendants of Confederate Veterans. He began identifying more and more with his ancestors, and through Civil War reenactments he began seeing the war differently—not as a struggle to liberate slaves by a benign North as he had always been taught but instead as a struggle for Southern freedom in the face of blatant Northern aggression. As he looked at the world he lived in, he couldn't help but recognize the forces that drove modern US ambitions in the world as the same ones that fueled the Civil War: not benevolence but a malevolent hunger for power.

His newfound southern identity was causing friction in other areas of his life. He still went to meetings at the Socialist Student Union at Towson, but he fretted that they were getting caught up with small issues and not focusing on anti-imperialism. Gay rights and feminism were all well and good—Matthew was still an atheist at that time, and the culture wars didn't really interest him, except for the abortion issue, on which he was vehemently on the side of the right to life—but what good was social justice in a fundamentally unjust world where the United States trampled around like a bull in a china shop? He had also been reading about how immigration was really no more than a tool developed by capitalists to further their own agenda, so it frustrated him when his socialist friends took up issues such as immigration reform when it seemed so clear that immigration and socialism were mutually exclusive. As he saw it, immigrants from developing countries provided cheap labor for the fat-cat capitalists, and he was flabbergasted that his fellow socialists couldn't see that.

He was also becoming increasingly frustrated with the petty and meaningless squabbles within the group that made it all but impossible to get anything done. There were Trotskyites who were endlessly preoccupied with the Spanish Civil War, Leninists who went on and on about the need for a Bolshevik revolution in the United States and about how the Trotskyites fundamentally got the role of the proletariat wrong, Marxists who felt like the Leninists had perverted Marx's vision of Marxist Bolshevism, and finally the Maoists who said they were all wrong and that the revolution needed to come from the rural districts of America and not the urban workforce. Matthew didn't know how to fight US imperialism, but he felt that if there was going to be any chance of success, one would need to reach regular, working people, not sitting around a campus discussing the finer points of General Francisco Franco's fascist regime.

During a visit to the library Matthew picked up a copy of a book that would solidify his political shift. *Death of the West*, published in 2001, was Pat Buchanan's polemical tirade on how everything from socialism to immigration was ensuring the death of the white race. Buchanan was a former power player inside the Republican Party, advising both Presidents Nixon and Reagan, but when he failed to secure the GOP presidential nomination in two primaries running—1992 and 1996—Buchanan veered to the right, leaving the Republican Party in 1999 and warning that "this year I believe is our last chance to save our republic before she disappears into the godless New World Order that our elites are constructing in betrayal of everything for which our Founding Fathers fought and lived and died."

Railing against both Democrats and Republicans as unable and unwilling to "drain this political swamp"—a debut of what would become a mantra in a successful presidential campaign sixteen years later—Buchanan went on to defeat his biggest rival in the Reform Party primaries and the person who would eventually go on to use much of his rhetoric to win the presidency: Donald J. Trump. Although his campaign after the primaries went nowhere, his rhetoric and ideas not only inspired a generation of far-right activists but also gave rise to a new American nationalism.

Paleo-conservatism has deep roots in American society, with much of its ideological detritus going back to the Old Right—the conservative movement that fought hard against Roosevelt's New Deal—and the wildly isolationist and anti-Semitic John Birch Society. The John Birch Society (JBS), named after an American missionary killed in China whom its founder, Robert W. Welch Jr., believed to be the first casualty of the Cold War, was a fiercely anticommunist proponent of very limited government.

Founded in 1958 by Welch—a man so eminently paranoid that he once accused President Eisenhower of being "a dedicated, conscious agent of the Communist conspiracy" and alleged that the US government was "under operational control of the Communist Party"—the JBS institutionalized the virulent xenophobia and isolationist tendencies that would later propel Pat Buchanan to fame and Donald Trump into the White House. Although the JBS is remembered primarily for its members' inveterate fear of anything that smacked of communism, it reserved much of its ire for the fight against civil and equal rights in America. Even this, however, was couched in an ostensible fight against the Soviet menace. In an advertorial in the *Palm Beach Post* from October 31, 1965, a JBS representative explained that while the Society had nothing against civil rights per se, the Civil Rights Movement was founded by communist agitators acting on behalf of the Soviet regime, much like future paleo-cons and nationalists would dismiss both feminism and social justice movements as false-flag operations instigated by the insidious skullduggery of global Zionism. Indeed, the JBS took an early stand against the so-called New World Order, a perceived global, socialist world government led by liberal *financiers*, a common code word for Jews. To this day remaining JBS members warn of the dangers of the United Nations as a first step toward a complete loss of US sovereignty.

The rise of Barry Goldwater—no stranger to race-baiting himself—coupled with the ascendancy of the brand of conservatism espoused by the *National Review*, temporarily broke the back of the John Birch Society and, by extension, paleo-conservatism in America. By that time, however, many of the Society's most ardent zealots had moved on, building a radical and at times violent strain of white nationalism upon the foundation of America First xenophobia. For example, after leaving the JBS, Robert Matthews became one of America's most notorious far-right terrorists, performing a streak of violent robberies and, in 1984, killing the Jewish radio host Alan Berg. Gordon Kahl was also a member of the society before his foray into the antigovernment world of the

Posse Commitatus ended with the death of two federal agents as well as the firefight that, in 1983, took Kahl's own life.

The same forces that had vanquished the JBS almost three decades earlier fueled the rise of Pat Buchanan's brand of paleoconservatism. Weary of the neocons' interventionism and worried about rising immigration, the Republican base was ready to accept a more isolationist strain of conservative politics, and Buchanan, having been a vocal critic of the first Iraq War and a furious opponent of the North American Free Trade Agreement (NAFTA), was able to capitalize, despite the racism and anti-Semitism running through his politics.

Matthew found himself enthralled by the urgency of Buchanan's message. He not only shared Matthew's sense of moral decay but also railed against US leaders' policies in a way Matthew had never read before. In *The Death of the West* Buchanan argued that socialism, liberal values, and expansive government had led America down a road to ruin from which there was almost no escape without major upheaval. Then, in his book *A Republic, Not an Empire*, Buchanan scolded American policy makers for their jingoistic ways, arguing that the United States had no place meddling in other nations' affairs. According to Buchanan, the baby boomers, complacent from a childhood in front of the TV and with no great war to forge them like their parents had, were as decadent as they were entitled, demanding equal rights not just for African Americans but also—and in Buchanan's view perhaps more shockingly—women. Weaving an intricate web of cause and effect, Buchanan claimed that women's rights not only led to promiscuity and moral collapse but eventually the very demise of the white race. According to him, "doing one's own thing" had subverted the perpetuation of the white race.

Although Matthew wasn't particularly concerned about promiscuity and declining morals, he was concerned about US imperialism. In Buchanan he found a kindred spirit and, more importantly, a guide to the world of right-wing politics. He left the socialist group at Towson behind and instead focused on organizing at his own high school. In 2008 the first Black Student Union was formed at Poolesville High School, and Matthew decided to form a White Student Union in response. In his mind he formed the White Student Union out of a sense of fairness: if the African American kids got their own union, then so should the white kids. Fair's fair, political correctness be damned. Besides, Poolesville was an overwhelmingly white town, and all the black kids sat together in the cafeteria anyway, so if the races were segregating themselves naturally, then it followed that the white students should have all the same things that black kids had. But the school didn't see it that way. Matthew had gathered the requisite number of signatures to form his union, but the school's principal, Deena Levine, still refused permission, saying that the very notion of a union for white students was offensive. Matthew was furious. The school leadership, he determined, was made up of a bunch of weak cowards. Of course, he realized that a white student union would offend some people, but wasn't that the point of fairness? Nobody deserved special treatment, and if that pissed some people off, that was just too bad.

During his senior year Matthew's parents split up and his dad moved in with his new girlfriend, pretty much severing all ties with Matthew, his brother, sister, and mom. A devout Catholic, Margaret never agreed to the divorce, even keeping her ex-husband's name, despite the ignoble nature of the breakup. Matthew was crushed. He'd been close with his dad and looked up to him, and now his dad was out of his life. It would be years until they spoke again. Matthew was seventeen and becoming increasingly ardent in his views. He lived in a good school district and hated the sight of kids from poorer neighborhoods being bused in. He resented the rich, DC families in his town and assumed they resented him too. Once, during a school debate on immigration, he called his Hispanic opponent a "wetback" and told him to get the hell out of his country. He recognized Buchanan's writings in the world around him. If race really wasn't important, then why did black kids mostly hang out with black kids, white kids with white kids, and Hispanic kids with Hispanic kids? Also, why could black kids talk about black power, but that one time he wore a T-shirt with a Confederate flag a black kid called him a racist and smacked the back of his head?

By fall of 2009, when he enrolled at Montgomery College in a neighboring town thirty minutes away, Matthew was an avowed paleo-con. He'd also started making his way back to Catholicism, realizing that although faith wasn't key to who he was as a person, Christianity nevertheless formed the foundation of the white race. His politics had hardened into a worldview in which the white race represented the pinnacle of human endeavor, and he believed that most if not all major human achievements in the last centuries could be attributed to whites. Eventually, he believed, the world would see a clash of civilizations. There was no getting along with other cultures and religions because the future was a zero-sum game in which the white race either prevailed or vanished. That is why he started coming to school with a T-shirt that said, "Everything I Need to Know About Islam I Learned on 9/11."

He majored in history and was vocal in class. He liked to provoke, and according to his teachers, he wasn't very popular with the other students in class, save for a couple of friends who hung on his every word. Sitting behind a laptop that had a sticker that said, "If I Knew the Trouble They Would Cause I Would Have Picked the Cotton Myself," he would lob racist and incendiary comments around no matter what topics the class was discussing. Once, during a lecture on lynchings in the South, he said that at least the lynching saved the state the expenses of a trial.

One of his professors, Dr. Joseph C. Thompson, remembers him as a clever kid who liked to argue but whom he could never quite figure out. Matthew wasn't the first conservative kid to walk through his door nor was he the first antigovernment or racist kid, yet Matthew didn't fit any of the regular boxes. Sure, he was far right and conservative, but he was also fiercely pro–workers unions. Also, for an arch conservative, he had little interest in the culture-war issues—beyond abortion—that normally animated conservatives. What drove him seemed to be a profound worry for the future of the white race. Once, Dr. Thompson told him that demographers estimate that by sometime between 2040 and 2050 Caucasians will no longer be in the majority in the United States and asked Matthew what he thought about that. "That terrifies me," Matthew had said. "Does it not scare you?" Matthew would often spend hours in Dr. Thompson's office, arguing with his liberal professor. "He was always polite during our discussions," Dr. Thompson recalled, "and it was never ugly." Most of the time they discussed race or history, and Dr. Thompson sometimes got the feeling that Matthew was using their meetings to hone his arguments, often coming in and blustering about one thing or another, then becoming quiet when his professor gave him a rebuttal. Other times he wondered if Matthew was perhaps using their meetings to talk him off the ledge. Dr. Thompson suspected that Matthew's politics were taking him in a direction he didn't necessarily want to go in. He had noticed that Matthew's clique of fellow conservatives had begun peeling off as Matthew's viewpoints became increasingly outrageous, and he wondered whether perhaps Matthew was looking for someone to tell him that he was wrong emphatically enough to make him change course.

Another of Matthew's teachers, Dr. Kurt Borkman, one of the only conservative professors at Montgomery and a devout Lutheran, remembers Matthew as an "intellectual arsonist," seemingly more interested in provoking than convincing others. Both Thompson and Borkman regarded Matthew as "smart" or "clever," but neither was ever sure he was intelligent. Dr. Thompson said he was smart because he could recite facts but perhaps not intelligent because he never seemed to give the facts his own interpretation. Dr. Borkman saw him as someone who was clearly clever but wondered how he wasn't intelligent enough to see through the blatant pseudoscience behind the paleo-conservative arguments.

As with Dr. Thompson, Matthew would spend hours in Dr. Borkman's office discussing history, and like his colleague, Dr. Borkman would try to steer the young ideologue away from his increasingly racist and hardline views. In particular he felt that Matthew could be guided away from the path he was on and tried to push against Matthew's most bombastic arguments. But despite the best efforts of the teachers Matthew most looked up to, it wasn't enough. Matthew continued to move steadily further right.

In his sophomore year Matthew discovered Youth for Western Civilization (YWC), a national organization with local chapters that perfectly summed up his politics at the time. Not only were they against immigration and multiculturalism, but they also saw odious forces working to undermine Western society by advancing both.

Formed in 2005 by student activist Kevin DeAnna, YWC sought to "defend Western culture" from the perceived threats of immigration and liberalism. Although the organization claimed it wasn't racist, its fetishization of Western (i.e., white) culture and close association with known racists placed it far to the right of other paleo-cons. In many ways YWC, which boasted a few hundred members when Matthew discovered it, was a precursor to what would become the alt-right movement.

Matthew met DeAnna in 2010 at CPAC, an annual convention for conservatives outside Washington, DC, and was immediately inspired. YWC was expanding, adding chapters at universities all over the country, and Matthew wanted to set one up at Montgomery but couldn't get the faculty sponsorship required to start an official student group. Matthew would have better luck when he transferred from Montgomery College to the larger Towson University at the start of his junior year. There he threw himself into YWC. He eventually managed to recruit a professor to serve as their faculty adviser and soon was the head of the brand-new Towson University branch of YWC.

Politically YWC was far to the right of mainstream Republicans but shared almost no ground with the thuggish skinheads and Nazis on the outer fringes. For one, they were supportive of Israel. Rather than stern speeches, their activities, although offensive to most and certainly racist, were tongue in cheek, and their goal was as much provocation as it was political advocacy. Once, they held a "Straight Pride Parade" in open mockery of the gay civil rights movement. Another time they hosted an "Affirmative Action Bake Sale," where they sold cupcakes to students at varying prices, depending on who the buyer was. White males were charged $2, Hispanics $1.50, African Americans $1, and Jews 75 cents. The student body was outraged. Various student groups organized protests, including Jewish students at Montgomery who weren't buying YWC's stated support of Israel.

Matthew had been pondering the so-called JQ—the Jewish question—for some time. The Jewish question has, for centuries, been used as a handy tool to disguise blatant racism in ostensibly anthropologic curiosity. The question, throughout its many iterations, boils down to whether Jews should be considered white and what their place in (white-led) society should be. Matthew was now beginning to believe that not only were they not white, but they were also not friendly to whites like him.

He had been reading revisionist history about World War II and the Holocaust that, to him, seemed to prove that the murder of 6.6 million Jews was not only likely an exaggeration but probably a fabrication that in large part benefited its supposed victims. A popular number thrown around in revisionist circles is roughly a tenth of the number historians agree upon, often even lower, although no serious scholarship supports this. The higher number of 6.6 million is, according to some Holocaust deniers, not only wildly inflated but also a tool used by Jews ever since in order to guilt the world into giving them what they want.

Matthew had now moved on from Buchanan and was testing the much more frigid waters of far-right writers such as David Duke. Duke—a former Grand Wizard in the KKK, former one-term representative in the Louisiana House of Representatives, twice-failed presidential candidate, demagogue, talk show host, and strident Holocaust denier—pinned on the Jews not only the woes of the world but also many of the societal advances he and his fellow arch-conservative racists so loathed. According to Duke, both abortion rights and the feminist movement are schemes hatched by the Jews to decimate the Gentile populations of the world. Not only that, Duke claims that Jews were behind communism and, by extension, the Gulag, once again in a brazen attempt at undermining white, European culture.

Matthew embraced Duke's ideas. For a long time he felt that Jewish groups on campus vilified him, even though he had—ostensibly—supported Israel. In his mind he had never had a problem with Jews, but they seemed to have a problem with him, attacking him at rallies, calling him a Nazi, and threatening him and his family. Once the YWC were attacked for protesting the University Muslim Society over their invitation to a speaker whom Matthew and his friends saw as a radical Islamic. Matthew believed the ringleaders behind this attack were Jewish, and he struggled to understand why Jewish students would have a problem with the YWC protesting radical Islam. Why should Matthew go out of his way to support a people who clearly hated him? As a child he had always been taught that Jews were God's chosen people and that he had to be on their side, but the books he was reading proved that God's chosen people were the enemies of his race.

Being the leader of the Towson chapter of YWC was Matthew's entrance into the public political arena, and as the leader of a group basically known as "the campus Nazis," it was a baptism of fire. Other students hurled abuse at him in the quad, and he was deeply unpopular in class. Except for his regular posse of hangers-on who had followed him from Montgomery, he didn't have many friends at school, and the few friends he did have outside of YWC were distancing themselves from him. One of his friends in YWC suffered a nervous breakdown and left school. Matthew was threatened, and his family received abusive phone calls. His mother begged him to stop, but despite being ostracized and ridiculed, he kept at it, convincing himself that his work was far more important than his own comfort.

He started going to church again, at first on Sundays and then every day. He read old religious texts, soon reaching the conclusion that the weakness and fecklessness that had made him despise the Church was a result of modernity. The Church wasn't weak, only the people who had been running it for the last five hundred years, ever since the East-West Schism that divided the Roman Catholic Church and the Eastern Orthodox Church. Orthodoxy felt right to Matthew. It was strong and often merciless. It was masculine for men and feminine for women, celebrating the differences of the genders rather than claiming that genders were equal. Every day he knelt by the statue of his favorite saint, St. Michael, who in the orthodox faith is invoked for protection against invasion from enemies. As he prayed, Matthew looked up at the statue, the great archangel holding a flaming sword, and imagined himself the protector of his people and his race.

After being condemned by the Southern Poverty Law Center (SPLC), a nonprofit based in Alabama that specializes in monitoring far-right activity in America, the faculty sponsor withdrew his support, and YWM at Towson folded. Once again Matthew was outraged by what he saw as a refusal to support basic fairness. He couldn't for the life of him understand the furious and sometimes violent reactions to YWC. Every kind of minority got to organize, but as soon as white students organized in a way that signaled pride in their race, everyone was suddenly all up in arms about Nazis on campus. The fact that Towson University was more than two-thirds white and that student unions had been formed for groups who found themselves in the minority was not something Matthew considered.

Throughout its brief existence YWC had been called the White Student Union by its critics, and so Matthew decided that if that was what people decided they were, that was what they would be. With that, the White Student Union (WSU) was born. The organization, which had seventeen members at the time it was founded, was meant to be a safe space from what Matthew had come to believe was deliberate anti-white discrimination at Towson. Somewhere over the course of his time with YWC, Matthew had decided that Towson was becoming increasingly hostile to whites, particularly white women, who he believed were targets of racially based slurs and sexualized violence. Matthew believed that, like St. Michael, it was his job to protect his kin from the predatory nature of other races.

Having washed its hands completely of YWC, Towson University wanted nothing to do with Matthew's new group, but that didn't stop him from staging protests on campus and arranging nighttime patrols in search of crime. Despite a complete lack of evidence, Matthew believed that the school was in the middle of a dramatic crime wave and that white students often were its victims, so he and his friends armed themselves with Maglite flashlights and pepper spray, stalking the campus grounds looking for evildoers. Although no delinquents were ever foiled, Matthew did find plenty of national attention, landing him on newscasts and in articles almost overnight, announcing him as the new face of racism in America. Journalists and pundits liked him because he was gregarious and affable and always willing to talk to them while at the same time putting a new spin on old clichés about racial separation. It was in the WSU that Matthew first debuted his signature "live and let live form of racism," describing later, in a documentary produced by Vice, how he believed that "especially the black community will find areas in the South, areas like Detroit, where they can have their own homelands, we don't have to be antagonistic toward them. And if you want to sell yourself and your children down the river of multiculturalism, you can do that. But we deserve the right to exist, deserve the right to defend our culture, and deserve the right to have a future for our culture."

The attention amused Matthew, but his family had had enough. Matthew had been regularly making the news, and it was causing friction with his mother and siblings. During Easter in 2012, Matthew's senior year, at a family gathering he got into an argument with his aunt about the Trayvon Martin shooting, in which he firmly defended the shooter, George Zimmerman. After that Matthew's aunt made it clear that she no longer wanted to be in the same room as Matthew, and as a result, he was asked to stay away at Thanksgiving. Matthew's grandfather died the day after. Although his mom asked him not to come to the funeral, Matthew, who had loved his grandfather dearly, still showed up, sitting awkwardly with his family who didn't want him there. He left after the funeral without saying good-bye. It would be the last time he saw his family.

He returned to Towson and threw himself into his new venture, the WSU. He would take what he learned about organizing during his time with YWS and use it to expand his group to colleges across America. And from there he would build a movement.

CHAPTER 4

Kiggy

Souvenir collectors cut pieces of clothing from the two bodies
and bark from the lynching tree. One person took a shoe
home to display. . . . The most prized souvenir was rope, cut
in small segments: dozens of spectators took pieces home.

—James. H. Madison, *A Lynching in the Heartland:*
Race and Memory in America, chapter 1

"They're all criminals, and that's just about all there is to it," Doll
Baby said. She was sitting by a table overlooking the parking lot
of a Shoney's Restaurant in Johnson City, Tennessee, talking ani-
matedly, throwing her hands into the air as if what she was saying
was a complete no-brainer, and she couldn't believe she even had
to explain the many reasons why black people were more likely

to be a burden on society than white people. Her real name was Andrea, but for as long as she could remember everybody had just called her Doll Baby, so she had gotten it tattooed in big, pink cursive just below her belly button, next to a couple of Hello Kitty tattoos. She was twenty-five years old, but her bubbly voice and quick, sing-songy laugh that opened her face in a wide smile made her seem younger. She had a sweetness about her, at least when she wasn't talking about marauding black people, a subject that greatly upset her. It was the end of summer 2015, and Doll Baby and her boyfriend, Dan Elmquist, had driven to Tennessee from Kentucky in Dan's old BMW to take part in a funeral for the son of Gary Delp, the Grand Wizard of the Virgil Griffin White Knights. Matthew was there, and for the last thirty minutes I'd been listening to the three friends discuss the Baltimore riots after the death of Freddie Gray in police custody, while another friend of theirs, Eric Woodzell, a former neo-Nazi turned Klansman, shuttled back and forth to the buffet, loading up monstrous servings of scrambled eggs and gravy.

Matthew wasn't really keen on the Klan scene and had mostly stayed away since the rally in North Carolina where I'd first met him in 2011, but he and Dan were buddies, and if Matthew was serious about being the one to finally unite the disparate groups of the far right, he'd need to suck it up and see if the Klan had something to offer. Since our trip to Tennessee and Tom Pierce's flag rally, Matthew had been hard at work trying to build a coalition of sorts under the Traditionalist Workers Party. He'd made some headway, recruiting the Keystone State Skinheads, a crew from Pennsylvania, as well as their counterparts in Oakland, Golden State Skinheads, but it was hardly enough to call it a grand alliance, and he needed to cut a wider swath through the far right. As much as he disliked the KKK, he certainly wasn't above hearing what they had to say, and who knows—they might be persuaded to come around to his way of thinking.

"All I'm saying is the way these black folks are misusing the welfare system and looting and misbehaving, they should be arrested," said Doll Baby in an exasperated Kentucky drawl before taking a swig from a tall glass of sweet tea. "They should be made to suffer the way they make us suffer, and then they should be killed. Now, I'm sorry, I don't mean to get upset or angry about this, but I just can't help it."

I asked Doll Baby how they were making her suffer.

"Well, we're paying for their welfare, aren't we?" she said. "That's coming out of my paycheck."

Dan shook his head. "See how she gets?" he said. "When she's like this I try and stay out of it or she'll tear me a new one."

"You like it when I get all racist," Doll Baby laughed and pouted.

"Damned right, I love it," he said.

Dan and Doll Baby had been dating for a while, and things were going well. Doll Baby was his first girlfriend who had been raised in the white power movement, and Dan loved that about her. For the first time, he had been able to sit down with his in-laws and discuss his political beliefs without getting chased out of the house.

Matthew sat across from him and made a slight grimace as Doll Baby spoke. His problem with the Klan wasn't necessarily their racism—Matthew had told me time and time again about the problems of living in a predominantly black part of Cincinnati; instead, it was the completely overt nature of that racism. If nationalism was ever to become palatable outside the boundaries of the far right, they would need to change some of their messaging. White supremacy would never attract a wider audience, and it was counterproductive to what he was trying to achieve. He firmly believed that nationalism didn't need to be racist and that once he explained to blacks and browns that his nationalism was also their nationalism—it was about the right to self-determination for races—then real change might be achieved. However, it would be a tough sell if his comrades in the movement ran around shouting slurs and claiming that whites were the master race. The Klan was pure white supremacy, and Matthew knew that it was an anchor that would drag the entire movement down.

Unlike most Klansmen, Dan hadn't grown up in the Klan nor did he have relatives who were members, but he claimed to have ancestors who were in the German Luftwaffe, although he never expounded on it. Sometimes he joked that he was the latest in a long line of hateful people. According to Dan, he was a mess before joining the Klan. After high school he had followed the remaining members of the Grateful Dead around the country, doing whatever drugs he could get his hands on and getting into fights. He claimed that Jesus and the Klan had saved him.

When I first met him he was married and miserable. His wife was making him choose between the Klan and her, and divorce was clearly coming down the pike. On top of that, he had just lost his second job in two months. He'd been a loader at the local Walmart but got fired due to downsizing. During his time there he'd thrown out his back doing thirteen-hour shifts loading and unloading boxes, and his doctor prescribed painkillers. He got his next job, sandblasting paint off sheets of metal, through a temp agency, but the agency had neglected to tell his new employer about his pain medication, and when his drug test came up positive for opioids, they let him go. Broke and about to lose his house in a divorce, Dan's only network for support was his Klan family. Since then his divorce was finalized, and his ex-wife had taken the house. He'd been doing odd jobs, but the back injury made manual labor—pretty much the only jobs around—painful, and the pain medicine made him loopy. Still, he had found Andrea, and he had his Klan. Nothing else, he decided, was really all that important.

The marginalized, disaffected, and lost were the radical right's ideal audience, and Dan was far from the first person I'd encountered who had found a sense of purpose and belonging within the open arms of extremist groups. A study by the British Council found that one of the major drivers of extremist recruitment was the desire to be a part of something bigger and to no longer "feel invisible." On a larger scale this was much the same sentiment that would fuel Donald Trump's victory among those large parts of the electorate who increasingly felt alienated and forgotten by politicians. Matthew hoped it would provide fertile ground in which he could sow the seeds of his nationalistic movement.

I'd spent some time with Dan since he first invited me to a rally with his former group, the now-defunct Imperial Knights of America. Since joining the Virgil Griffin White Knights he'd been excited to show me what a "real" Klan group was like. Much like National Socialist groups, the Klan measures their "realness" in terms of lineage, placing a premium on groups with direct lines to a perceived legitimate leader or some kind of event that cemented the forebear as a committed Klansman.

The Virgil Griffin White Knights had taken their name from Virgil Lee Griffin. Griffin, who died in 2009, was the leader of the Greensboro White Knights, famous in Klan circles for their role in the Greensboro Massacre of 1979. On November 3, 1979, industry workers and members of the local Communist Party gathered in the outskirts of Greensboro to rally against the Klan. The Communist Party had been feuding with the local chapter of the KKK ever since some of its members had interrupted a screening of *Birth of a Nation* a few months before. For over a hundred years the movie has been a staple with Klan groups all over the country, and interrupting a screening of it was a slap in the face to the members of the Greensboro White Knights.

The protestors had called out the Klan and stood in the streets holding signs and shouting "Death to the Klan" as an armada of cars carrying armed Klansmen, among them Doll Baby's dad, slowly rolled through. At one point the demonstrators attacked the cars, and suddenly shots rang out. It's unclear who fired first, but it whipped the demonstrators into a panicked frenzy. As they ran, one of the cars carrying the Klansmen, a powder-blue Oldsmobile, slammed on the brakes, and four Klansmen jumped out, brandishing pistols, rifles, and shotguns. They fired into the crowds, and some of the demonstrators who were also armed fired back as the Klan crouched for cover behind the car. Soon the shots died down, and the Oldsmobile fled the scene. Five bodies lay in the street. Eventually fourteen members of the Klan and the American Nazi Party were charged with the murders but acquitted by all-white juries.

Since then the massacre had become a point of pride for members of the Virgil Griffin White Knights, some of whom claimed to have taken part in it. Rather than a massacre, the Klan saw it as a glorious battle in which the Red Menace was beaten back by American Patriots, marking the first of what was surely to be many battles to come before America was restored to its former glory. To Gary Delp's group, it was a badge of honor, signifying that they were the real deal. Dan wouldn't say if Gary Delp had been involved, but he alluded that the Grand Wizard, who'd only been a regular foot soldier at the time, had been involved in "some serious shit in his day." "These guys don't F around," he'd warned me. They were a group that would not modernize or soften, because they were a group that had fought and killed for the white race.

These days, of course, they were not fighting any battles. The Virgil Griffin White Knights were getting old and were not likely to shoot anyone, for the white race or otherwise, and the same could be said for the other Klan groups scattered around the country. What had once been a national organization with more than 5 million members had atrophied into a handful of more or less defunct chapters more preoccupied with squabbles and infighting than protecting the white race from imagined threats. According to the SPLC, there were 130 active Klaverns (Klan terminology for local chapter) in the country in 2016, but it is impossible to say how many members each group has or how active they are, as groups fold and re-emerge incessantly. Most members would swear up and down that the Klan was in every state of the Union, but this was true only if you counted as a New York Klan the couple who sometimes made the trek to Kentucky to hang with Dan but mostly didn't. In 1925 almost fifty thousand Klansmen marched up Pennsylvania Avenue in Washington, DC, but in 2015 anyone holding a rally would be ecstatic if even fifty members showed up.

EVERYTHING YOU LOVE WILL BURN

Throughout its 150-year history the Klan has ebbed and flowed. Each ebb marked the end of an era, and each flow marked the beginning of a new one. The history of the Ku Klux Klan is one of rampant domestic terrorism, barbarity, and white supremacy, all performed with near-complete impunity. But it is also a history of ignominious failures.

Born out of boredom more than ideology, the Klan first saw the light of day on Christmas Eve, 1865, in Pulaski, Tennessee. Six former Confederate officers decided to form a fraternal club to alleviate the tedium of peacetime. They chose the name Ku Klux Klan, an Anglicization of the Greek word for "circle," *kyklos*, and "clan," and set about entertaining themselves by riding around at night in silly costumes, announcing that they were ghosts of the fallen soldiers of the Battle of Shiloh and that they lived in Hell. To this end they made elaborate costumes, with sheets and hoods meant to make them look like ghosts, some even including fake heads that could be removed to further the ghoulish impression. To their delight they discovered that their exploits had the added benefit of terrifying the credulous former slaves, and they realized that they had stumbled upon a powerful tool to control them. The group grew rapidly, and in 1867 the KKK formalized its structure with a centralized management overseeing a scattered collection of local franchises. On top of this organization sat Nathan Bedford Forrest, once a famed Confederate general, presiding over a network of underlings with titles that could easily pass for characters in Dungeons and Dragons. Bedford Forrest was given the title *Grand Wizard*, and his domain, divided into *realms*, *dominions*, *provinces*, and *dens*, were populated with *Grand Dragons*, *Cyclops*, *Titans*, and other vassals with more gibberish-sounding titles such as *Kludds*, *Klailiffs*, *Klokards*, and *Kligrapps*. Alliteration was big.

The Klan grew for years and, as it did, became increasingly difficult to control. Its decentralized structure, where the local chapters were free to interpret the Klan's chartered mission of protecting "the weak, the innocent and the defenseless" however they saw fit, meant that many descended into terror and brutality. In the beginning at least, the Klan was typically made up of the "best" people of the areas in which it operated, meaning its members were often former officers of the Confederate army, law enforcement, or other reputable citizens. Their actions, in their eyes at least, were seen as keeping order and not breaking the law, and they went about it with abandon—shooting, beating, hanging, stabbing, flogging, and exiling anyone they felt deserved it.

By 1869 most of the more respectable members had left, and Bedford Forrest, fed up with trying to maintain control over what by then was basically a terrorist organization, decided that the time had come for the KKK to close its doors. The Klan survived locally for a couple of years before the government, unable to turn a blind eye to the marauding bands of violent vigilantes any longer, finally shut it down.

Almost fifty years later, however, D. W. Griffith's *Birth of a Nation*, arguably the first blockbuster in movie history and a complete hagiography to the Klan, showed virtuous hooded riders rescuing a poor, desperate white woman from depraved African Americans, and the country loved it. The movie was a gigantic hit, and its popularity to a large degree relaunched the Klan. Once again the KKK was presented as the protector of morals, values, and the innocent, and again its membership drew from the leaders in the community, giving its members a self-perceived notion of authority. Members of this second-era Klan included senators and governors, with many of those elected to Congress in the 1924 elections owing their seats to the Klan's endorsement. At the height of its power in 1925 it is estimated that membership in the Klan was around 5 million people nationwide, and on August 8, 1925, fifty thousand of them paraded down Pennsylvania Avenue in an unprecedented show of force.

But once again the decentralized structure of the Klan made it difficult to control, and their penchant for violence eventually made it impossible for law enforcement, even those sympathetic to the Klan, to look away. By the end of the 1930s only fractions

were left of the once-mighty Klan. In 1944 it was finally eutha-
nized when the Internal Revenue Service filed a massive lien for
back taxes on revenue earned in the 1920s.

In the 1960s the Civil Rights Movement led to a resurgence of
Klan activity in the South. Headquartered in North Carolina, the
United Klans of America (UKA) was by far the largest group in
the country, boasting twenty-five thousand members across ten
states. But the political winds had shifted since the Klan's heyday of the 1920s, and although still a sizeable group capable of
untold mayhem, the UKA of the 1960s was but a shadow of what
the KKK had been four decades earlier. The UKA nevertheless
murdered, beat, threatened, bombed, and harassed in large parts
of the American South, but they could no longer count on the un-
wavering support of white communities nor complete impunity
in the eyes of the law. As the Civil Rights Movement fought on
through the 1960s, the increasingly desperate and brutal actions
of the Klan became untenable for authorities. What's more, the
passage of the Civil Rights Act (1964) and Voting Rights Act (1965)
put an end to most of the region's Jim Crow laws, rendering moot
the Klan's spurious claims of upholding the law of the land. Declining memberships led to declining revenue, which in turn led
to infighting and fractures. By the end of the decade the UKA was
decimated. Once again the Ku Klux Klan as a force of any consequence was dead.

When I began reporting on them it had been decades since
the Klan had had any relevance as a political force in the United
States. But apparently nobody had told the Klan, and they seemed
as convinced as ever that the organization was poised for a comeback. People in America were waking up to what was going on,
Dan would tell me, what with immigrants and such, and he firmly
believed that whites in America would soon realize they needed
the KKK. He had invited me to come to the funeral of Gary Delp's
son to show me evidence of what he had been talking about.
"There's going to be big things coming up for us," he said. "There's
going to be some important people at this funeral, and they are

going to be planning something that's going to bring us out of this funk we've been in."

By that time I had been to a few Klan meetings, mostly smaller affairs that felt more like family gatherings than rallies, but the fascination with the Klan stayed with me, more because of their outsized role in American mythology than their actual political clout. Decapitated and broken as the Klan was, it still had an uncanny ability to stoke fear and outrage in the American public. Every so often a newspaper or local TV station would break the news of KKK flyers found on cars, with a reporter breathlessly describing how the Klan might possibly be making a comeback. The Klan was the quintessential face of hatred and racism in America. The image of the white hood and fiery cross took people back to a time when no African American was safe, when churches burned and strange fruit dangled from southern trees. It seemed almost impossible that these robed devils were still around, yet here they were, and I wanted to find out what they wanted.

"GODDAMMIT, MATTHEW," SAID DAN. "Are you kidding me, dude?" He had just noticed Matthew's T-shirt featuring a print of three skulls, the middle one looking dead at you while the two other ones looked off to the sides. All of them had daggers between their teeth. Above them were the words "Orthodoxy or Death."

"What?"

"Matt, I love you, but you're killing me. 'Orthodoxy or Death' at a Klan event? Can you please make a little bit of an effort not to pick a theological fight with these guys?"

"What's wrong with my shirt?" asked Matthew.

"These guys are good, Protestant Christians," said Dan. "If you come waltzing in with your 'Orthodoxy or Death,' they just might kill you."

"Then I'll be the first white guy to get lynched at a Klan event."

Dan rubbed the bridge of his nose. Matthew loved a good argument—especially about religion.

"Darnit, Matthew," said Dan. He was training to be a Kludd, the Klan version of a preacher, and was trying to wean himself off swearing. This weekend was a big deal for him, and he could easily see it go down the drain because he brought a quarrelsome Christian Orthodox, a lapsed neo-Nazi, and a journalist along. The fact that he seemed more worried about Matthew than about me said something about Matthew's fondness for disputes. "Can you just do this for me, please? We're going to a funeral. Just be cool for once."

"Fine," said Matthew. "I'll change into another T-shirt. But I'm warning you right now—it's going to be a *Star Wars* T-shirt."

Dan's phone rang, and he talked quietly for a moment before hanging up with an "I'll be right there."

"Come on, Doll Baby. We have to go," he said. "One of the older guys had a stroke this morning, and it looks like he might not make it. His wife's asked for a Kludd, but none of the other Kludds are in town yet, so it's just me." He threw a twenty-dollar bill on the table, grabbed Doll Baby's hand, and headed for the exit. Dan was serious about his Klancraft in the same way an ex-junkie is serious about yoga or whatever else he had taken to get himself off drugs, and he wanted to prove to his new Klan group that he had what it took to shepherd a flock. "You guys go without me. We'll catch up!" he shouted as they left the restaurant. "I'll text you the address. Tell them you're with me."

"Are you really going to wear a *Star Wars* T-shirt?" Eric said through mouthfuls of eggs.

"Heck yeah, I'm wearing a *Star Wars* T-shirt," Matthew said.

On the way to the rally site we stopped at the Red Roof Inn, where they all shared a room. Matthew ran in to get changed while Eric and I stayed in the car. Eric, who was of Irish descent, slipped a CD with IRA music into the rental's stereo and hummed along. "I think I'm the only Klansman in America who's also an IRA supporter," he said. "I know I was the only skinhead."

I'd met Eric a few months before when he was the president of the Aryan Terror Brigade (ATB), a small band of skinheads who, like so many others on the far right, suffered from a collective delusion of grandeur. As president, Eric boasted of member chapters and affiliates all over the world, yet whenever I asked him if he could put me in touch with other members, he invariably became vague and dismissive, prompting me to think that his group was nowhere near as ubiquitous as he would have me believe. I did, however, meet his friends John and Josh, two hapless neo-Nazis who spent most of their time shooting guns in the woods and fighting each other. Once, John made me hold his gun because he knew he was going to have to get into it with Josh and would rather not end up shooting his friend in the heat of the moment. Having met them only a couple of hours earlier, I suddenly found myself holding a 9mm pistol as the two skinheads grappled in the mud because Josh had accused John of not knowing how to reverse a pickup out of a mud hole. Another time I spent a day at Josh's trailer in the hills outside of Kuttawa in southern Kentucky as he sprayed bullets into the woods from his stoop while shouting warnings at imaginary communists approaching his house. When John went to prison on a gun charge, the membership in ATB was effectively cut by a full third, so Eric decided to shutter the organization and join the Klan instead. I once asked him how a former skinhead with no religious beliefs could join a strictly Protestant organization, but Eric only shrugged and said that maybe they wouldn't notice.

Matthew came back wearing a *Star Wars* shirt as promised. As we drove, Eric sang along atonally to a song about Bobby Sands, the IRA martyr who died following a hunger strike in 1981.

"Ugh, IRA," said Matthew dismissively. "If there was ever proof that violent resistance doesn't work, the IRA is it. Decades of war, and look what it got them. At the same time Scotland almost just broke free peacefully. That's how we have to do it."

"My dad was in the IRA," Eric mumbled and switched off the music.

"Well, then, your dad was a fool," Matthew said.

We drove out of Johnson City along the freeway before pulling off where a large billboard advertised a corn maze. A narrow road wound its way along the foothills of the Great Smoky Mountains at the edge of Cherokee National Forest. Finally we got to the address Dan had texted us, which turned out to be a barn just off the main road. Someone had left a metal gate open, so we drove through and parked. A sign nailed to the gatepost warned, "Trespassers Will Be Shot. Survivors Will Be Shot Again." Underneath it read, "ABSOLUTELY NO ALCOHOL, DRUGS, AND WEAPONS OR FIGHTING!" The sign had been decorated by a white X in the middle of a red circle. In the center of the X was a drop of blood. It was known as the MIOAK—the Mystic Insignia of a Klansman— and the drop of blood represented the blood of Jesus Christ. As I was about to find out, only the part about drugs was a firm rule.

We got out and looked around, feeling slightly intimidated on the private property of a Klansman we didn't know and, more importantly, who didn't know us. There was no one around, and all we could hear was the buzz of a riding mower somewhere in the distance. It was one of the first really hot days of the year, and the morning had brought the kind of southern heat that trickles from the dirt and grass and kudzu, bringing with it ticks and chiggers that crawled across our shoes. The barn was small, with an opening on each side so we could see through it. Bales of hay were stacked up against the back wall. Along the side wall was a raised area with a table and a few chairs. A noose hanging from the rafters swung in a gentle wind. Matthew frowned. "A bit on the nose, isn't it?" he said.

A gentle slope led up from the barn, past the rusted-out husk of an old Brockway truck that had plants growing out of the engine bay. The field was an oblong triangle narrowing as it ran down to the barn. Along one side was a small creek that ran in a pipe in some places and bubbled lazily in others. The hypotenuse was fenced off against a row of low bungalows with neat backyards littered with children's toys.

A hundred yards or so toward the middle of the field a figure was hunched over, working on something with an axe.

"Who's that guy?" asked Eric.

"Beats me," said Matthew.

It was a large man, tall and heavy set, and he stared in our direction as he placed his hands on the small of his back and stretched. He was wearing a beat-up cowboy hat made of straw, a tattered undershirt, and filthy jeans at least two sizes too big that he had stuffed into massive, leather boots. His hair and beard were long and tussled and had turned almost completely gray except for streaks of strawberry blond. It was a thick and dirty beard, completely obscuring his neck. His eyes narrowed when he saw us. He dropped the axe and started toward us, walking with a limp and using a hand on his thigh as support.

"We're with Dan," I said.

The man grabbed my hand and twisted it a couple of times as he shook it.

"Kiggy," he grunted, and he repeated the handshake with Eric and Matthew.

"Nice to meet you, Kiggy," I said. "As I said, we're here with Dan. He had to go to the hospital but said it was okay that we come out."

Kiggy scowled. "My name's not Kiggy," he said. He spoke in a deep, moist rumble, with a heavy southern drawl. "It's Randy. Who the hell are you guys?"

I explained to Randy that I was working on a book about the far right and was hoping to spend some time with them that weekend. Randy stood completely still, his scowl fixed on me.

"So yeah," I said. "Hopefully we'll have a good weekend."

Randy moved closer, placing a large hand on my shoulder while he breathed into my face. "I didn't invite you here," he said finally.

"I know," I said. "Dan, he . . ."

He cut me off. "I didn't invite you. And I don't want you here." He reached for something in his back pocket. "You shouldn't be here." In his hand was an old 9mm pistol that he brought up under my chin and held there as his body swayed drunkenly. "You should know," he said slowly. "I've killed more people than I've been in prison for. And I've been in prison for killing people. Maybe I ought to kill you."

Matthew and Eric stood frozen a few steps over. The moment dragged on. Randy's watery eyes were half closed, staring at me from behind heavy lids. The whites in his eyes were yellow. Something greenish had coagulated in the corners. His lips moved soundlessly under his bushy moustache, wet and sticky from warm beer and chewing tobacco. Finally he gave my shoulder an affectionate squeeze and holstered the gun in the lining of his pants. "You can stay," he said. "I don't give a fuck. Just stay the hell out of my way." With that he turned his back and walked down toward the barn. "Keep an eye on the cross there," he barked.

"Crap," said Matthew. "That was fucking terrifying." I watched as Randy waddled away, and I felt my stomach drop from my throat to somewhere around my ankles. Although it hadn't felt truly life threatening—I was fairly certain that even within the confines of Randy's confused and angry mind the logistics involved with killing and disposing of a journalist on a field in broad daylight were confounding enough to stop him from pulling the trigger—the sensation of a loaded gun pushing against my jaw had turned my mind blank, and as he left, everything was slowly coming back into focus. Clearly Dan had been right when he'd told me that these guys weren't fucking around, but I still hadn't expected to be held at gunpoint.

We all looked at the parts of the cross laying on the wet grass that Randy had told us to keep an eye on, not knowing what to do next. It looked like it would be close to thirty feet tall.

"Does he want us to finish it?" asked Eric.

"Beats me," said Matthew. "I don't know how to wrap a cross. Do you?" Matthew plonked down on a large cinderblock next to some of Randy's tools. Eric halted a trickle of sweat on his shaved head with the back of his hand before he too sat down. The riding mower could still be heard off somewhere in the distance, but apart from Randy, the field was empty.

"What do we do now?" asked Eric.

"I guess we wait."

"YOU CALLED HIM KIGGY?" Dan said when he joined us a while later. Matthew, Eric, and I had been sitting next to the cross, quietly hoping that Randy would never come back.

"That's what he told me his name was," I said.

"Dude, *KIGY*," said Dan. "It means 'Klansman I Greet You.' He thought you were in the Klan. No wonder he was pissed. Stay away from Randy. That guy's a sweetheart, but he will kill you."

KIGY is only one of a myriad of codes used by the KKK to separate members from civilians. The proper response to Randy's greeting would have been "AKIA," meaning "A Klansman I Am." Watching members of the KKK comment on each other's posts on social media was more often than not completely incomprehensible.

Johnny Miller, the man who owned the property, eventually joined us. Johnny was short and round, with beady but friendly eyes and a bushy beard. He was the one who had been riding the mower we had heard earlier, and he was still on it. He laughed when he heard about our introduction to Randy. "Pay it no mind," he said. "Randy's been drinking, and he's a little crazy. He'll come around."

Johnny's property was less private than one might think would be suitable for a KKK cross lighting. The field backed up to his neighbors' properties, and the cross would be pretty much in their backyard. Johnny explained that it wouldn't be a problem and that his neighbors were used to it. Besides, many of them were going to take part tonight anyway. The people who lived in the neighborhood used to say it was God's country, but it would be closer to the truth to call it Klan country. Most of the houses along the road flew Confederate flags, both a sign of allegiance to the South and a code to those who knew how to read it. Some of the front yards had small porcelain statues of robed Klansmen, sagely studying passersby through white picket fences. On the other side of the field, through the hickory trees and across the small creek, lived the only Yankee for miles. He had called the cops on Johnny a few times during cross lightings, but the complaints had stopped when the neighbor realized that the police had no interest in breaking up the parties. In fact, Johnny's closest neighbor across from the field was a cop, his Charger parked in the driveway, and he didn't seem to mind. Besides, Johnny said, it was all on private land anyway, so what the fuck was he going to do about it.

Dan looked at the unfinished cross on the ground. "You guys haven't wrapped this thing yet? Don't tell me you don't know how to wrap a cross."

"Not in the Klan, remember?" Matthew said.

Dan grabbed a bag filled with old clothes and threw it to Matthew. He picked up a stapler from the ground and, along with Doll Baby and Matthew, began stapling old sweaters, jeans, and T-shirts to the cross.

"Here. Make yourself useful, commie," he said and passed me a spool of metal wire. I gingerly strung it around the beam and wondered briefly about the ethics of helping the Klan wrap a cross when Dan grabbed it out of my hands.

"Utterly useless," he said. "There's a way of wrapping these things right. Clothes first to soak up the kerosene so it doesn't all just drip down onto the ground. Then a layer of rough burlap, and then the real trick is making, like, a ribbon of burlap and wrapping it around the cross from the bottom to the top to make a path so that the flames spiral up the cross."

Doll Baby got some thick bailing wire and ran it tight around the vertical beam of the cross. "You want it tight, but not too tight," said Dan. "The burlap needs some breeze through it to catch the flames, and we don't want the wire to smother it."

All day Klansmen and women arrived at Johnny's property as the trio worked on wrapping the cross. Dan assigned Eric to be the "Nighthawk," or Klan security, so it was his job to make sure everyone who came had been invited. Billy Snuffer, Imperial Wizard of the Rebel White Knights, showed up with his daughter. Richard Preston, the leader of the Confederate White Knights, had driven in from Maryland with a few of his guys. As the day wore on, around twenty people had showed up and were milling

Dan Elmquist, Doll Baby, and Matthew Heimbach wrapping a cross in discarded clothes on the morning of Brian Delp's funeral.

around outside Johnny's garage, drinking sodas and talking, most of them wearing the black casual shirt uniform of the Klan, decked out in various patches and pins. Johnny got a barbeque going and handed out hamburgers while his wife, Rachel, drove back and forth between the barn and the main house fetching coleslaw, more sodas, chips, dips, and hotdogs. She wasn't in the Klan herself but had been married to Johnny for a long time and was sort of a den mother to the Virgil Griffin White Knights, making sure they were fed and happy.

Eventually Dan and Doll Baby finished the cross, and Johnny attached a drill to his little tractor and started making a hole in the moist dirt where the cross would go. Randy, apparently forgetting his disdain for me and now teetering precariously after a long day of drinking in the sun, guided the drill, all the while telling everybody that they didn't know what the fuck they were doing and that they should all step back a fucking ways and let him take care of it.

"Watch out for that big nigger head there," a guy said as the drill struck a large, brown rock, shooting off sparks. Randy suggested he go fuck himself and declared that the hole was sufficiently deep. Somehow the guys managed to drag, lift, and heave the cross into standing position.

"Now we can have us a fucking funeral," Randy said.

BRIAN DELP HAD DIED of an aneurism at the age of forty-four on a Wednesday in April 2015. His daddy, Gary, and his mother, Becky, both pushing eighty, had him cremated and kept his ashes in a small Tupperware container in their house because Gary felt he should get a Klan burial, where his ashes would be spread at the foot of a fiery cross. Their son's death had hit them hard. Not only the son of the Grand Wizard, Brian was also a youngish member of an aging organization that desperately needed fresh blood.

While the Klansmen wandered around, getting burger juice on their uniforms and talking about how the blacks in this country "were getting out of fucking control," Gary mostly sat in an old rocking chair in the barn, thanking those who offered their condolences. Becky was ashen and gray, hunched over even more than usual, most of the time sitting next to either her husband or Rachel, murmuring quietly and every so often emitting low wails of grief.

I sat down with Karl Viddig and some other Klan elders around a table in the barn and listened as they explained why the seemingly dismal number of members in the Klan might all be a ruse designed to trick those of us not in the Klan. Karl was the Kludd of the Virgil Griffin White Knights and whatever other Klan group was interested in hosting him. He was short and squarely built, with a raspy voice and a perpetual mischievous grin on his face. I asked him what the point of remaining in the Klan was, seeing as how their membership had almost completely atrophied.

"Of course that might just be what we want everyone to think," he winked. "Why is it that the media always portrays the Klan as nothing but a bunch of backward hicks barbequing in the woods?" he continued. "Well, if you want the answer to that, you'll have to ask yourself who runs the media. Now who do you suppose that is?" I told him that I didn't know, although I suspected what his answer might be.

"The Jews," a couple of the guys standing around him mumbled.

"That's right. The Jews! Now we've been assholes to the Jews for 150 years, and so we had to expect them to sting us right back, and that's what's happening now. They are running things now, and they are giving as good as they got. But people don't know how powerful the Klan is. We're called the Invisible Empire for a reason. All they see is the people we want them to see."

"Amen," said Pastor Gregory Martin Beckett. Tall, completely bald and with large eyes peering out from behind round spectacles, he was Karl's opposite, quiet and collected where Karl was quick and gregarious. In addition to being a Kludd of the KKK, Pastor Gregory claimed to actually be a certified pastor, and like Karl, he traveled the various Klan groups, trying to make sure everyone was on the same theological page. "Just like the CIA don't send their people overseas holding signs that say they're CIA, we don't disclose our members, and we have people that they don't know about and when our people get their assignments, they know who their enemies are."

"So you're saying that you might very well have thousands of sleeper cells throughout the country?" I asked.

"That you will never know," Karl said. "Well, that is, until we decide to make ourselves known."

This was almost certainly nonsense. The idea of a vast cabal of secret Klansmen biding their time in the wings until such a time when the white race was in its darkest hour belonged with theories of the Illuminati, secretive Zionist occupation governments, and other cast members of Dan Brown books. Still, Karl seemed convinced.

For the last couple of years he and Pastor Gregory had been on a mission to promote unity within the different Klan groups scattered around the country and, as they said, "bring God back into the Klan." It was only going so-so. Many Klan groups had found it necessary to join forces with what Karl and Pastor Gregory saw as more unsavory elements of the white nationalist movement. There was Ron Edwards, Imperial Wizard of the Imperial Knights of America, who, before going to prison for selling prescription drugs, had held an annual festival called Nordic Fest on his Kentucky compound that drew skinheads, Nazis, and even Odinists. Then there were Chris Barker's Loyal White Knights out of North Carolina, which made no bones about working with the neo-Nazis of the National Socialist Movement. To top it all off, it had recently come to light that Barker was, in addition to being a Grand Wizard, also a federal informant, feeding information about the Klan to the feds. To Karl, Pastor Gregory, and many others in the Klan, associating with these kinds of characters just to boost membership numbers ruined the purity and strength of the Klan. As Richard Preston, Imperial Wizard of the Confederate White Knights and close friend of both Karl and Pastor Gregory, often said, "I would rather have two good men than twenty weak ones." To their minds the Klan had to get back to its core. Every time the Klan had strayed into terrorism and violent racism in the past, they were removing themselves from what it meant to be a Klansman. A Klansman was white, Christian, patriotic, and American. There was nothing in the bylaws that said you had to hate blacks, Jews, and Mexicans; you just had to be proud of who you were and promise not to have anyone of your kin mix with other races. To Karl and Pastor Gregory this had nothing to do with racism and everything to do with racial pride and self-preservation. Still, old habits die hard, and even Karl had to admit that there were those in the organization who took a dim view of those who they deemed nonwhite.

"Say what you want about these niggers," said Richard Preston a little later outside the barn. Richard, who lived right outside Baltimore, had been patrolling the city in an attempt to keep the peace as the Freddie Gray riots escalated but eventually realized the situation was getting too hot even for him and his heavily armed boys. "They are out on the streets throwing fucking spears, like goddamned Zulu warriors. If we don't stop them, these fucking coons are going to take over everything. This is what they've been waiting for, I can promise you that, and goddamned Barry Soetoro is just itching to let them and ISIS have the whole goddamned thing."

Barry Soetoro was President Barack Obama. A few years into his presidency an image started popping up online of a student ID from 1981 of a Columbia University exchange student named Barry Soetoro. The picture on the ID was of a young Barack Obama, and although it was quickly proved to be a fake, to many on the right the ID became just more proof of what was so crystal clear to them: Barry "Barack Hussein Obama" Soetoro was a pawn placed in the White House by a nefarious cabal of international bankers—shorthand for Jews—already working on setting up the New World Order by way of an intricate plan involving, among other things, the cultivation of ISIS via US shell companies and the complete disarmament of the US population in advance of an invasion led by UN forces.

"Our whole country is going to shit, and we're just standing by like assholes watching it happen. We let scumbags like Lil Wayne step on our flag when what he should be is strung up for treason. The problem is we're not proud anymore. We don't stand for anything. During the Civil War people died for the Confederate flag because their rights were being taken away from them. It was never about slavery. The race issue was a distraction, and it still is." Richard had a theory that most if not all acts of terrorism in recent history had been red herrings designed to draw attention away from the diabolical machinations of our government. "Take Sandy Hook," he said, a throbbing vein becoming visible on his neck as he found his speed. "Never happened, and I can prove it." His proof was a handful of websites all claiming to have found evidence of so called crisis actors, people deployed by the government to play bereaved relatives, shocked victims, or horrified witnesses to whatever atrocity the government had concocted. Even as conspiracy theories went, the crisis actor theory was pretty left of field, but Richard claimed to have amassed sufficient evidence that it went all the way to the top. "Why is it that one of the women that supposedly died at Sandy Hook all of a sudden shows up at the Boston bombing, huh? You tell me that," he went on. "It's all designed to take attention away from Barry Soetoro, the closet Muslim. Mohammad was nothing but a child-raping, goat-molesting piece of garbage, and one of his followers has taken over the White House. It's fucking disgusting." With that, he left to get one of the burgers that Johnny was cooking up on the barbeque.

Matthew had stood off to the side as the Kludds and Richard ranted. He'd mostly kept his promise to Dan, avoiding topics that might get touchy, such as theology, but he was having a hard time masking his disdain for the KKK.

"It's not that they're bad people or anything," he told me. "It's just that they have nothing to offer. They're all about 'Murica that hasn't existed for decades, whereas I want to build a modern nationalist movement." He'd been pleasant and gregarious all day, but as far as I knew he hadn't made any real effort to share his vision with the Knights. I didn't blame him. From what I understood about what Matthew was trying to do, I found it difficult to imagine Randy having a place within his plans. He waved his hand at the Klansmen robing up around him in preparation for the cross lighting. "I mean this is all well and good, but it has nothing to do with saving our country. It's a hobby. It's playing dress-up."

Randy limped up, more than a little drunk, and put his arm around me. "I'm sorry for trying to shoot you earlier," he said.

"That's okay," I said. "You didn't know who I was."

"Still, that's no excuse for shooting a guy."

His eyes were tearing up.

"Do you know I was in Vietnam? I did two and a half tours before they sent me home. I did recon. First one in and last one out. You might not believe it, but I was good. I killed a lot of people."

Randy giving the sign of the three eras of the KKK.

Randy held me tighter as he spoke, his mouth only inches from my face. "I lost my wife too. I mean, I lost both of them, but I recently lost my second wife."

He told me about coming home from Vietnam not able to talk to his family anymore because they had no idea what he had done or gone through and so they left him. Before leaving for Vietnam Randy had been a member of the Ku Klux Klan, and when he came back he joined up again. When his family left, the Klan became his family, and when he went to prison for reasons he wouldn't tell me, the Aryan Brotherhood became his family even though he hated Nazis. In prison your race was your first line of defense, and the Aryan Brotherhood decided who was and who wasn't white, and if you didn't cover your body with tattoos of swastikas, then you might as well be black, or worse. So he covered his body with tattoos of swastikas.

"There was no ink," he said, showing me a grubby, faded swastika on his arm. "We used charcoal and piss."

When Randy got out he rejoined the Virgil Griffin White Knights, who, he said, he did some bad stuff for. He remarried and had several kids and grandkids. Then, two weeks ago, his wife had died suddenly. Now, again, all he had left was his brothers in the Klan. A family he seemed to love and hate at the same time.

"I joined the Klan when I was nine," he said, openly weeping. "What kind of people let a nine-year-old boy join the Klan? A young boy shouldn't have to do the things I did. I never had a chance."

He let out a deep sigh and shuffled off.

Later, having filled up on burgers and Mountain Dew, the elders at the gathering—Karl Viddig, Pastor Gregory, Richard Preston, Gary Delp, and Billy Snuffer—retired to discuss the state of the Klan. All of them had grown sick and tired of all the bickering and infighting paralyzing the Klan for as long as any of them could remember, and they wanted to do something about it. Karl and Pastor Gregory both agreed that at some point the Klan had gotten away from God, or perhaps it was the other way around. Either way, something had to be done about the KKK's theological underpinnings.

Richard saw the problem as more acute. After all, it was painfully clear to anyone who bothered to look that Obama was gearing up to hand over the country to a UN/ISIS coalition before he left office. Richard had been talking about this regularly for a while, even going so far as mapping out what he suspected were FEMA camps (Federal Emergency Management Agency) where political dissidents such as him would be taken when Obama showed his true colors. Of course, he could only suspect their use because he was unwilling to get close enough to find out for sure. At any rate, there were large white buildings surrounded by tall fences, so whatever they were, it had to be bad. Richard wanted to prepare and to build an army of patriots ready to take the fight to the government. His first plan of action was to gather incontrovertible evidence of Obama's machinations and take it to Congress within the year. If he could get Obama impeached before leaving office, that would mean that every executive order the president had ever signed would be null and void. This wasn't true, of course— executive orders stand regardless of impeachment—but Richard was unconcerned with such details. Perhaps he believed that the crimes he would uncover would be so egregious that everything Obama had ever done would need to be revisited. Richard would have foiled the Jewish plan and prevented the destruction of America.

Richard was a realist, however, and was under no illusion that things would go as planned. That was why he needed Gary Delp and Billy Snuffer. They would provide the manpower needed if things went south and Obama started rounding up patriots. At some point Americans would need to stand up against their corrupt government, and then they would finally turn to the Klan for leadership, Richard was sure of it. He was ready, and he needed his Klan to be too. He knew very well that he might die in the struggle, but it was worth it if it meant exposing or defeating Obama.

When they returned, Richard winked and told me that he couldn't say much but, suffice it to say, they'd hatched a plan that would be set in motion immediately and that the world would soon know. It was all very hush-hush, and the whole thing was to be revealed at a rally at Richard's place later in July.

UP BY THE CROSS, which was now doused in kerosene, Dan and Doll Baby were robing up for the memorial service. Dan had his black sunglasses perched on his forehead and was smoking a cigarette while he brushed some of the wrinkles out of his white and gold robe.

"Lord I swear my robe gets more creased the more I iron it," said Doll Baby, wrapping a red and white robe around her body. On the left side of her chest she had sewn on a Confederate flag, and over her heart was a white shield with a red cross, the insignia of the Women of the KKK. She had taken off her black combat shirt but was still wearing camouflage fatigues and heavy boots under her robe.

"Baby, did you sew my badge on straight?" said Dan, fingering the MIOAK stitched onto the left side of his robe, covering his heart. "It looks a little crooked."

"Then it's your eyes that are crooked," Doll Baby said. "I always sew everything on straight."

"You're right," said Dan.

The Klansmen were all dressed in ceremonial robes when they filled Johnny's garage for Brian Delp's memorial. Johnny covered a beer cooler with a piece of cloth to serve as an altar of sorts, and on it Brian's family had placed pictures of him with his kids and his nieces. Fluorescent tubes flickered overhead and reflected from the aluminum siding walls. Karl and Greg stood next to the cooler/altar, their arms around Gary and Becky Delp.

Becky was ashen, her face immobile as she clung to her husband to keep herself from collapsing.

"I sure hope you folks will join me in a song," said Karl, "because I'm going to sing anyway, even if I have to do it myself." The mourners shuffled their feet. Karl went on alone.

> *Though none go with me,*
> *still I will follow.*
> *Though none go with me,*
> *still I will follow.*
> *Though none go with me,*
> *still I will follow.*
> *No turning back. No turning back.*

His voice was crisp and clear. Brian's sisters stood in the doorway and shook between sobs. Two of his nieces played hide-and-seek in the robes of the Klansmen standing in a line looking somber.

Members of the Virgil Griffin White Knights at Brian Delp's funeral.

Gary wore his purple and gold robes, and large tears were dripping from his nose and onto the lush silk.

> The cross before me,
> the world behind me.
> The cross before me,
> the world behind me.
> The cross before me,
> the world behind me.
> No turning back. No turning back.

Then we all walked in procession out onto the field. The sun had set behind the trees, and the last bit of light was just kissing the tall cross. Fireflies danced across the grass, chased around by some of the younger kids, too hopped up on Mountain Dew to sleep.

Karl was preparing the torches for the cross lighting. A dozen or so sticks, each around five feet long, were standing in a bucket, and Karl was dousing them in kerosene.

Eric was in charge of handing out the torches. It was to be his first time doing it, and Karl wanted to know that the former skinhead knew what he was doing.

"So they'll all form a circle around the cross, then walk past me. I'll ask each of them if they accept the light of Christ. When they say yes, you hand them a torch."

"Got it," said Eric.

"Now mind you that you don't hold the torch too low and put it out on the grass, or too high so the kerosene drips onto the robes and sets them on fire. That would be bad."

"Got it," said Eric.

Dan was leading the ceremony, and as he always did, he carried with him a small portable CD player on which he had cued up a version of "Amazing Grace" that he liked. The Klansmen, roughly fifteen of them, circled the cross slowly, stopping at intervals and shouting "For God! For Race! For the Klan!" They did this three times before Dan held his hands out and announced "Klan! Approach the cross!" The circle tightened, and the men of the Klan put their torches to the base of the cross, flames suddenly snaking around the vertical beam and racing upward, just as Dan had intended. The Klansmen made an opening in the circle, and Gary and Becky, clinging to each other and carrying the Tupperware box containing their son, made their way slowly to the cross. Becky stood back as Gary moved to the base of the cross, opened the container, and poured the beige powder that had once been Brian Delp onto the ground. He took a couple of steps back and stood silent. Randy, teetering dangerously, limped to his side.

"My wife is dead!" he shouted in a slur. "I'm going to sing for her."

Members of the Virgil Griffin White Knights surrounding the fiery cross.

He launched into a heartbroken version of "Too Ra Loo Ra Loo Ral," and the Klan joined in. Randy's song was loud and off key, more a barely melodic series of sobs than actual singing. It soon ended, and as the Klan stood in silence watching the fiery cross sending sparks high up in the air and raining back down on Gary Delp's family and friends, all that could be heard were Becky Delp's soft whimpers and Randy's desperate howls.

CHAPTER 5

————

The NSM Turns Forty

If a grasshopper tries to fight a lawnmower, one may admire
his courage but not his judgment.

—Robert A. Heinlein, *Farnham's Freehold*

The National Socialist Movement had seen better days, that
much was clear. Not by much perhaps, but still . . . better than
this. The few members who had shown up to the National Socialist Movement's grand fortieth anniversary celebration in 2014
were gathered in the far end of the meeting room of a hotel on
the outskirts of Chattanooga, making the small, dingy space look
positively cavernous. Compared to 2011 in Trenton the turnout
was dismal. Since then membership, or at least turnout for the big
events, had been in a death spiral. I'd gone to their last event too,

a fairly underwhelming gathering in Atlanta where all the members, Commander Schoep in particular, had gone to great lengths explaining that the low turnout was merely a lull and that he could feel it in his bones that things were going to turn around. In April of 2013 we were a few months into the second Obama administration, and the NSM was in a slump. A year later that slump was not only ongoing; it seemed to have deepened.

At one end of the room was a large white, black, and red banner made especially for the event, announcing the momentous occasion. If the NSM's forty-year history had been glorious, as much of the printed material claimed, these were certainly not glorious times, and the handful of members sitting glumly in the conference room made little effort to pretend otherwise.

In front of the banner was a small lectern that one of the members had brought. It was a narrow pillar of dark wood, slightly scuffed from transportation and adorned with a small swastika flag. Next to it, to the side, was the usual table covered with neo-Nazi knickknacks and Third Reich memorabilia, manned by an impossibly tall figure with long, thinning hair carefully collected into a greasy ponytail. He wore a Brownshirt uniform adorned with all manner of Nazi trinkets and baubles. His sleeves were too short for his long arms, and as he stretched, the fabric rose up to reveal a tattoo of a full-figure Adolf Hitler giving a roman salute, although Adolf's head had been eaten away by a severe case of psoriasis on the man's elbow.

Two years had passed since the weekend in New Jersey, which had since been dubbed "The Battle of Trenton" in NSM circles. More than a few faces were missing. A couple of months after New Jersey Duke Schneider emailed to tell me that Schoep was about to make him a major and that he would be put in charge of rebuilding NSM into a full-scale empire. Whatever that meant.

Then a few months went by during which all my emails and texts went unanswered until he finally got in touch and invited me back to the diner. Just like old times, I waited for his old Hyundai under the overpass, only this time we didn't drive to the usual diner but to his house in Sheepshead Bay. There, over tea in a small, tidy living room, he told me that he went by the name Keith now and that he had left the movement after a brush with cancer had led him to Jesus and an African American wife. His daughter Kate was still in the NSM, but all things considered, he was happier than he'd ever been. He was active in a local church and had decided to pursue acting, landing a few walk-on parts on low-budget horror films. From the shelf along the wall he picked out a DVD and slipped the disc in the player before handing me the cover. The movie was called *The Ghost of Angela Webb* and looked very much straight to DVD. Keith fast forwarded through most of the movie, then hit play just as a puzzled-looking woman on the screen entered a dark, spooky barn. "She's a detective," Keith explained. "But she can also see into the spirit world."

"This room has an overwhelming sense of sadness," the woman said as she noticed the inanimate corpse of Keith hanging from the rafters by a noose.

He switched the movie off. "I didn't use a harness or anything for that," he said, slapping his massive neck. "All muscles."

The issue of Duke/Keith leaving was not one the NSM wanted to discuss. When I asked Schoep about it his face got hard. "We don't talk anymore," he said.

Wilson, the sergeant who loved to fight, was also AWOL, and no one seemed to know what had happened to him. Some said he had just up and left. Others told me he had been a federal informant and was swept away into witness protection. Exactly what he had been snitching about was unclear, but the rumor about witness protection seemed hyperbolic, as I seriously doubted that the NSM had any secrets that would warrant murdering a person for revealing them. As far as I could tell, there was very little mystery left to the NSM. They hadn't even bothered to warn me about cameras and cell phones.

Jeff Schoep was standing close to the door, looking impatient. He had filled out since last time. He was less scrawny, and his suit, a glistening three-piece number in a charcoal gray, seemed to

actually fit his frame. Still, he looked out of place among the uniformed Nazis, most of whom had fashioned their own uniforms out
of shirts and pants bought at the store because even the most basic replica uniforms were expensive. Jeff had also shaved his head
since last time and left his wife for an attractive but stern-looking
woman in a pretty dress.

He looked at his wristwatch, then at the doors leading to the
parking lot, and back to his wristwatch. Butch Urban, the NSM
captain from Tennessee, came in and shook his head somberly. "I
think that might be it," he said in a low voice.

"Really? All right, fine. Let's just do it. Stay outside and keep an
eye out for stragglers. There should be more coming."

"Ten-four, Commander," said Urban. He gave a curt nod and
something that almost looked like a click of his heels, then backed
out the door toward his post in the parking lot.

JEFF SCHOEP WAS only twenty-one years old when he took over an
organization in tatters. In 1994 the NSM was struggling under the
laborious name National Socialist American Workers Freedom
Movement (NSAWFM) and boasted fewer than a handful of members despite having been founded on the remains of the once-
notorious American Nazi Party.

Before taking over the NSAWFM Jeff had steeped himself in the
ideology of the far right for years. Growing up in the almost uni-
formly white rural Minnesota, he spent his adolescence obsessed
with World War II history and Adolf Hitler. Members of his family
had fought for Germany during the war, and as a kid he poured
over World War II documentaries, imagining that the faces of the
German soldiers he saw on the screen might be those of his ancestors. It filled him not only with pride but also an insidious dread
that vengeful Jews might one day target his family.

The 1980s, when Jeff was growing up, were heady times for the
far right in America. The Aryan Nations was growing both in size
and notoriety, Robert Matthews and his Order were in the midst of

a national crime spree that made them heroes in white supremacist circles, militia groups were popping up like toadstools, and the
skinhead movement, recently imported from Europe, was becoming a vital force in cities across the country. Part of the reason for
all this was the conservative resurgence brought by the election of
Ronald Reagan in 1980 and the stubborn lingering effects of the
late 1970s rise in unemployment. Another equally important fac-
tor was a shift in mindset that had occurred on the far right. What
had once been a struggle to maintain white supremacy in America
had turned into a fight to retake what was once theirs. The civil
rights era was over, and in the minds of many on the far right, the
white race had lost, despite the efforts of the KKK, the White Citizens' Councils, and other segregationist groups. Everywhere they
looked they saw evidence of their defeat. Not only could African
Americans vote, but many had even been elected to office. The
feminist movement had, in the eyes of many white supremacists,
upended the traditional family in America, and affirmative action
had caused great friction between the white nationalist movement
and a government they felt was no longer on their side. This provided ample recruitment tools for nationalist leaders as well as
fertile ground for new groups to set root and thrive in.

Although there were plenty of groups active in the Twin City
area when Jeff was growing up, he was in high school and far removed from where the action was. One day he saw a piece on the
news about William Pierce's National Alliance hosting an event
in Minneapolis. A poster with the group's mailing address flashed
across the screen but was gone before he could write it down, so
he waited until the news came back on again later that night, hoping for a repeat of the story. When the poster flashed again he
was ready with pen and paper. He wrote to the National Alliance,
and they sent him leaflets and various propaganda pieces, but Jeff
was disappointed by their lack of real-world action. To him they
seemed more like a book club than an actual political group. He
wanted to belong to a group that got things done. Almost by chance
he came across a book in the local library that contained a list of

far-right groups active in the United States, along with a short description of each group. Jeff took the book home and then set about introducing himself to the white nationalist movement in America.

He contacted everyone from skinhead crews to Aryan Nations, skipping only the KKK and Christian Identity groups because he didn't consider himself religious. He told them about discovering *Mein Kampf* when he was fifteen, about his family fighting for Hitler, and how he was looking for a group with which he could do something real and tangible for the white race. For a while Jeff thought about joining the skinheads, but he discarded the idea because of their apparent lack of any cohesive political strategy. He was briefly member number 203 of Aryan Nations, but he didn't see the point of staying in the group, because of their religion and their far-flung home base in Hayden Lake, Idaho. Eventually Jeff came across NSAWFM. Not only were they just a short trip away in St. Paul, but they were also unafraid to take to the streets and be seen. He liked that the group had a heritage, a direct line of ascendancy to the father of National Socialism in America, the American Führer, George Lincoln Rockwell.

IF ROCKWELL WAS ANYTHING, he was a man of wild ambition but with limited means to achieve those ambitions. Although he saw himself as the heir to Adolf Hitler and the kindling to what would no doubt be a glorious flame of white nationalism in America, he was in fact for most of his adult life the destitute leader of a handful of malcontents who lived off cereal and water in a small house in Arlington, Virginia.

His life, leading up to his murder in 1967 at the hands of a former comrade, was a long line of mostly failed endeavors. Yet what he built and those he inspired provided the foundation for the modern radical right movement in America today.

There was little in Rockwell's background that might suggest he would one day become the father of postwar National Socialism in America. He was born in Illinois in 1918 to parents who were well-known vaudeville performers. His father toured the country extensively, while his mother stayed at home with Norman and his younger brother and sister. The marriage eventually fell apart, and Rockwell spent his childhood summers at his father's new home in Southport Island, Maine, and the rest of the year living with his mother in Bloomington, Illinois, until the family moved to his aunt's house in Atlantic City, New Jersey. In his biography of Rockwell, *For Race and Nation: George Lincoln Rockwell and the American Nazi Party*, author William H. Schmaltz describes Rockwell as an extrovert and a daredevil as well as a boy who desperately wanted to please his aloof father.

Living with his overbearing mother and aunt was hard for Rockwell, and in his senior year of high school he moved in with his paternal grandmother in Providence, Rhode Island, where he spent some of the happiest times of his youth. He was active in school and sports and enjoyed reading. During this time he had a realization that would shape his work in the future: a skillful writer could manipulate the reader to believe almost anything and that this was not only an effective tool but also a dangerous one. "I sensed an attempt to convince me of social ideas," he wrote, "not by reason, but by emotional manipulations while my mind was hypnotized by my emotions. I didn't fully realize it, but I had discovered left-wing and communist propaganda."

Anti-Semitism in America was rampant during the interwar era when Rockwell was growing up. The KKK was at the peak of its power, with millions of members across the country. Father Charles Coughlin's virulently anti-Semitic radio show reached as many as 30 million weekly listeners, and Henry Ford published a highly popular newspaper that regularly warned of the dangers of the international Jewry. Yet Rockwell, whose entertainer father often hosted Jewish friends in his home in Southport—Benny Goodman and Groucho Marx were just some of the famous Jewish performers who visited—picked up little of this, remembering only that his father described Jews as a "sophisticated and smart people."

He was a smart kid and eventually got into Brown, where he excelled, working as a cartoonist for the college paper and majoring in philosophy. One subject, however, frustrated him deeply. As part of the required subjects he took sociology and found the experience confounding. Especially infuriating was the notion that all humans and civilizations were basically created equal and that any disparity in advancement was the result of external factors that had nothing to do with qualities inherent in various races.

"You can make a helpless boob out of a born genius by bringing him up in a dark closet," he insisted in his autobiography, "but you can't make a genius out of a drooling idiot, even by sending him to Brown."

At Brown Rockwell suspected that his professors all knew the absurdity of such a doctrine, but he also suspected that something dark and nefarious worked in the wings to make sure it remained dogma. Rockwell was still at Brown in 1941 when the war broke out. He despised FDR but hated Hitler even more, so he enlisted in the Navy and spent the war flying missions in both the Atlantic and Pacific theaters.

In the early 1950s, when serving as an instructor at a Navy base in southern California, Rockwell became increasingly convinced of the dangers of communism. He wasn't the only one, of course—the Red Scare was in full swing. Patriots all over the country saw the dark hand of communism everywhere, and Senator Joseph McCarthy was hunting for Soviet infiltrators in every branch of government. Rockwell became involved in the effort to nominate the fiercely anticommunist World War II general Douglas MacArthur for president and once tried to rent a hall in San Diego for a rally. Another MacArthur supporter told him that he would never be able to rent Union Hall in San Diego because of the Jews—apparently the Jews were in cahoots with the communists and would do whatever they could to foil a MacArthur candidacy. Rockwell was flabbergasted. The woman gave him several Jewish newspapers that all ridiculed and warned of the dangers of his hero MacArthur. It was to be Rockwell's first peek through the looking glass.

As he wrote in *This Time the World*, "I had suddenly been exposed to a whole secret world which the average American never even imagines and never sees: the world of the Jews."

In the time that followed, Rockwell disappeared down a rabbit hole of nationalist literature and thinking, until he finally ended up at Adolf Hitler. Having read and reread *Mein Kampf*, Rockwell became convinced that National Socialism was "the only thing which could save man from his own degradation in luxury, self-seeking short-sightedness and racial degeneration."

For years he struggled to put together some sort of outlet for his anti-Jewish ideas, dabbling both in publishing and political organizing, but time and time again he found himself penniless, friendless, and destitute following his latest failure. In 1958, after having lost almost everything he owned except for the lease of a small, two-story house in Arlington, Rockwell founded the World Union of Free Enterprise National Socialists (WUFENS). The group, consisting of a handful of "troopers" who had sought Rockwell out following one of his many public forays into nationalism, was as ambitious as it was incapable of following through on those ambitions. Rockwell had come up with a seven-point manifesto for WUFENS, including a promise to "investigate, try and execute all Jews proved to have taken part in Marxist or Zionist plots of treason against their nations or humanity." Rockwell believed that millions of Americans would embrace National Socialism once they woke up to the degeneracy of modern, liberal values.

Still, for all the anti-Semitism, anticommunism, opposition to desegregation, and explicit racism that existed in America at the time, National Socialism was too much for most people. The Nazi concentration camps were still fresh in peoples' minds, and many of those who Rockwell sought to convince had, like himself, fought against Hitler less than two decades earlier. If National Socialism was to succeed in America, Rockwell needed to convince the public that, in fact, it wasn't as bad as they had been told.

In a minor stroke of genius that would foreshadow the fake news epidemic sixty years later, Rockwell fabricated a US GI by the name of Lew Cor ("Rockwell" phonetically backward) and, under his new pseudonym, made up grotesque stories from the Holocaust that Cor supposedly had witnessed during the war. He then sold it to pulp magazine *Sir!*. His plan was to muddy the waters of the Holocaust. Awful stories about the conditions of the concentration camps abounded, but if Rockwell could point to one of them and say, "This one is all lies, and I should know because I made it up," then it would taint all the other stories about Nazi atrocities. If one story was fake, wasn't there a chance all of them were? Rockwell explained his plan later in an interview with *Playboy* magazine: "Here's my ultimate proof of just how utterly ridiculous all the anti-Nazi literature you've read really is. . . . I wrote the vilest lies I could think of! And here they all are in print in this magazine. Look at the photographs! These are supposed to be actual shots of Nazi victims mentioned in the article—victims that I invented!"

As the NSM would decades later, Rockwell's WUFENS troopers mounted demonstrations designed to attract the ire of protesters. They marched in replica SS uniforms, relying heavily on pantomime and pageantry to get the public's attention. The idea was that it would attract only those most dedicated to the cause, and as such, it was a resounding success. The handful of people who joined WUFENS were certainly dedicated, but one might wonder if Rockwell's organization would have been more successful had they toned down their most overt Hitlerisms—the same might be said for today's NSM. As it was, Rockwell's operations were mostly small fry, with questionable results. Once, after having been refused service at a local pizzeria, Rockwell rallied his troops to picket the pizza parlor. They retreated after about an hour when the pizza parlor's owner turned the hose on them, but back at HQ Rockwell turned defeat into victory when he speculated that they had probably reduced the pizza place's business for the duration of the hour they were there.

Membership in WUFENS rarely exceeded twenty troopers, and by mid-1959, having lost the lease on his house and all but a couple of troopers, Rockwell decided he had had enough. He disbanded the organization and founded the American Nazi Party (ANP). If people thought he'd been extreme in the past, he would show them what extreme meant.

Rockwell met William Luther Pierce in 1965. Fifteen years Rockwell's junior, Pierce was a physicist working for the defense industry. As a student and then assistant professor at the University of Oregon, Pierce claimed to have had no time to pay attention to the outside world but that the world, with its ascendant civil rights battles, eventually demanded it. Pierce struggled with what to think about civil rights. On the one hand, he believed firmly that African Americans had every right to do whatever they wanted so long as they didn't bother anyone, but on the other, he also strongly believed that white Americans had every right to not eat with them, hire them, or send their kids to school with them.

Much like Rockwell, Pierce didn't buy into the notion that all humans were created equal and that blacks were the same as whites. However, where Rockwell firmly believed that whites were superior to blacks in every way, Pierce at that point hadn't really thought about it in qualitative terms; he simply believed that the two were inherently different. He sought help at the John Birch Society but found their mindless blaming of everything on the communists unhelpful. He suspected that somehow the Jews played an outsourcing role in the civil rights struggles, but he didn't know to what extent. In his autobiographical essay *The Radicalization of an American*, Pierce writes, "I could hardly help noticing that the shrillest and pushiest of those demanding 'equality now' for Blacks, both on the Oregon State campus and in the media, were not Blacks but members of another minority group—which raised, for the first time in my life, the Jewish question."

He read extensively and eventually came up with his own patchwork of historical facts and interpretations that formed a profoundly racist worldview, at which Adolf Hitler sat at the center. It was this ideology, coupled with a move from Oregon to Connecticut, that brought Pierce and Rockwell together.

Although skeptical of Rockwell's "flamboyant tactics"—meaning the ANP's penchant for SS uniforms and marching—Pierce nevertheless admired the commander's courage and idealism in the face of public outrage. More a thinker and ideologue than a jackbooted stormtrooper, Pierce was put in charge of editing the publication *National Socialist World*, in which Rockwell spread the word of National Socialism to a national audience.

Meanwhile the civil rights fight had greatly energized Rockwell, giving him a specific enemy to fight rather than a nebulous Jewish conspiracy. He got his hands on a bus that he decorated with swastikas and dubbed "The Hate Bus," and he and his troopers followed the Freedom Riders around the country, trolling and harassing them endlessly. More than anything Rockwell despised Martin Luther King Jr., who he called "Martin Luther Coon." Segregationists at the time saw their struggle as a zero-sum game, and to Rockwell and his cohorts, the struggle was nothing short of existential. Every right and liberty gained by African Americans was at the expense of white Americans, and rather than African Americans climbing out of oppression, Rockwell saw the Civil Rights Movement as blacks dragging whites down into the dirt.

At the same time, Rockwell greatly admired Malcolm X. Although he despised the Civil Rights Movement, Rockwell saw Malcolm X as a fellow warrior and respected him for it. In an interview in *Playboy* magazine he predicted that by 1972 whites in America would be clamoring for a leader with "the guts of Malcolm X." He aspired to be that leader.

On August 25, 1967, Rockwell was doing laundry at a laundromat in Arlington when he realized he had forgotten the bleach, and decided to go home and get it. He got into his car and pulled out from the curb when two shots rang out, hitting Rockwell in the chest and head. He managed to leave the car before he fell, dying in a swirl of laundry detergent. His killer was John Patler, a former member of the ANP who carried a grudge after Rockwell dismissed him from the group.

Members of the National Socialist Movement and the Loyal White Knights of the KKK.

Rockwell's death set off a series of rifts inside the party, eventually splitting it into several factions, all of which claimed to be the true torchbearers of Commander Rockwell's legacy. Pierce stayed with the largest faction but was increasingly frustrated with the group's fetishization of everything German. More and more he came to abhor the pageantry element of the party and felt that although Rockwell had been correct that the current political system in the United States was fundamentally broken and needed to be replaced, what was needed was not a German solution but an American one. Writing in his manifesto "Prospectus for a Nationalist Front," Pierce explained the problem of relying on symbolism and rhetoric that, he rightly assumed, the vast majority of the United States public found abhorrent: "We do have to avoid isolating ourselves from the public with programs and images so radical that only a small fraction of one percent will respond."

Pierce soon left the party and set out to look for something that better suited his uniquely American style of white nationalism, and soon he found it. He would go on to become the most influential white supremacist in American history and would be indirectly responsible for the deaths of hundreds of innocent Americans.

"I THINK WE HAVE SOME WORK to do, guys," Schoep said. It was late Saturday night, and he was reclining on the bed in Gunner's hotel room, resting against the headboard and nursing a beer. He'd been quiet and withdrawn since the rally earlier that day, only making halfhearted declarations of victory that everyone knew weren't true and that he didn't really mean. The anniversary weekend had been a dud. Hardly anyone had showed up. In fact, there hadn't even been a person for each of the forty years the organization had been in existence. The rally itself in downtown Chattanooga had been an embarrassing medley of technical difficulties and frustratingly accurate heckling from the crowd. The NSM's sound system hadn't worked, and the audience had brought bullhorns that very much had, so the NSM cut the speeches short to spare themselves the indignities of having to listen to protestors mocking their anemic attendance. To top it all off, they'd gotten lost heading back to their cars and someone had spat on Gunner.

The year before in Atlanta they had almost twice as many members show up, and the year before that, at the glorious battle of Trenton, more still. Now Wilson was gone, and Schneider was a traitor—and that was just from the ranks of leadership. Last year they had families, people with young kids, marching through downtown Atlanta. They'd even signed several new members. Now most of the new guys from last year were AWOL, many of them disappearing almost immediately after signing up when they realized there would be membership dues. At this rate the NSM would be finished in a couple of years. The glorious work Commander Rockwell began in 1958 would have been for nothing, and the two decades Jeff had put in as leader of the NSM would have been a waste.

When Jeff joined the NSM in the early 1990s he quickly proved himself an able and eager young activist, and he had plenty of ideas he worked to implement in order to revive the party from the shambolic state it found itself in. He printed and handed out flyers, distributed literature, and put on rallies. He also worked tirelessly to reach out to younger skinheads and nationalists. Like Rockwell, he wanted the party to be in the vanguard of white nationalism in America. He would let the ideologues pontificate and ruminate; his was to be the party of action. He'd kept up his correspondence with many of those he had reached out to before joining the NSAWFM, and now he used them to spread the word that the party was growing again and the time had come to collaborate.

His star was rising, and in 1994 he was invited to address the crowd at the annual Aryan Nations World Congress, traditionally *the* place to be for white supremacists in America. At the same time, Chris Herrington, who had founded the National Socialist American Workers Freedom Movement on the ruins of the American Nazi Party in 1974, was teaching the young nationalist the ropes, describing the various pitfalls that could end a career and even a group. The number-one thing to watch out for was government ruses designed to entrap him. Members of the far right in America had a long history of getting locked up for things they had said to undercover federal informants. The FBI perfected their methods on black activists in the 1960s and 1970s and had, for decades, employed them with great success on the far right and antigovernment fringes. Herrington explained how any stranger offering weapons or advocating violence was most likely an undercover law enforcement officer or an informant.

One of Jeff's first goals when taking over as leader of the NSM was to grow the organization not only by attracting new members but also by explaining to other players on the scene that the only way forward was through collaboration. He came up with an umbrella organization he called the United Patriot Front and reached out to a host of other nationalist groups. Nobody took him up on his offer. There was just too much ego and too many old grudges that would need to be set aside before the groups could come together. Besides, despite his rapid ascension to leader of the NSM and speaking slot at the Aryan World Congress, Jeff was still largely unknown to other groups. He may have been a young talent, but asking established groups to join forces with a rookie commanding a tiny outfit in the Midwest was simply too much.

It was a rude awakening for Jeff, who had always believed he could overcome the petty and sometimes outright violent inter-group skirmishes. He had been in his share of fights with other nationalists and even had his nose split open by a steel-tipped boot to the face, but he'd always believed it was possible to rally together in the face of a common enemy. They were all white people, and that had to count for something.

Disillusioned but undaunted, Jeff set about revamping the NSM to attract a younger crowd. He released "The 25 Points of American National Socialism," a list of 25 demands that he had lifted almost verbatim from Hitler's "Program of the National Socialist German Workers' Party," with only a few modernizing flourishes. For instance, where Hitler demanded that "no Jew can be a countryman," Jeff maintained that "no Jew or homosexual may be a member of the nation." He also included a demand for national universal healthcare, the outlawing of abortions, and the right to bear arms. He established the Viking Youth Corps, which focused on recruiting angry teens, and he launched a special Women's Division of the NSM. He also founded NSM88 Records, a label releasing only white power music, and bought the neo-Nazi social networking site New Saxon.

He even fielded a political action committee, 88 PAC, designed to fund the campaigns of pro-white candidates. Although the PAC failed to have much impact—its activities peaked in the 2006 election cycle when it raised $660 and spent $652, which included a single campaign contribution of $10 to a failed campaign in Tennessee. Jeff's other endeavors helped the NSM become the largest

Cake commemorating the forty-year anniversary of the NSM.

and most visible neo-Nazi group in the country. It also didn't hurt that both the National Alliance and Aryan Nations, two of the leading far-right groups in the country, folded during the first couple of years of the new millennium, leaving the NSM to soak up some of the homeless members. By 2009 the NSM boasted sixty-one chapters in thirty-five states, and although they were mocked and ridiculed for their fondness of dressing up in the style of German troops, no other groups could claim to be bigger.

Still, having hundreds of members on paper counted very little when only a dozen or so showed up when called upon, and in 2014 the NSM would have had difficulties mustering sufficient bodies to even field a soccer team. Something needed to be done, and Jeff believed he knew just what that was. So in the summer of 2016 he called Matthew Heimbach and set up a meeting.

CHAPTER 6

The Soldiers of the Earl Turner

Enemies of mankind. You cannot slaughter innocent men, women, and America's kids and get away with it. We will not rest or have peace until this crime against humanity is adjudged and punished.

—Then FBI director Louis Freeh, atop the rubble in
the wake of the Oklahoma City bombing, 1995

Matthew believed that whites in America were at the cusp of waking up and fighting back. In a term favored by the alt-right and lifted from the movie *The Matrix*, he believed that more and more people were becoming "red-pilled." In the movie the main character, Neo, played by Keanu Reeves, gets offered a choice between two pills from the mysterious hacker Morpheus. "You take the blue pill, the story ends. You wake up in your bed and believe whatever you want to believe. You take the red pill, you stay in Wonderland, and I show you how deep the rabbit hole goes." Matthew knew how deep the rabbit hole went. Like in *The Matrix*, the real world—the one that most people didn't see—was an elaborate machine designed to suppress people like him. In order to get free, white people needed to destroy the machine. There was no piecemeal solution. The whole rotten thing had to go and be replaced by a new system, one that didn't hate people like him, that didn't actively try to destroy the white race. There could be no bargaining and no compromise because those in power wanted him and his kin dead. There were those before him who had believed the same thing.

On April 19, 1995, as ashes and debris were still raining from the sky in Oklahoma City, a forty-three-year-old highway patrol cop pulled over a yellow 1977 Mercury Marquis sixty miles north of the city for driving without a license plate. Inside the car was a twenty-seven-year-old Timothy McVeigh, wearing a T-shirt with the words "Sic Semper Tyrannis" (Thus Always to Tyrants) and carrying a loaded Glock under his windbreaker. On the dashboard under the windshield was an envelope on which McVeigh had scribbled, "Obey the Constitution of the United States and we won't shoot you." Inside were various racist, apocalyptic ravings that had informed McVeigh's murder of 168 people, among them clippings from a book called *The Turner Diaries*, written by a man called Andrew Macdonald.

Masquerading as the discovered diary of one Earl Turner, *The Turner Diaries* describes a dystopian future (the book was written in 1978 but set in the early 1990s) in which draconian laws have made gun ownership illegal and forced a small band of white, patriotic Americans known as "The Underground" to fight back. The diary begins as the new laws have led to marauding African Americans attacking law-abiding, disarmed whites—"Robberies of this sort had become all too common since the Cohen Act, with groups of Blacks forcing their way into White homes to rob and rape"—and ends with the global eradication of all Jews. *The Turner Diaries* perfectly encapsulated the zeitgeist of the nascent antigovernment patriot movement in the United States in the late 1970s and inspired countless aspiring right-wing radicals to organize. The man behind the pseudonym "Andrew Macdonald" was William Luther Pierce.

After being ousted from the ANP—which by that time had changed its name to the National Socialist White People's Party (NSWPP)—in 1970 Pierce searched for a group for which his evolving politics were better suited. He was in no way moderating his views—in fact, during his tenure as leader of the NSWPP he had frequently made public death threats against prominent politicians. For instance, he once suggested that President Nixon should be "dragged out of his office and shot." He was growing frustrated by the ineffectiveness and disparate nature of the radical right in America and in an essay titled "Prospectus for a National Front," published in August 1970, he wrote,

> Instead of genuine political organizations the groups which constitute "the movement" are, in most cases, clubs, cliques, societies, or cults. They each tend to have quite narrow and specific organizational personalities to which they require every new member to conform. They each have a unique "way to do it," which they insist is the only correct path to salvation. As a matter of fact, these various programs for victory seldom have much to do with reality. They are based more on daydreams and theory than on hardheaded political thinking.

Almost fifty years later Matthew would use much the same rhetoric, even borrowing the name of Pierce's prospected alliance when he launched the Nationalist Front.

Much like Matthew discovering Youth for Western Civilization, Pierce eventually found a group whose ostensible conservative politics belied a profoundly racist bent he could exploit and shape. The National Youth Alliance (NYA) had grown out of Youth for Wallace, which had supported the wildly segregationist 1968 presidential campaign of Alabama governor George Wallace. When Pierce learned of the group in 1970 it was under the control of Willis Carto, an influential conservative publisher who had also founded the Liberty Lobby, a lobbying group with anti-Semitic and racist views. But Carto's leadership was weakened from infighting with the pro-Wallace faction of the NYA, who disagreed with the fiercely anti-Semitic leanings of Carto's supporters. Almost immediately friction arose between Carto and Pierce, the latter espousing a much more militaristic form of white supremacy. Carto, furious at the upstart who believed he could hijack his group, accused Pierce of stealing the Liberty Lobby mailing list, and Pierce in turn accused Carto of using this list to mount outside attacks on the NYA. Eventually Carto filed theft charges against Pierce, while Pierce maintained that Carto was secretly being controlled by Jews.

Pierce was also frustrated by the NYA itself, believing the members to be too timid on their politics and unwilling to recognize the solutions needed to address the racial issues in America. During his tenure as leader he used the NYA's publication *Attack!* to alienate and push out those he felt didn't have the stomach to do what he believed was necessary to save the white race. In an essay from 1978, as he changed the name of the publication from *Attack!* to *American Vanguard*, Pierce boasted about how *Attack!*'s increasing calls for military revolution—"revolution becomes every patriot's duty, and mindless support for the new masters of the citadel is treason"—drove away the NYA's conservative, weak-willed members in droves.

But shedding weaker members wasn't enough for Pierce, and in 1974 he left the NYA and formed a new group on its remains: the National Alliance, which would go on to become one of the wealthiest and most influential neo-Nazi organizations in America.

At the same time Pierce was building his National Alliance (NA), a fifty-five-year-old aeronautical engineer from Denver,

Colorado, Richard Girnt Butler, moved to the picturesque area of Hayden Lake, Idaho, to enjoy his retirement. He'd lived in Lancaster, on the outskirts of Los Angeles, for most of his adult life, and he yearned for fresh air and open spaces. Hayden Lake fit perfectly. However, there was another reason for his relocation. Butler had always held anticommunist convictions, and in the early 1960s, while active in efforts to ferret out communist schoolteachers in the local community, Butler had met William Potter Gale. A retired colonel and World War II veteran, Gale was virulently anticommunist and, in the 1960s, argued that the government had no right intervening in civil rights issues. He introduced Butler to Wesley Swift, a pioneer of the so-called Christian Identity (CI) movement, and Butler, who until then had been a secular man, found God. CI is a deeply warped form of Christianity that holds that whites are the true Israelites and that Jews were the offspring of Eve mating with the Serpent in the Garden of Eden. Through CI Butler soon came to believe that the corrupting hand of the Jew sullied every aspect of society and that escaping its influence would mean creating a new homeland for whites. When he retired in 1974 he and his wife, Betty, set about making his dream a reality in Hayden Lake.

If Swift's CI lay the theological foundations for Butler's life in Hayden Lake, it was William Potter Gale who provided the political brickwork. Gale spent most of the 1960s and early 1970s coming up with a framework for his by-then antigovernment, tax-protesting, anti-Semitic, and white supremacist worldview. Fiercely racist, he advocated violence against Jews and was obsessed with racial warfare. In 1982, in his regular radio address broadcast across eastern Colorado, southwestern Kansas, and northern Oklahoma, he advocated both the lynching of African Americans—"How do you get a nigger out of a tree? Cut the rope."—as well as coordinated attacks on Jews—"You're damn right I'm teaching violence! You better start making dossiers, names, addresses, phone numbers, car license numbers, on every damn Jew rabbi in this land . . . and you better start doing it now.

And know where he is. If you have to be told any more than that, you're too damn dumb to bother with."

In 1971 Gale, under the pseudonym Colonel Ben Cameron, a name derived from a character from *Birth of a Nation*, wrote an article that laid out his politics. He railed against the United Nations, unlawful taxation for the support of foreign governments, civil rights, and the income tax, which he claimed was communist inspired. Further, he wrote that there should be no higher seat of power than the county level, and that the sheriff was the only legal law enforcement officer in the country. Gale called his ideology the *Posse Commitatus*, Latin for "power of the county," and it quickly spread from his base in Mariposa, California, throughout the Northwest.

Butler was an early adopter of the Posse Commitatus ideology and moved to implement it at his growing compound in Hayden Lake. Idaho, like many western states, was fertile ground for separatist communities. Butler was quickly able to start a Posse chapter in a region with a deep-seated skepticism of the federal government, rooted not only in its geographical distance from Washington, DC, but also its continued frontier mentality and ever-present disputes with the Federal Bureau of Land Management over land use. By 1977 Butler had formed his own Christian Identity church, called the Church of Jesus Christ Christian. One part of his work would be to spread the word of the white God to his congregation. Another would be to form a political arm with the purpose of implementing that word. This he called the Aryan Nations. And as the Church followed a tortured version of the Christian God, Aryan Nations revered a man who had never professed a religious belief in his life: Adolf Hitler.

Much like Matthew more than three decades later, Butler dreamed of bringing the various elements of the ascendant far-right movement together, and in 1981 he hosted the first annual Aryan World Congress. Among the guests were luminaries of the far right at the time, including Tom Metzger, former Klan leader who would go on to found White Aryan Resistance (WAR), and a young Don

Black, then a Klansman as well. Eventually word of Butler's church reached a man who, like Butler, had moved to the Northwest to escape society's corruption and was building himself a homestead only two hours north of Hayden Lake: Robert Jay Matthews. Like many who would eventually join the far right, Matthews had been passionate about the fight against communism. At fifteen he sent a check for $5 to the John Birch Society in California in payment for their manifesto, *The Blue Book*. Eventually his involvement in the John Birch Society led him to see the government's activities as anti-American and communist in nature, none more so than the collection of income tax. He saw the creeping hand of socialism in most aspects of American society, and when he was nineteen years old, with some friends he formed a militia, the Sons of Liberty, with the stated objective of fighting back the communist takeover of the US government. Matthews was still active in the John Birch Society and was even a member of the Young Republicans, but any faith he still had in the government was shattered as Nixon, once as fierce an anticommunist as any, sought closer bonds with the mortal enemy of Matthews and the John Birch Society: China. For Matthews it was proof that the global communist takeover that the Society had warned about for decades was coming to pass and that the time for politics was irrevocably over.

Believing that the collapse of society was imminent, Matthews instilled as strict an order on his militia group as someone in their early twenties can. He created a list of weapons that it was incumbent on all his members to procure, and they trained rigorously—that is, until Matthews lost interest and moved to Metaline Falls, Washington, in 1974. It seems he had left the militia movement behind as he settled in the lush wooded hills of Washington.

Richard Butler wanted to expand his ministry in Hayden Lake. Shortly after establishing the Aryan Nations he began selling family memberships for $15 per year in order to encourage not just men who wanted to fight for the white race to come but also wives who could instill Butler's values into the minds of young children to grow up to be proud, white warriors. To the men who joined he gave the uniform of the Aryan Nations: crisp, sky-blue shirts emblazoned with the logo of a crowned Christian cross on a blue shield as well as a swastika armband. He was building a church and an army. Part preacher and part huckster, he also sold an impressive array of merchandise and books, all to fill the coffers and build his white homeland. Much like the far right would decades later and even claiming the same proof, Butler claimed that the government of America was actively trying to emasculate and destroy the white race. Millions of white babies were being butchered by the Jewish abortion mongers, and because of affirmative action, white men were being discriminated against at every turn. His plan was to attract white people to the Inland Empire—an area spanning Idaho, Washington, and parts of Montana—and then eventually spread into Wyoming and Oregon in sufficient numbers to take over the state legislatures and eventually carve their new homeland out of the United States.

Butler began by reaching out to other Identity churches across the country, inviting them to annual gatherings for communal lectures and services held by the churches' elders, but he soon realized he needed to look outside the relatively limited world of Christian Identity if he truly wanted to expand his flock. He reached out to neo-Nazi leaders, other leaders of the Posse Commitatus, and Klansmen, reminding them that despite their differences, they shared an Aryan heritage that should be more important than any ideological or theological differences. It was a pitch that many aspiring unifiers on the far right would give, including Matthew Heimbach, but unlike Matthew, Butler wanted the symbols of hate—the swastika and the worship of Adolf Hitler—to be front and center. After a 1980 bombing of his church, where nobody was arrested and nobody injured, Butler increased security on the compound. He built a guard tower with a cat walk where armed guards patrolled, and he added a sign at the bottom of the drive that said, "Whites Only."

As Butler was growing his organization, adding soldiers to his church, Robert Matthews worked on the hillside property he'd bought two hours north of the Aryan Nations compound. He was still antagonistic to the government, whose taxation he believed was a treasonous affront to American values, but he was no longer involved in any militia activity. By all appearances he was living a quiet life.

But his reading habits were becoming more radical. He joined William Luther Pierce's National Alliance after reading *Which Way Western Man*, a monotonous tome written by one of the earliest adherents to white supremacy in America, William Gayle Simpson. The book was a wordy diatribe against the ills that have fallen on the white race, even when it was at the peak of its influence in the mid-twentieth century. It argued that liberal values and zero population growth were the weapons with which the white race was committing suicide. "In this light, birth control is seen to be the knife by which civilized White man is cutting his own throat," Simpson railed. And as it so often was, the nefarious force behind it was the vicious Jew, who, according to Simpson, believed that "Earth was made for them to rule, and gentiles to be their servants and slaves, their milk cows."

"Race consciousness, and discrimination on the basis of race, are absolutely essential to any race's survival, and to any nation's survival," Simpson concluded, and Matthews agreed. Simpson's case had been made before—and wasn't any truer for it. Future white nationalists would make the argument again. His lament for an emasculated race, made to be ashamed of what it was, would become a staple with nationalists and white supremacists in the years to come. In fact, his writings echo in the very justification made for marches like the one in Charlottesville in 2017 and in the arguments for keeping Confederate monuments:

> Thus the White man has been left not only split and confused but frustrated and even ashamed of himself—ashamed of his mastery, ashamed of his empires, ashamed even of the very ancestors to whom he is supremely indebted for all that he is and for all that he has. He, the White man, sprung from one of the greatest warrior

races of history, instead of leaping to assert himself, and to defend himself, and to press firmly for what he needs for his survival and for the realization of the greatness that is in him, sits in a corner, and hesitates, and mopes, and apologizes not only for being what he is but for what his ancestors were.

Matthews discovered the Aryan Nations in 1982. He began attending services there, and although he had no time for the Christian Identity aspect of the AN, he agreed with Butler's vision of an Aryan homeland in the Pacific Northwest. His increasingly radical reading habits had led him back to the militant frame of mind he had once left behind when he moved to Metaline Falls, and more than ever he felt the need to take action against the government. In AN he recognized a good place to scout for like-minded men who were as ready as he was.

There was much talk of action at the compound, but to Matthews's frustration, it never went beyond words. For all their talk of creating a white homeland, there were very few actual steps being made toward realizing the plan. Even more frustrating to Matthews was the fact that while he and the Aryan Nation did nothing, the radical left had a long history of flamboyant actions. The Weather Underground had detonated a bomb in Chicago in 1969, and the Black Panthers had shaken the nation with their militant tactics throughout the early 1970s. Then there was the issue of money. To mount a revolution you needed money for guns and supplies. Here too the radical left had done what the far right so far had only dared to talk about. In 1981 members of the Black Liberation Army as well as former members of the Weather Underground, now calling themselves the May 19th Communist Organization, robbed a Brink's armored car, killing one guard and gravely wounding another before getting away with $1.6 million.

It was as if it had been lifted from the pages of *The Turner Diaries*, only with leftist radicals in place of white supremacists, and it was precisely the kind of activity Matthews had envisioned for his army. Relatively low profile but perfect to raise the funds and the army that would be needed for bigger operations to come. Pierce's book inspired him, and he handed out copies of it and other NA literature to potential conscripts. Soon he and some friends had built a house next to his own on his property in Metaline Falls. They would serve as barracks. Just like in *The Turner Diaries*, Matthews envisioned an army made of small cells, capable of quick, devastating blows against the enemy. And just like the organization in Pierce's book, Matthews named his "The Order." Between 1983 and 1984 the members of The Order, which Matthews later renamed the Silent Brotherhood, went on a murder and crime spree, eventually killing three people and stealing millions of dollars, most of which Matthews redistributed to other far-right leaders he deemed worthy. He was eventually felled by an informant in his own ranks who the FBI had turned, and after one of the largest manhunts in American history, he was cornered in a house on Whidbey Island in Washington State. After a protracted firefight Matthews was killed when the house burned down around him. He died on December 8, 1984, thirty-one years old, with a gun still in his charred hand when authorities found him. His death while fighting the FBI instantly made him a martyr to the American far right.

A few months after Matthews' death one member of his gang, David Lane, who had been the getaway driver during the murder of Jewish radio host Alan Berg on June 18, 1984, was arrested. For his role in the actions of The Order—counterfeiting, robbery, and murder—Lane received a total of 190 years in prison. He died in prison in 2007, but not before having become an influential writer in his own right, publishing several screeds in the ideological vein of William Luther Pierce. His most influential work, however, became famous for its short length: the fourteen-word sentence, "We must secure the existence of our people and a future for white children." This sentence would become the mantra for white nationalists of all bents in the years to come and eventually gain such ubiquity that the entirety of the sentence would no longer be needed. The phrase "fourteen words" became shorthand, a code by which nationalists, neo-Nazis, Klansmen, and other white supremacists identify each other.

Through The Order and Timothy McVeigh's bombing in Oklahoma City, right-wing terrorism entered the public consciousness in the 1980s and 1990s in a way it hadn't before, even when the KKK was at its abominable height. "Sovereign citizens," and "patriots" became terms that captured the imagination of the country and struck fear into the hearts of citizens and concern from those in law enforcement.

Only a year after the Oklahoma City bombing the FBI and Bureau of Alcohol, Tobacco and Firearms (ATF, now the Bureau of Alcohol, Tobacco, Firearms and Explosives) led a weeks-long siege of a piece of land outside Jordan, Montana, where a Christian antigovernment patriot group had holed up after its members had been charged with counterfeiting. Four years after Oklahoma City the authorities finally arrested "The Unabomber," Ted Kaczynski, after his homemade letter bombs had killed three people and injured thirteen. In his remote Montana cabin police found bomb-making equipment as well as a thirty-five-thousand-word antigovernment manifesto.

The McVeigh bombing in particular brought into sharp focus the need for law enforcement to develop a cohesive plan for dealing with terrorism, both foreign and domestic. To this end President Bill Clinton signed Presidential Decision Directive 39, officially making the FBI the head agency in investigating terrorist attacks against Americans. However, a changing trend in the nature of domestic terror made the FBI's work more difficult. The years following the Oklahoma City bombing saw a marked increase in attacks by so-called lone-wolf offenders, perpetrators who operate outside of groups, making their activities more difficult to spot for law enforcement. The most shocking acts of politically motivated terror committed by domestic terrorists since McVeigh have all been lone wolves. Some of the most influential writing advocating lone-wolf terrorism comes from those who were close to AN and inspired by Pierce. In May of 2000 Tom Metzger, the neo-Nazi and former Klan leader who was present at the inaugural Aryan World Congress in 1982, published in his magazine, *White Aryan Resistance*, a manifesto from an ostensibly anonymous author called "The Lone Wolf Creed." It stated,

> I am the Lone Wolf; I am covert. . . . I do not join groups and/or organizations due to informants, agent provocateurs and troublemakers. I avoid being on a list. I have studied and researched people like the Unabomber, BTK Wichita, Kansas serial killer, Eric Rudolph, Robert Matthews and others and learned from their errors. I am preparing for the coming war. I am ready when the line is crossed. . . . I am the underground insurgent fighter and independent.

Louis Beam, a member of the AN, saw the promise in unaffiliated terrorists even sooner and, in 1992, published an essay called "Leaderless Resistance" in the antigovernment newsletter *The Seditionist*. In it he warned that groups and organizations were easy for the government to kill and that smaller cells would be needed.

> Leaderless Resistance leads to very small or even one man cells of resistance. Those who join organizations to play "let's pretend" or who are "groupies" will quickly be weeded out. While for those who are serious about their opposition to federal despotism, this is exactly what is desired.

Their call to action and the allure of the lone warrior found an eager and receptive audience, often with devastating results. Wade Michael Page, the skinhead who killed six people in a Sikh temple in Wisconsin on August 5, 2012, was a member of the Hammerskin Nation, but there is no evidence to suggest that his fellow skinheads were aware of his plans. Dylann Roof, who killed nine people at an African American church in Charleston, South Carolina, showed Confederate and white supremacist sympathies online but did not belong to a group, nor did any group admit knowledge of his actions. Anders Behring Breivik, who detonated a bomb in Oslo, Norway, before going on a shooting spree at a summer camp for the governing Labor Party's youth arm, eventually killing seventy-seven people, was also active on far-right forums but did not belong to any group, nor did he share his intentions publicly.

The actions of Timothy McVeigh also brought *The Turner Diaries* to a new generation of antigovernment activists and white supremacists, and the years since have seen a slew of acts of brutality inspired by the work of William Luther Pierce. In 1998, when three white men dragged James Byrd Jr. to death behind their pickup truck, one of the perpetrators, John King, allegedly said, "We're starting the Turner Diaries early."

Still, the lasting legacy of *The Turner Diaries* upon the far right in America wasn't just violence but also an ideological agnosticism that would one day give birth to the modern-day nationalist movement, a movement in which ideology mattered less than a sense of racial dispossession and the looming threat of "white genocide." As J. M. Berger, an associate fellow with the International Centre for Counter-Terrorism, The Hague, explained,

> *The Turner Diaries* is notable for its lack of ideological persuasion. At one point in the novel, its protagonist, Earl Turner, is given a book to read. Turner claims the book perfectly explains the reasons for white supremacy and the justification of all of The Order's actions. Importantly, this magical tome's contents are never specified. Although the novel's epilogue broadly hints at a Nazi orientation, the book never explicitly identifies The Order with a specific movement.

According to Berger, the lack of ideological specificity of Pierce's work has two benefits: it allows nationalists and white supremacists of all stripes to superimpose their own beliefs onto the protagonists in the book, but, more importantly, *The Turner Diaries* inspired leaders in the movement to "take a more carefully generic approach, playing on racial fear and resentment as they existed, rather than attempting to manufacture doctrinaire justifications."

This would become a key part in the relative success of the alt-right leading up to the 2016 election and was fundamental in Matthew Heimbach's approach to building his grand alliance. Particular ideological quirks and doctrines were detrimental to building a movement. Rather than focus on what separated them—skinheads and KKK would never agree on most things, nor could the alt-right have played a part in the election of Donald Trump if they were specifically neo-Nazi or specifically anything else—they highlighted their common struggles and upcoming battles. As Berger points out, "While it would be a mistake to credit *The Turner Diaries* for the entirety of this transition in white nationalism, the novel demonstrated how to successfully leverage racial fears and resentments in the service of violence, without a call to a specific ideology."

I came across *The Turner Diaries* many times while writing this book. Once, I was given a copy at a Klan rally and told it would change my life. I saw it at NSM conventions, skinhead gatherings, and even gun shows, and it seemed like J. M. Berger was right: it didn't matter that the groups agreed on almost nothing—*The Turner Diaries* spoke to all of them.

Matthew had, of course, read it and dismissed it as a juvenile fantasy, a daydream for those who had no idea how to actually get anything done. But for all its ridiculousness, Matthew said the book served a real purpose, albeit one that William Pierce hadn't intended.

"We use it as a red flag," he told me once. "If someone comes up and says they want to join our group, then starts talking about *The Turner Diaries* and all that nonsense, it means that the guy is probably an informant or an undercover cop. There's no group out there that talks about doing *Turner Diary* stuff. That is guaranteed to get you a domestic terrorism charge."

Jeff Schoep told me similar stories about guys talking about bomb plots or acts of terror and said he learned quickly to steer clear. He knew that the government was looking for ways to entrap white nationalists to become informants, and talking about terror

plots was an easy way to get in trouble. Although this seemed paranoid, there was a long track record of the FBI using informants to
gain knowledge of the workings of radical groups. Wayne Manis,
a retired FBI agent who had been in charge of the Bureau's investigation into AN in the 1980s and 1990s, confirmed this when I
spoke to him about my reporting for this book. He estimated that
a good 20 percent of everyone I'd interviewed was probably some
kind of federal informant. "We have them everywhere in these
groups," he said.

"That *Turner Diary* stuff might have worked in the old days,"
Matthew said. "Back when people actually met face to face, but
now, when people talk over the internet, everything is monitored.
Besides, violence doesn't work. We know this. Violence doesn't
create converts; it just makes you an asshole."

CHAPTER 7

National
Kill-a-White-Person Day

All through my life I've had this strange unaccountable
feeling that something was going on in the world, something
big, even sinister, and no one would tell me what it was.
"No," said the old man, "that's just perfectly normal paranoia.
Everyone in the Universe has that."

—Douglas Adams, *The Hitchhiker's Guide to the Galaxy,* chapter 30

Dan Elmquist woke at dawn on the day of his wedding. His fiancée, Doll Baby, was still asleep as he threw on a black hoodie
and a black leather vest with patches that said "KKK Life Member" and "Bureau of Negro Control" and left the campervan he had

EVERYTHING YOU LOVE WILL BURN

borrowed from his friend Johnny Miller. The morning was gray and oppressive. It had been raining when the couple arrived at Johnny's property the night before, and it was still drizzling now. Dan gingerly placed his bare feet onto the wet grass and walked over to a low-slung towing trailer by the side of the barn, where he brushed off some dew and sat down. The chill from a night in the campervan had seeped into his bones, and he fought off a shiver, wrapping his arms around his torso and peering up toward the fog that was rolling menacingly down from the Great Smoky Mountains in the distance. He fished a menthol cigarette from his breast pocket, lit it, and inhaled deeply, then sat quietly for a while and smoked, blowing silvery plumes of smoke into the still air. He finished the cigarette and lit another with the butt of the first one. "Can I have a drag?" asked Doll Baby, sidling up next to him, their dog Leroy at her feet. From inside the trailer they could hear Jim Sheely, Dan's mentor in the Klan and former Grand Wizard, snoring softly on a narrow sofa. Dan put a hand on her belly and passed her a smoke. She was pregnant with a boy who Dan had already decided would be named Odin, after the Norse god.

"You ready to get married, Doll Baby?" he asked.

"I've been ready for a long time," Doll Baby said and kissed him on the cheek. Leroy jumped up onto the trailer, and Dan scratched the dog's head absentmindedly as they smoked in silence for a few minutes.

"This is all I want," Dan said after a while. "You, Odin, a double-wide trailer, and a gun for hunting. We'll grow old together, and one night I'll die in my sleep. Then Jesus will give me a good job in heaven, and I'll be useful forever."

Doll Baby didn't say anything, just chuckled like she usually did when Dan got overly emotional.

Dan hadn't seen much of Matthew during the six months since Brian's funeral, and it seemed as if they'd had an unspoken parting of ways. As Matthew had become increasingly determined to build a far-right coalition of some political value, one that eschewed the old white supremacy of the radical right, Dan had withdrawn into tradition. The more he thought about it, the less he wanted any part in politicking. As far as he was concerned the Klan should stick to what it did best, being a spiritual sanctuary for white Americans who cared for their race. The rest of the world could go to hell for all he cared. The KKK would endure like they always had.

By the time their host came and joined them, they were sitting on camping chairs by the van drinking coffee. Dan's friend Dustin was there too, drawing illegible shapes in the dirt with a stick. "When did you guys get in last night?" Johnny asked.

"Around two," said Dan. "Was it a quiet night? Did you see anyone?"

"I sat on the porch until about 1 a.m. without seeing a soul," said Miller.

The black civil rights leader Louis Farrakhan had made a speech a couple of days before, where he said that black people should fight back against those who tried to kill them. Members of various far right groups, believing that Farrakhan had encouraged African-American death squads, were on high alert. Supposedly today was the day when blacks would rise up, so October 10, 2015, had become known, by some at least, as "National Kill-a-White-Person Day." Outside of a misconstrued Farrakhan quote, there was no evidence this was a real thing. There were no grand plans of killing white people, but the idea fit nicely into the besieged frames of mind of Ku Klux Klan members. If they weren't living under an existential threat as white people, then was there really a point to what they were doing?

"Did you hear Richard Preston went nigger hunting last night?" Dan said.

"Did he get any?"

"I don't think so. Old Richard is all talk. He probably just rode around for a bit, then he'll be talking up a storm later."

"Yeah, we haven't seen him for a while. He's too busy having Obama arrested. Nothing ever seems to happen though."

Richard had been at the last cross lighting at Johnny's property, the time they had spread Brian Delp's ashes, when the KKK leaders had all snuck off to discuss ways to bring the Klan back to its former glory. Dan had hinted at something big going down but refused to give me specifics. In October, when the results of those talks were finally unveiled, Dan's predictions turned out to be overblown.

Since the Delp funeral, for reasons I never quite understood, Richard Preston had gotten into the habit of calling me a couple of times a week. He seemed to get a kick out of explaining the degree to which the wool of liberal lies had been covering my eyes. Most of the time he wanted to talk about something that Obama had done to piss him off, like discussing gun legislation or addressing racial issues in America. He once called me up to describe in intricate detail how the Sandy Hook massacre, in which twenty children and six adults were killed at their school in Connecticut, never took place and that it was all a ruse by gun control lobbyists and foreign influencers. "There are videos where you can see it—I mean actually see it with your own eyes—that the so-called victims are nothing but actors. Take the one dad, David Wheeler. Grieving dad, right? He spoke in front of Congress and met with Barry Soetoro Obama, and boo-hoo, right? Wrong! The guy's a damned actor. There's footage of him from the day of the massacre where he's an FBI agent! They used the same damned actors twice!"

There was no evidence of this other than the homemade videos that were flourishing in the conspiracy happy corners of the internet, but Richard would keep me on the phone, often for more than an hour, explaining how this was all part of the Muslims' plan to disarm America so ISIS could swoop in and take over.

"Listen, I have some news for you," he said one day when I picked up the phone. "We're launching a new thing next weekend, and you should come down. It's going to be big." Apparently whatever he had discussed with Billy Snuffer and Karl Viddig at Brian Delp's funeral had been percolating for long enough, and he was now ready to unveil what they had come up with. I drove down I-95 into the rural, forested parts of northeastern Maryland, where I found Richard's two-story wood house on a narrow, isolated street. He'd bought the house a few years ago and was still in the process of renovating it. Through the front door was a small room in which he kept his KKK keepsakes—a small KKK folding knife, some old KKK calling cards, and other assorted knickknacks. There was a small kitchen off the front room and a spacious living room in the back, dominated by a giant recliner. When I arrived and knocked on the door I heard Richard calling me in from somewhere inside the house. A low buzzing noise came from the kitchen, and there was Richard, his T-shirt off, leaning back on a rickety chair while a friend of his gave him a tattoo. "What do you think?" he asked, proudly displaying a half-finished and bleeding patch of ink. "We're all getting these. The Klan is finally coming together."

He'd designed the tattoo himself. It was a circle with blue and yellow rays shooting from it. Around the inner edge of the circle were the words "IMPERIAL SEAL. Americas [sic] Ku Klux Klan," and in the center were the iron cross of the KKK and a baffling collection of seemingly random numbers. The roman numerals I, II, III, and IV were written around the cross, signifying the four levels of Klancraft—K-uno, -duo, -trio, and -quad. Richard explained that much like Scientologists, the KKK also had ranks that its faithful could rise through. Then there were two instances of the numbers "03," which signified the three eras of the KKK as well as the three Klans—the Confederate White Knights, the Virginia Knights, and the Rebel Brigade—that had come together to form the new group. Their leaders were characteristically coy about revealing membership numbers. Karl hinted of members in the tens of thousands, but from what I'd seen at their rallies I would be surprised if they could muster more than a few dozen. In the tattoo there was also the number 15, which signified both 1915, the year the movie *Birth of a Nation* came out—to many the founding moment of the second-era Klan—as well as 2015, the founding year of this new Klan. Then there was the number 65, meaning 1865, when the first Klan was founded in Pulaski, Tennessee, and finally, in the dead center of the cross in bold letters, 150, signifying the 150-year anniversary of the KKK. The name *America's Ku Klux Klan* was, I gathered, aspirational and in no way reflected reality.

Richard used the original drawing to explain everything, as most of his tattoo was currently seeping copious amounts of blood on account of the fairly rudimentary equipment they were using.

They finished the tattoo, and Richard draped a stained T-shirt over his torso and went outside. In the yard next to a shed where Richard kept a couple of dirt bikes lay a cross made of steel pipes that was hinged at the bottom so Richard could erect it or lay it flat whenever he wanted. The pipes had small holes drilled into them, and Richard had connected the whole thing to a gas tank, which meant he didn't need to fuss with cutting a tree and wrapping a cross whenever he felt like having a lighting ceremony. "This is the future of the Klan," he explained.

Karl Viddig was there as well as Billy Snuffer, who had come up with his daughter to inaugurate the new family of Klans. Finally there was Travis, Richard's giant of a Nighthawk, who held an old rifle at his side while he goose stepped absurdly back and forth in Richard's yard. There seemed to be no immediate risk of attack or infiltration, but Travis clearly enjoyed the marching, so Richard let him have it. The nearest neighbor was Richard's friend Gary, who had a small gun range set up in his backyard where he and Richard shot Barack Obama targets. If there ever was such a thing as a Klan-friendly neighborhood, this was it.

"This new family of Klans we're starting is about being prepared," Billy Snuffer said. He was sitting in a white, plastic lawn chair, fingering a battered SKS assault rifle, which he explained was for the coming race war. Karl was talking about Bruce Jenner, the transgender reality show star and former athlete who had recently become Caitlyn Jenner, while Richard was busy admonishing him for never picking up the damned phone when he called.

"That's only because I don't have three hours to spend on listening to your nonsense," Karl said.

Shooting targets decorated with Barack Obama's face in the backyard of Richard Preston's neighbor.

We sat around for a couple of hours while Richard explained how the signs of the impending cataclysm were everywhere. There were secret ISIS training camps in Appalachia funded by Obama, and the UN was clearly just months away from launching an all-out assault on America. Then there was the FEMA camp not far from his house, which Richard had been obsessing about for as long as I'd known him. Apparently it had recently accepted a shipment of crates, which, to Richard's eyes, looked a whole lot like coffins, which led him to believe that they were to be used for people like him when the government started interring and executing patriots who dared to stand against the Obama/UN/ISIS coalition.

A few stragglers showed up later in the afternoon, among them a woman who wanted to be brought into the KKK. Still, there were only five or six people there, and Richard, having promised dozens of Klansmen, was visibly upset. "Goddammit," he said. "If you can't even trust your own goddammed guys, then who can you trust?" Dan Elmquist had also promised to make the trip but claimed to have had to cancel at the last minute when he didn't have gas money. "There was a pileup on I-95 coming up here," Billy Snuffer said helpfully. "Perhaps they're stuck in traffic."

"Are their phones stuck in traffic too?" Richard snorted. "Goddammit. Nobody can ever just make a goddammed phone call."

The whole thing was doubly infuriating because he had invited a British news crew from ITV to document the momentous occasion, and at the moment there were more journalists than Klansmen in attendance. What's more, he had to figure out how to navigate the tricky waters of having a camera crew at an ostensibly secret ceremony. There are some rituals within the Klan that are more sub-rosa than others, and a naturalization ritual, which is what the Klan calls the induction of new members, was a closely guarded event—or at least it had been for decades. Richard and Billy went behind the shed to confer before returning with a decision.

"We've all discussed it and decided that you guys won't be allowed to film the naturalization ceremony," Richard said.

The Brits pushed back.

"We need something to show the vitality and might of the KKK," said the director, painfully aware that the so-called might of the Klan as far as this gathering was concerned consisted of a handful of people, one of whom was still goose stepping in the yard. Billy came over and pulled Richard away, and together they huddled for another thirty seconds behind the shed before Billy came back. "Okay, we've decided that you can film the beginning of the ceremony but not the end."

Karl Viddig explained how the oath was a matter of great secrecy and that no one outside the Klan could ever witness it but that they could film the first part of the naturalization because it pretty much only entailed marching blindfolded down a path. "So here's what's going to happen," he said, pointing to a small patch of grass behind some trees a little ways back. "Jen here is going to be blindfolded and led over there by two Nighthawks and two Imperial officers. Now, you folks don't need to know what kind of Imperial officers we are . . ." he paused for a while, letting the mystery take hold, "but it just so happens that Richard here is an Imperial Wizard and I'm an Imperial Kludd, so that's . . ." He trailed off and nodded with significance. The whole time he spoke, a white tassel mounted on the tip of his hood danced happily as if to emphasize his words. It was clear that we should be awed.

Richard fastened a piece of beige fabric around Jen's head, blindfolding her, and another man, wearing wraparound sunglasses and black robes with the skull insignia of a Nighthawk, took her by the arm. Richard and Karl went ahead into the thicket and placed a small folding table on the ground over which they draped an American flag with only the thirteen stars of the early colonies. On top of it they placed a copy of the Kloran—the KKK handbook containing detailed instructions to rituals and ceremonies—and a small knife.

"Y'all good to go?" the Nighthawk yelled from the yard.

"Yeah," Karl hollered, concealed by the bushes.

"All right, let's go."

Jen was led through the thick grass and the small trees, while the Brits trailed her with cameras. As she approached the makeshift altar Karl told the crew to turn the cameras off. Jen went down on one knee, and Richard placed a sword on her shoulder.

"Are you a white American?" he asked.

"Yessir," Jen said.

Satisfied by the answer, Richard went through the holy oath. "I swear to God that I will never divulge anything that takes place here today. I'm willing to die before I reveal such secrets." As he spoke this last sentence he shot a glance at the camera crew. They were clearly still filming. He soldiered on. "I will be truly Klanish toward any Klansman."

He splashed some homemade holy water on her and told her to rise, and then the Confederate White Knights had grown by one member.

"I told you that you guys couldn't film that part," Richard fumed to the director as they headed back to the yard. "You promised."

"We didn't film," the director said.

"Then why was the camera on the guy's shoulder and he was looking into the little thing the whole time?"

"That's just the most comfortable way to hold a camera."

Richard didn't seem convinced but told them that they could stay, but no more funny business—he'd gone out on a limb inviting them here.

He dragged a small podium from the shed and set it up in the yard. Karl was first to speak and led the small congregation in the Lord's Prayer followed by the Pledge of Allegiance.

"They call us a terrorist organization," he said. "But I don't know of a single terrorist organization that starts their meetings with a prayer."

He spoke for a while about the Christian values of the KKK and how everyone got them wrong when it came to race. "We don't mind other races," he said. "We just don't want them mixing." While the latter was true, I had heard plenty of things said that made it graphically clear how they felt about other races.

When it was Richard's turn he expounded on the whole alleged misunderstanding, addressing the camera directly, presumably because the four members sitting in lawn chairs knew better.

"They call us a hate group," he said magnanimously. "But all they really know is that a few bad people did a few bad things. We had soup kitchens for the poor in the 1920s. We provided food. Granted, blacks weren't allowed in, but they still got food and they could sit by the door. And the 1960s had nothing to do with race but about integration. After all, it says in the Bible that mongrels are damned by birth."

This led Richard into his favorite topic, and his voice rose with enthusiasm.

"We have a mongrel in the White House! We have a Muslim in the White House! Muslims believe that if you kill an infidel, you get seventy-two virgins. What do you get if you kill an entire

Karl Viddig and Richard Preston burning the UN flag at Preston's home in Maryland.

nation? Why do you think ISIS hasn't invaded us already? First, because we already own ISIS, but second and more importantly, we have guns! But that might not last. The UN has been training on our soil for two years, and why do you think that is? They are going to take our country away from us!"

On cue Richard reached inside the podium and fished out a large UN flag, waving it over his head in disgust as he went on. "When they come for our guns, they won't get them!" He was shouting into the camera at this point. "Our guns are what have kept us safe. Once Obama has our guns he will let ISIS loose, and they will kill all Christian Americans! We will fight hard! We will fight well! And we will . . . . wait, do you have a lighter on you?" He turned to Karl, who frantically searched his robe until he came up with a box of matches and some lighter fluid. "Thanks. . . . And we will not bow down!" With that he set fire to the blue and white flag, which promptly flamed and melted.

He was screaming now, throwing the flag to the ground and howling triumphantly. "Far as I'm concerned the United Nations can burn in hell! Along with every Muslim, including Barack Obama, including ISIS. Every last one of these Muslims can die in my country or get out!" He spat on the flag at his feet. "Come for my guns, Obama! I guarantee you'll get the ammo first!"

Burning the flag apparently held some cathartic value, and Richard calmed down slightly as he continued. "What Obama has to understand is that when the war that he so wants comes, our people will come from the mountains and hollows and the cities, and we will fight back," he said.

"That's right," said Karl. "Regular folks have no idea how many people are in the Klan. We all know, Richard and Billy and I, and we're here to tell you that our numbers have been doubling and tripling."

Apparently the lackadaisical showing today was no indication of the KKK's true membership because, as Karl had told me before, there were public members and there were secret members. There was zero evidence to support his claim, but in a way—and according to the Klan's nebulous logic—wasn't the absence of proof really all the proof you needed? Not according to the SPLC, who put the Klan's membership throughout the country at between five thousand and eight thousand. Even this seemed generous to me. Although Richard's group, judging by those who had bothered to show up, was tiny by any standard, other groups I visited were hardly much bigger. Even at the rallies I'd been to where the organizers were pleased with the turnout—these were exceedingly rare—I'd never seen more than fifty Klansmen in one place.

"Listen," Richard said, leaning in. "There are issues with race in this country, but you have to believe me when I tell you that we in the Klan are trying to solve it. We don't want marshal law, and if you were president and you knew our true numbers, I promise you that you would think twice about giving the country over to the Muslims."

According to Richard, Billy, and Karl, there was currently a struggle happening within the Klan in which one faction, close to 70 percent of its members, wanted to start a race war—"And remember, these people are armed to the teeth"—while a smaller faction, of which the three were a part, favored temperance. Apparently it was a struggle they were losing.

"I tell you," Richard continued, "We don't know how long we can hold these people back. They are rearing to go to war." As he saw it the only thing standing between peace and outright race war was the case he was currently compiling against Obama. "It's all on me," he said. "I have to take my evidence to Congress, and when they drag that disgusting mongrel out of the Oval Office, I'll tell them what has to change for the country to get back on track: NAFTA has to go. The Federal Reserve needs to be shut down. We got to get the steel mills working again and back on American soil." It was all run-of-the-mill Tea Party rhetoric, the kind that Donald Trump would use to great effect a year later. Richard, though, seemed to believe he was alone in having figured out what needed to be done.

He lost his train of thought and went back to shouting. "Sandy Hook was staged, and the elites hate us! The Charleston shooting was a fake, and I'll tell you why: they interviewed a woman on air thirty minutes after her mother got shot and she wasn't crying. No tears. Tell me how that is possible."

Eventually they got to lighting the cross. The Brits felt it would be better for their cameras if Richard would light it before it got too dark. The fiery cross symbolizes the light of Christ in the dark, not the light of Christ in the still pretty bright dusk, but Nathan Bedford Forrest, the first Grand Wizard of the KKK, never had cameras to deal with, so Richard made an executive decision. Billy called bullshit on the whole thing and refused to robe up if Richard was going to make him do it in daylight. Karl was pragmatic about it and said the important thing was that they lit the cross, and besides, it would be dark soon anyway and went to his car to retrieve his robes from the trunk.

"Come on, Billy," Richard implored. "If you don't robe up, it won't look right."

"I don't give a rat's ass," said Billy.

"Can you give us a ten-minute warning before lighting the cross? We need to set up lights and cameras," said the producer.

Billy spat.

They started to do the ceremony, walking around the unlit cross, chanting their oaths of loyalty to God, their race, and their Klan, but they didn't get to lighting it because the camera crew thought it might look better if they redid it going the other way around the cross. "You got it," Richard said, putting on a brave face. Billy looked like he was ready to leave.

They were finally able to light the thing but were then made to stand awkwardly around it, holding their arms outstretched as the TV presenter did his closing statement a few yards away. "Did you guys get it yet?" Karl shouted.

"Just give us another thirty seconds! Keep your arms out! No talking!" The presenter took on a serious tone as he looked into the camera. "Given the secrecy surrounding these Klan gatherings, it is extremely difficult to know the strength of the KKK in the country today."

"How long are they going to make us stand like this?" Karl muttered under his breath before a camera man shushed him. The Brits did another couple of takes before the presenter nailed his line.

"All right, guys! We got it! Thanks!"

They did an interview with Richard, then quickly packed their gear into a station wagon and left, leaving the boys of America's Ku Klux Klan in the dark, sitting on Richard's rickety lawn furniture.

"I thought that went well," said Richard.

"Yeah, I thought so," said Karl.

Billy didn't speak and soon got in his car and drove back to Tennessee.

"It's about getting the word out," said Karl. "To let people know that the Klan will protect America."

"But isn't the point of a secret organization that you're secret?" I asked. I told them that I found it a little strange that they had invited a bunch of journalists to see a ceremony where the oath literally promised death to anyone revealing it.

"Well, you see," said Karl, "it doesn't have to be a secret that we are secret. A secret organization has no value unless people know there's a secret organization there. Besides, they don't know the secret, just that there is one. That's the power of it."

"And the time has come for the KKK to step out of the shadows and lead," said Richard.

NOTHING CAME OF Richard's plans to bring the KKK back to its former glory, at least not at the time of writing this. Shortly after the event in his yard he stopped calling me and also seemed to lose touch with other Klan groups around the country. As we sat outside Johnny Miller's barn on the day of Dan and Doll Baby's wedding three months later, no one had really heard from Richard in a while, except for finding out through others that he was doing patrols in Baltimore, hunting for rapacious African Americans. For all their talk about bringing the Klans together, it seemed like all they had gained from America's Klans were matching and poorly executed tattoos. The next time I saw Richard was in Charlottesville in August of 2017, where he drew a gun and fired into a crowd of protestors. No one was hit, and he quickly gave himself up to law enforcement. At the time of writing this he's still in jail awaiting trial.

Billy Snuffer was hosting an event down in Martinsville on Dan's wedding day, and Dan was a little peeved about it. In these days of meager memberships, the KKK in large part measured the loyalties of others by who showed up to events, so Billy setting up a rally on Dan's wedding day was a slap in the face.

"We were never really asked to join his Americas [sic] Ku Klux Klan," said Dan. "I don't think we would have if we did. We don't want to get involved in all his politics. I want my Klan to be traditional, to be about community, not politics. Besides, I can't listen to all his bullshit about impeaching Obama for another second. I mean, we all hate that nigger in the White House, but damn, talk about something else for a second."

As they talked, Gary Delp came through the gate and sat down. His long hair had grown stringier and grayer since the funeral, and his leathery skin had taken on the color of ash. At the same time, Jim Sheely clambered out of the campervan and sat down with a cup of coffee. He was already in a crisp, beige shirt and his usual riding pants. "We were just talking about Richard's Klan army," Dan said.

"Oh yeah, that old nonsense," said Jim. "I get that he wants the Klan to be a force to be reckoned with," he said. "But I don't think we need to be involved in all this politicking. The Klan should be about tradition and communion. We shouldn't be out in public. Our power is in rallying white people together and teaching them about tradition."

At the moment there seemed to be two differing schools of thought within the Klan, and they were not, as Richard claimed, a militant wing and a temperance wing; rather, members disagreed about whether the KKK was a community or a political group. It had been decades since the KKK had any form of centralized guidance, and since then it had fallen into complete disarray. Groups spend most of their time claiming to be the true heirs of the original Klan, and the various groups often demonstrated wildly different visions of what the modern KKK should be. It didn't help that some of these groups were tiny and that there are no prerequisites to start a Klan group. At the time the Rocky Mountain Knights out of Montana were making waves because their leader had encouraged black, gay, and Jewish people to join. Although this was clearly a publicity stunt, the very idea was enough to have other Klan groups fuming. Frank Ancona and his periphrastically named *True* Invisible Empire Traditionalist American Knights of the Ku Klux Klan saw the KKK's role as that of a community group, at one time planning to build a soup kitchen for the poor—until, that is, Ancona was killed, allegedly by his own wife. Jim Sheely didn't buy into the notions of the Klan as a community group or a political entity; their power was in fear, and people wouldn't fear them if they handed out free soup every which way.

"The Klan has always been feared," he said. "That's how it should be. Blacks have to fear us for the Klan to serve a purpose, but that doesn't mean we have to be violent. At home I have an old nigger doll hanging from a noose, but those are just decorations to send a message. I don't hate anyone. I just want to be around my own people.

"I don't believe in slavery," he continued. "One human being should never own another, but we need apartheid for the same reasons you don't see fish and mammals mix. Why do people have to mix the races? Every time I leave the house I see a nigger and a white woman dragging some mud child behind them. No immigration, no race mixing."

"Amen!" said Doll Baby. "They're not like us. I have black folks coming into the store to buy chitlins from me, and I'm, like, 'If you ain't a slave no more then why are you eating like one?' I don't get why people assume it's such a good thing that we all mix. I refused to learn Spanish in high school, and I told the teacher that she better fail me because there was no way I was learning that goddammed language. I know 'puta' [whore] and I know 'pendejo' [stupid], and that's all the Spanish I'll ever need."

Dan was nursing a lukewarm coffee as he searched his pockets for some painkillers. He'd thrown his back out a while ago and was on some fairly heavy sedatives. At the moment they were the only drugs he took, and he hated how they made him sluggish and disoriented.

"When I was younger I was really into weed," he told me. "And I was just bumming around, getting high and checking out the Grateful Dead. My dad had been in the Tenth Mountain Division, and so he tried to get me to join up, but when I got to the recruitment office wearing a weed T-shirt, the recruiter must have known something was up. He asked me if I really wanted to be in the Army, and I told him "Hell, no," and the Army said they didn't want me either, so we parted ways." In hindsight Dan almost wished he had joined up, as it would probably have saved him a lot of years doing nothing, but he also hated what his country had become and had no interest in fighting for it. The Klan was his way of fighting.

"We're becoming mixed, bastardized, and mongrelized," Dan said, "and our government sure as shit ain't going to do anything about it. They want to see the white man on his knees. The other day I was laying floors at this sand nigger's house, and his place was nicer than mine. You tell me how that's right that we save these fucking people down in Iraq, but they still live better than us."

"And still they're fucking bitching about everything," Dustin said, finally speaking up from his dirt drawing. "We gave them their freedom, we integrated them, and they're still pissed. Just what do these fucking niggers want?"

"Lord knows," said Gary in his desert-parched, angle-grinder voice. "They say they're African Americans, but I say either you're African or you're American. Either way, you're a nigger. Now I give niggers every right to be human, but the fact remains that they're black and I'm white."

Johnny had built them a good cross of firm, young birch and had dragged it down to the barn so they could put it on the towing trailer to wrap it. Becky, Gary's wife, had brought large sacks of discarded clothes to wrap it with, and soon they were all busy tearing denim and cotton into long rags. Doll Baby had a vampy piece of lace that she tied around the birch beams. "It is a wedding, after all," she smiled, an L&M cigarette dangling between her lips.

"It's your day, baby, and you're going to look so pretty," said Becky.

"Thank you, mama," said Doll Baby, who had known Becky since childhood.

Dan pulled a large red sheet from the bag. "This looks like cotton," he said.

"If it is, then maybe save it for the torches," rasped Gary. "They'll burn for longer if we wrap them in cotton."

Dustin was fingering a shiny piece of blue garment he'd found when Becky snatched it out of his hands and threw it on the ground. "Don't use that," she said. "It's polyester, and it'll just melt all over the place."

As the day wore on, more and more guests arrived, kissing Doll Baby and shaking Dan's hand. A Klan wedding was a relatively rare occasion, and Klansmen from all over the South showed up to pay their respects. One person who hadn't showed up, however, was Dan's best man and personal Nighthawk, Scott, and it had Dan fuming.

"I'm getting real sick of his shit," he said. "Tells me he can't do it with no good excuse. It's my wedding day, and I don't have a best man, and it's National Kill-a-White-Person Day, and I don't have a damned Nighthawk."

Jim Sheely was in the barn decorating a cross that Dan and Andrea would be married in front of. One by one, he lit thirteen candles and placed them on the cross. Thirteen is an important number in Klan lore because it symbolizes both Jesus and the twelve disciples as well as the eleven southern states and two northern states that fought in the Civil War. "I find it just looks really pretty too," he said. "What's a wedding without candles?"

Gary sat in a rocking chair next to him smoking a cigarette. I'd been talking with the two of them about how the Klan had changed in their time. Both had been in the KKK for decades, Gary joining up as an enforcer during the civil rights era. It had been his job, he said with pride, "to knock some sense into those who needed some sense knocked into them," and back then, in the later days of the Civil Rights Movement, there had been a lot of folks who had needed it. Both seemed a little baffled as to what the Klan's role should be today. In their day the Klan had been all about preserving the place of the white man at the top of the food chain, but these days everything was upside down and nothing was sacred anymore. Interracial dating could get you killed back when they joined the Klan. So could homosexuality, feminism, and everything else that seemed to be encouraged these days. If everything was natural and right, then nothing was natural and right. Gary would never use a term like *moral relativism*, but that was what lay at the root of their problems with the modern world. They—and, by extension, the KKK—were of a time when there were moral absolutes set by people like them: white, Christian men. Back then there was no racism because, to the minds of those who made the rules, African Americans weren't equal and so the idea of treating them as equals was as laughable as giving dogs the right to vote. There was no feminism because why would women need rights when it was the job of the man to protect her? The KKK had thrived during a time when they felt it was their duty to uphold these sacred pillars upon which society was built.

When William J. Simmons founded the second-era Klan in 1915 it was clear he saw African Americans not so much as a threat but as a pest that needed to be controlled, writing that the Klan favored "keeping the Negro in his place." He marketed the Klan as a fraternal order, and unlike its predecessor, the collection of militia groups that had been terrorizing freed slaves in the antebellum South, the new Klan would be "a classy order of the highest class." It was also fiercely anti-Catholic, as Simmons saw Catholicism as a much bigger threat to America than African Americans. Yet, as with the original Klan, its stated principles of serving as only defenders of virtues and morals translated into a free pass to harass, murder, and terrorize anyone who disagreed with them. Like the First Era Klan, this second incarnation KKK got away with it for decades because it was men like them—or, more often than not, its actual members—who set the rules for what was right and just in America. They were the protectors of the status quo—until suddenly the status quo started slipping out of their hands because of uppity civil rights activists, defiant women, and traitorous liberals.

As the absolute hegemony of the white male started to slip, the KKK struggled to fight back. Theirs had been an existence founded on sacred principles of white supremacy and Protestant

Christianity, and suddenly they found themselves in a world where these principles no longer dictated what was right. For decades they had been floundering, unable to recapture the glory of the former KKK, and the 1960s saw them reduced to a terror organization, effective at spreading fear but forced to do it in hiding and out of step with mainstream opinion. In 1963 members of a Birmingham, Alabama, chapter of the KKK bombed the predominantly black Sixteenth Street Baptist Church, killing four young girls. In 1964 the Mississippi White Knights of the Ku Klux Klan were behind the murders of civil rights activists Andrew Goodman, Michael Schwerner, and James Chaney as well as the burning of twenty black churches. These acts struck terror into the Civil Rights Movement but were not enough to turn back the tide of progress. The KKK, accustomed to operating with impunity, found that their actions sparked outrage and national attention, and in the summer of 1964, less than two weeks after the murders of Goodman, Schwerner, and Chaney, President Johnson signed the Civil Rights Act, a major step toward ending the Jim Crow era. Like the KKK then, Jim and Gary struggled to make heads or tails of the world they currently found themselves in. They didn't know how to stop it, only that the world was becoming ever more inscrutable.

"It's not the niggers I'm worried about," Gary said. "I worry for the white children who are growing up without any understanding of what it means to be white, without pride in their race. All other races show pride in who they are, but the second a white man says that he is proud to be white, then he's labeled a racist. It didn't use to be like that."

Outside the barn the members of the Virgil Griffin White Knights were busy piling potato salad and hot dogs onto paper plates and trying to not spill their Mountain Dews as they mingled. Dustin, Dan's friend who'd come with him from Kentucky, was standing next to a bucket of long sticks that were going to be used as torches later. "We're going to have him direct the lighting today, since I'm getting married," Dan explained. "How are you doing, Dustin? All set for this thing?" Dustin looked frazzled.

"I'm not so sure, Dan," he said. "There's a lot of stuff to keep in my mind."

On his lower arm he'd written the words "Klansmen at?" with a pen.

"It's 'Klansmen at ease,'" Dan said.

Dustin crossed out the question mark and wrote the word *ease*.

"Then you just hold the torch with a straight arm and guide the members around the cross clockwise and say, 'Klansmen! For God! For race! For . . .'"

"Wait, I have to say all that?" said Dustin. He was scribbling furiously on his arm, rapidly running out of skin. "I thought I only had to do the 'at ease' thing."

"Only the . . . ? Come on, man. Of course you have to say the whole thing. Who else is gonna?"

"All right, just tell me what to say and I'll say it."

Dan told Dustin the ritual of lighting the cross, and then he told him again, slowly and patiently so Dustin could get it all down on his lower arm, which at this point looked like a pen had exploded on it. "You'll be fine," Dan said after making Dustin recite it for him. "We're all brothers here. You're good with what to say when you light the torches, right?"

"Yeah, it's just 'Do you accept the Light of Christ?'"

"Klansman," said Dan.

"What?"

"You have to say 'Klansman': 'Klansman, do you accept the Light of Christ?'"

Dustin looked down at his arm. It was clear that he was unprepared for more lines, and there was no more room on his arm.

"What if it's a woman?"

"Well, then you say 'Klanswoman.'"

Dan's back was starting to act up, so he popped a couple of pills, washing them down with coffee and cream. Soon his eyes got drowsy and his speech slurred. He walked somewhat unsteadily down to the campervan where Doll Baby was preparing her red

Leroy, the white power cockerpoodle.

and white satin robe. "How are you feeling, baby?" she asked as he sat down next to her.

Leroy the dog was resting in a deep chair in the shade of the barn. Doll Baby had made him a red robe for the occasion with the words "White Power" embroidered on. "That there is the world's first and only white power cockerpoodle," Dan said proudly. "He even barks at niggers, just like I do." He laughed a sedate laugh.

Doll Baby shook out some creases in the red cape that she would drape over her shoulders, then moved on to Dan's robe, a white cotton one with bright green trimmings on the sleeves and hem. "This feels so good, doesn't it, baby?" Dan said as he struggled to keep his eyelids open. "Just me and you. Growing old together. Leroy's going to grow old too, but probably faster than we will."

Jim Sheely walked past, heading up the sloping field past the barn to where some guys were erecting the cross. Dan tried to grab him and almost fell out of the chair. "Hey, Jim," he said, composing himself with some effort. "I'm glad you're here, man. I'm glad you're enjoying yourself with these honest people. I hope you're enjoying yourself. Hey, man, let me help you guys with the cross. It's not right that you guys do it for me." He tried to stand up and teetered precariously. Doll Baby grabbed him by his collar and pushed him back down.

"No, baby," she said. "You sit down. You have to let the painkillers work. You're liable to fall and kill yourself." He flopped back down on the chair and reached over, grabbing a plate of potato salad that Doll Baby had been eating.

"You're right, baby," he mumbled. "There are other Klansmen to do it. Honorable Klansmen. Men who . . . God, Doll Baby, have you had this potato salad?" He brought the plate up to his face, studying the potatoes with sleepy-eyed awe. "Jim, try this here potato salad."

Jim took a bite and nodded. "It's good potato salad. You should try mine. It's my mother's recipe."

Dan made a noise of excitement. "I love your potato salad, Jim. I wish I had some."

"I try and stay away from potato salad," said Doll Baby. "Too much mayo."

"Hey, Jim!" said Dan, giggling. "Jim! My wife is racist against mayo."

Dan and Doll Baby got married in front of the cross, with Gary officiating. He was getting old and called Doll Baby, whose real name was Andrea, both Ashley and Amanda during the ceremony, but she didn't care. They said, "I do," and Gary declared them man and wife by the power given him as an Imperial Wizard, which, incidentally, the state of Tennessee didn't recognize, meaning that Dan and Doll Baby would have to go to City Hall at some point to make the thing legal. After the vows the congregation walked up to Johnny's field, where they had erected the cross and doused it in kerosene. They circled it, first clockwise, then counterclockwise, Dustin beaming with pride as he read from his lower arm, before gathering in the middle and putting the flaming, cotton-wrapped torches to the base until the flames caught. Then

Dan and Andrea get married.

they all stood around the cross, singing "Amazing Grace" while it burned to the ground. Afterward Becky and Rachel decked out the tables in the garage with cake and coffee.

"This is what the Klan is about," said Dan between mouthfuls of chocolate cake with blue frosting. "Being together with your family. That's all it is."

"That's right," said Gary. "We may never be as powerful as we once were, but perhaps we can open some eyes before the white race goes extinct. If you take clear, pure water and mix it with black dirt, then you're only left with mud."

CHAPTER 8

The ANA

Perhaps Evelyn Waugh could have gotten it down exactly
right: Waugh was good at scenes of industrious self-delusion,
scenes of people absorbed in odd games.

—Joan Didion, *The White Album*

One day early in July 2016 Matthew called me and said he had
big news: the Traditionalist Workers Party had been asked to en-
dorse a mainstream candidate for Congress, and after much discussion and vetting, they had decided to accept the invitation and
the whole thing was to be made public at the candidate's road-
side diner a short hour's drive west of Chattanooga, Tennessee.
What's more, it was to be the grand unveiling of Matthew and
Jeff Schoep's big collaboration, a new coalition of American white

nationalists called the Aryan Nationalist Alliance (ANA). "We're still working on the name," he added almost apologetically. "Jeff had to throw some meat to his guys, so I'll let him keep the 'Aryan' part—for now."

ANA was a brand-new affair and the result of many meetings between Jeff and Matthew. I knew the idea of collaboration between groups had been on Jeff's mind for a long time, but I wasn't aware he'd reached out to Matthew. On the face of it, the NSM and the TWP were diametrically opposed, the latter emphasizing a humane form of nationalism—humane being, of course, a relative term—and somewhat civil political discourse, whereas the former had been content, historically at least, to put on SS uniforms and salute pictures of Adolf Hitler. I was curious to know where exactly the meeting of the minds had happened. Later that day Matthew sent me a document he called a "statement of principles for the ANA." The document, a wordy tome coming in at just shy of sixteen single-spaced pages, acknowledged that although there was little common ground between the various groups making up the alliance, they shared one thing that made all other issues secondary: "nearly every single problem we have in our nation—from street crime to anti-White governmental policies, to attacks on our sovereignty and faith—can be answered in one simple phrase: '*If White people had a country of our own, this wouldn't be happening.*'"

Thus the foundational goal of the ANA, as stated in the principles, was also the foundation of the white ethno-state that Matthew had been pining for. Their thinking went that the establishment of such a white homeland would eliminate most problems plaguing modern society because most were caused by the inevitable friction of tribal intermingling.

Also—and most crucially—the principles committed every group joining the alliance to renounce the notion of white supremacy and embrace nationalism for all people and, what's more, made it incumbent upon the leaders of the groups to make sure their members kept their supremacy and racial slurs in check. For Matthew's group this was relatively easy, as they were pretty used to keeping their slurs private, but for the NSM it was a big deal. You'd be hard pressed to come by a single item of NSM merchandise that didn't have the swastika on it, so any attempt at renouncing white supremacy was going to take nothing short of a complete rebranding. Not to mention how fond its members were of their SS uniforms. "It's a big deal," Matthew said as he invited me down for the unveiling. "This could be what I've been working for all this time."

AFTER THE POOR SHOWING in Chattanooga at the fortieth anniversary celebration of the NSM two years earlier, Jeff had decided that if he was going to save the NSM—and, by extension, in his eyes at least, the white race in America—he'd need to go all in. The NSM alone wasn't going to cut it, and as much as he might wish it, the methods the NSM had inherited from George Lincoln Rockwell— marching in SS uniforms and molding the organization after its Third Reich counterpart—were perhaps not suited for the modern nationalist struggle. Once again he found himself toying with the idea of an alliance on the far right. The failure of the Unite Patriot Front was still fresh in his mind, but he'd chalked that up to him being too untried to inspire any confidence. That had changed now. Jeff was an old hand. Most of the guys who had been leaders when he came up were either dead or in prison. William Pierce had died in 2002, leaving his National Alliance leaderless, and 2004 saw the death of Richard Butler as well as the imprisonment of Matt Hale, leader of the hugely influential World Church of the Creator. All this had left a huge power vacuum on the far right as well as many now ideologically homeless nationalists, and several of them had landed within the NSM. Of course, that was many years ago now, and if the NSM had ever been a force on the far right, they certainly weren't one now. But at least Jeff was a known quantity. People knew he could organize and lead.

Many of the same old problems that sank the UPF still persisted. Some groups banned its members from mixing with other white nationalists. A couple of Klan guys had asked him not to tell anyone that they were at an NSM rally because they were afraid their Grand Wizards might find out.

He was frustrated but still couldn't get the idea out of his head that white nationalism could have a chance in the United States if the far right would just get over its pathetic and inconsequential infighting. He was seeing progress all over the world. The fascist party Golden Dawn was entering the mainstream in Greece, taking advantage of frustrations over EU-imposed austerity to accomplish real political power. At the same time, the nationalist National Front had become one of France's leading parties, taking nearly a third of the vote in the 2015 regional elections. Marine Le Pen, the party's president, would lose the 2017 presidential election to Emmanuel Macron, but only after forcing a runoff in which she took 33 percent of the votes. The Jobbik Party in Hungary had taken 20 percent of the vote in the 2014 parliamentary elections, and the nationalist Sweden Democrats had taken close to 13 percent of the vote in their election. In Germany, Norway, Britain, and Italy, whites marched in protest of immigration and Islam.

It seemed to Jeff that something was percolating in the West. White people all over Europe were becoming aware of their race and how the only way to save it, not only against a Jewish conspiracy but also against the flood of Muslim immigration, was to band together and put their differences behind them. It didn't matter that the situation was vastly different in the United States from Europe, where far-right parties in some cases had successfully managed to rebrand themselves into protectors of liberalism and culture—ideals that the average member of NSM found confusing and Jeff believed were signs of weakness; what mattered was that white people were waking up to the realities of the world. But while Europe was waking up, the United States remained in slumber. For the life of him, Jeff couldn't understand why America couldn't have a nationalist resurgence when it was happening all over Europe. Obama was nearing the end of his term, but Jeff felt pretty sure that whoever replaced him wasn't going to care much about white working-class people. Republicans and Democrats were all the same breed of traitorous scum.

At the same time, he saw how rough things were in America's white, industrialized heartland. The world seemed to be screaming out for nationalism and racial solidarity, yet his country was coming up with nothing, so Jeff decided to give the grand alliance one last try. He called around to a host of smaller groups as well as a couple outfits he had worked with before to pitch the idea of an alliance, and then one year after the Chattanooga debacle the NSM gathered in Rome, Georgia. Standing on the courthouse steps, flanked by security consisting of a grinning Gunner and his eternally scowling Lieutenant Schloer, Jeff announced the formation of his new alliance. "We're bringing together white organizations from all across this country," he shouted as the crowd booed. "You see the National Socialist Movement, with our brothers and sisters in the Loyal White Knights. With the Aryan Nations. With the SS Action Group. With the Rebel Knights from Texas . . . the Vinlanders."

At first glance it was an impressive list of organizations, ranging from skinheads to pragmatic nationalists, but a closer look revealed a profound birth defect in Jeff's baby. Out of all the groups on the initial list, only a few had more than a handful of members. Others would best be described as not extant, and some only joined the ANA because no other group would touch them. In the latter category were the Loyal White Knights and the Aryan Strike Force. The Knights hadn't gained a shred of credibility since I'd first encountered them in 2011 in North Carolina. In fact, it had recently been revealed that Chris Barker was an FBI informant who had helped the feds build a case against an LWK member who was conspiring to build a ray gun to kill Muslims. The fact that none of this technology existed hadn't stopped the LWK member, a Glendon Scott Crawford, from trying to get in touch with the Israeli national intelligence agency Mossad to offer them first dibs on his imaginary weapon of mass destruction. All this had taken a toll on membership, and although the LWK still maintained an active chapter of sorts, the only steady members seemed to be Chris and his wife, Amanda, who led a rotating cast of dropouts and hangers on.

Aryan Strike Force was Josh Steever's new outfit. After having been kicked out of the Aryan Terror Brigade for being—in the words of its new leader, then skinhead and now Klansman Eric Woodzell—"just too fucking crazy and stupid," Steever had married and promptly divorced Patrick Swayze's niece Danielle Swayze and founded the Aryan Strike Force. How many members Steever would bring to the ANA was never clear, but as far as credibility in the movement went, he might have been the only one with less than Chris Barker and the LWK.

Other members of the fledgling alliance included the America First Committee, whose sole membership seemed to consist of septuagenarian Arthur Jones and his wife, and, interestingly, a group called the Phineas Priesthood, which was less a group than a rumor within the far-right movement. The Priesthood is to the far right what fairies are to the rest of us: nobody really believes they exist, some claim to have met one, and every so often you meet a kook crazy enough to say he is one. Still, nonexistent, lackluster, and low-credibility member groups notwithstanding, there now was an alliance where before there had been none. Jeff, hungry to expand, soon reached out to several other groups, among them Matthew and his Traditionalist Workers Party.

The idea appealed to Matthew's sense of unity. Despite the ridiculous theatrics of the NSM, Matthew had always liked Jeff, and Jeff, for his part, saw in Matthew a younger self, a smart, headstrong leader who wasn't afraid to fight in the streets if needed. The two got together in Ohio in the early days of the summer of 2016 to hash out the details and soon announced that the TWP would be joining the Alliance. One of the conditions Matthew had set for joining was that the Alliance shed some of its more troublesome members, and eventually they also changed their name to something a little less white supremacist-y, deciding on the Nationalist Front. Anyone not on board was free to leave. A few groups, Werewolf 88 and the Authoritarian Party, took them up on the offer and exited, whereas the Loyal White Knights and the Aryan Strike Force were shown the door. Matthew was clear that he wanted a European-style movement where the most outlandish nods to Adolf Hitler and white supremacy would be removed and that this had to be more than just lip service. He couldn't have a movement that, publicly, was past white supremacy and then have its members Sieg Heiling and sporting swastikas in private.

Matthew wanted them to be taken seriously, so when a legitimate candidate running for election in a deeply conservative district reached out, it was proof that white nationalism was no longer anathema in mainstream political circles. It felt like just the shot at legitimacy the Nationalist Front needed.

"This guy's the real deal," Matthew told me on the phone. "His name is Rick Tyler, and he's solid. Small business owner, successful, racially aware, and he's the one who reached out to us. He wants the Nationalist Front to help out with his campaign."

I drove to Tennessee through Matthew's neck of the woods, south from Ohio, through the coal country of West Virginia and Kentucky. This was the part of the country where Matthew was trying to build his movement, and, incidentally, it was also the part of the country where Donald Trump was building his electoral victory. Presently there was an almost uncanny overlap between Matthew's politics and those espoused by the Republican front-runner for president, save for the fact that Matthew would never publicly accuse Mexican immigrants of being rapists. If anything, Trump often went further than Matthew, and he once told me how strange it was that, after a lifetime of being on the very far-right fringes of politics, he had found himself to the left of the leading GOP candidate on many issues.

The previous year had seen a symbiotic relationship develop between Trump and the far right, which by then had been renamed, by the media as much as by itself, the alt-right. Within the xenophobic, isolationist and misogynistic salmagundi of ideas populating not only the alt-right Twitterverse but also Trump's stump-speeches, it was hard to know who had come up with what. Trump, ever the master dog whistler, was careful not to openly embrace his most racist fan base, yet fed them just enough red meat to keep them motivated. As a candidate, Trump regularly retweeted alt-right Twitter users, among them a user called "WhiteGenocideTM" ostensibly located in "Jewmerica," and the blogger Jason Bergkamp, who writes for the website Vanguard 14—"14" being code for "14 words," the white supremacist mantra conceived by David Lane.

The relationship would soon become even closer when, in August of 2016, Trump made Steve Bannon chief executive for the campaign. The hiring of Bannon, the head of Breitbart News, a wildly conspiratorial and right-leaning website that Bannon himself proudly declared to be a "platform of the alt-right," not only seemed to pull the campaign out of the death spiral it found itself in but was also a not very subtle nod to the furthest right reaches of the political spectrum. Somewhere along the way Matthew became a Trump supporter. He still believed the GOP were a traitorous bunch of cowards and was convinced there was no way the establishment—by which he meant the Jews—would let Trump win, but Trump had made it abundantly clear that he was for the white working man, so Matthew was behind him. Also, he despised how liberal protestors disrupted Trump's rallies. Matthew had been on the receiving end of these kinds of protests many times and knew a thing or two about how to handle them, so whenever he could, he staged counter-protests at Trump rallies to let the liberals know he was onto them. This is how he came to be sued along with Donald Trump. At a rally in Louisville, Kentucky, he ended up shoving black protestor Kashiya Nwanguma as she was leaving the arena. Matthew first claimed he was only trying to stop her from tearing up Trump banners, but later, after the election, as he soured on President Trump, he would claim that if he had attacked Nwanguma—which he still disputed that he had—it was only because Trump had encouraged the crowd and he was merely following orders. If anyone was guilty of anything, it was Trump.

Richard Spencer, the man who had coined the term alt-right and, by 2016, had become its de facto leader and also a proud Trump supporter, once told me that he saw himself and the rest of the movement as the ideological kitchen for the far-right positions, which Trump, by osmosis, made his own. Even though Spencer and Matthew very much disliked each other, they agreed that the Trump campaign was co-opting their ideas. Others in the alt-right movement were more skeptical of Trump but still grateful for his candidacy, believing he would be a gateway drug to white nationalism. Whatever the truth of the relationship was, Trump's ascendancy had created a sense of urgency and vigor on the far right that its members had never felt before, and now they were all scrambling to capitalize before Trump inevitably screwed up and lost to Hillary Clinton. In separate interviews Matthew, Jeff, and Richard Spencer had all told me the same thing: this was their moment.

Much of the trip from Ohio down to Tennessee went through parts of the country I had driven with Matthew before. There were still the same payday loan storefronts and pawnshops littering the strip malls of northern Kentucky. In Ohio, billboards by the side of the road across from closed-down coal mines promised "Jobs! Jobs! Jobs!" and in lieu of money you could pay your bar tab with half a tablet of Oxycontin at the local Moose Lounge in Boone County, West Virginia. Appalachia was beaten and broken, and all that was left was a mangled sense of pride in its own brokenness. It had retreated into itself and turned itself off from the world.

The land was generational, as were the jobs. In almost any hollow, people lived alongside the dead. Small cemeteries insistently clung to the sides of steep slopes. In places the mountain around them had been stripped away, peeled off by coal companies that had been nice enough to leave the family grave plot as they sheared off the very mountains the plots were on, leaving behind bizarre tufts of grass and tombstones. The people in this part of the country were attached to their land. For generations their coal had built and powered America, their fathers and grandfathers had died deep in the mines, and every boy, upon finishing school, could go straight to the coal companies for a steady job. Life was a codependent and often abusive relationship, in which the miners' work was rewarded with broken bodies, blackened lungs, and a crippling addiction to painkillers from accidents in the mines and unemployment. But their entire existence was built on the jobs that coal had provided, and their identity was founded on hard work and sacrifice in the mines. The fact that they were now destitute couldn't be blamed on coal; in fact, many of them didn't even blame it on the coal companies who had left. No, the culprits were in Washington. In southern Ohio, not far from Matthew's new place in Paoli, I drove past a coal mine owned by Murray Energy. On the gate to the mine's office building hung a sign that said, "Save America. Impeach Obama."

"Obama said point blank that he wanted to put the mines out of business," Ken Mullet, the mine's foreman, told me. "These people don't give a shit about us."

"These people" were the coastal elites who dismissed the part of America that had built this country as "flyover country," an inconvenience and nothing more. They were the elites who, for decades, had taken the coal and hard work from Appalachia and thrown back scraps. This was where Lyndon B. Johnson's War on Poverty was launched in 1965, yet young mothers in War, West Virginia, were still begging for money to buy diapers for their kids. Conservatives were no better than liberals. *National Review* writer Kevin D. Williamson summed it up nicely when, in March of 2016, he wrote, "The truth about these dysfunctional, downscale communities is that they deserve to die. Economically, they are negative assets. Morally, they are indefensible. Forget all your cheap theatrical Bruce Springsteen crap. Forget your sanctimony about struggling Rust Belt factory towns and your conspiracy theories about the wily Orientals stealing our jobs. . . . The white American underclass is in thrall to a vicious, selfish culture whose main products are misery and used heroin needles."

The white people in Appalachia knew how the rest of the country saw them, and they didn't like it. It was this anger that Matthew wanted to harness.

"CHECK OUT THESE BANNERS," Matthew said as he unfolded a large vinyl sheet with the name of his party on it along with the cogwheel and pitchfork logo. "Isn't that some dank shit? I'm like a kid on Christmas." He was sitting in his usual cross-legged manner on a bed in a cheap hotel in Tennessee, showing me all the new merchandise the party had been coming up with. There were stickers, buttons, T-shirts, and, of course, the banner, which was big enough to more than fill the small hotel room. "All made in America, of course. It kind of hurts our image if we produced things in other countries. We actually had them done by a nationalist. It's pretty cool."

Earlier that evening I'd gotten to talking to a family from Mississippi who were drinking beers out of a cooler in the parking lot. They had told me that they were going to vote for Trump in the election not because he promised to bring jobs back to the coal industry but because he would be "tough on crime and tough on immigration, which by God the country needed because you saw these marauding hoodlums all over now, and I don't even know what's happening anymore."

This was, in a sense, Matthew's pitch as well. His was not just an economic argument about bringing wealth and dignity back to parts of America that sorely needed it; it was also an appeal to people's tribal nature. According to him, white people were being shafted by every kind of minority, and the wily Jew was orchestrating it all. The world as he saw it was getting worse, and white people were getting the short end of the stick. I told him what the family from Mississippi had told me, and he wasn't surprised. "People are coming around," he said. "The majority of births in this country aren't European American. There's no way to stop this thing, even if you were to ban all immigration. Whites will be the minority in twenty-five years, and people are beginning to see it now, but more importantly they are starting to feel it. Nobody wants to be a minority. Being a minority fucking sucks. Look at how we've treated black people. Don't for a second think that they'll treat us any better, which is why people are starting to realize that we need to think racially."

In Matthew's eyes his adolescent vision of a clash of civilizations was coming true. Everything was fraying and becoming unstuck. Globalism and liberalism had become the new gods that white people worshipped, and they didn't know that, by doing so, they were digging their own graves. His race was succumbing to white guilt on a global scale, where the white race, brainwashed by liberal values and notions of inclusivity, dove headlong into self-annihilation as they watered down their own gene pool. What's more, the white liberals' insistence that everyone is equal was eroding the very diversity it claimed to value. "Neoliberalism is the new colonialism," Matthew explained. "If everything is the same and equal, then there is no diversity." Globalism was a slow, relentless march toward base sameness, inevitable unless white people woke up to the realization that they were not the global hegemons that the elites would have you believe but rather a folk under siege.

"You just came from West Virginia," he said to me. "Tell me that we're not a people fighting for our very survival. You have looked into the eyes of broken people who have no hope. You have looked at destroyed communities and seen what the globalist agenda has done to break the very humanity of millions of people who are then spit upon by the elite. When Bernie Sanders gets up and says that white people don't know about poverty, and Hillary Clinton says that white people need to check their privilege, and then you go to West Virginia and you see this suffering that integration causes . . . how can you not be on our side?"

I told Matthew that I understood where he was coming from but that I disagreed with his conclusion that the problem was racial. To me his struggle to uphold the cause of poor white people had always seemed doomed because he insisted on focusing on white people rather than on poor people.

"I don't understand why you have to make this about race," I said. "Nobody's arguing that white people in Appalachia aren't suffering, but so are poor African Americans and Hispanics. If poor people of all colors would get together, then you would have something amazing, but all you're doing is splitting people up who might have the same interests."

"But everyone else has someone to speak for them," Matthew said. "It's just whites who have been left behind like this. So how can I not see the world in terms of race when every other group gets its place at the table? They all get advocates, but we, we get told that we're racist pieces of trash and to sit down and shut up."

To Matthew it was impossible to see the world in any other way than along racial lines because the people he identified with and the places they lived in were desperately poor and profoundly underrepresented and also happened to be overwhelmingly white. If that was all you knew of the world, you could be forgiven for believing that white people truly were a marginalized and persecuted people. But Matthew clearly did know more, so he conflated the fight for his people in Appalachia with nationalist struggles around the world. Appalachia was suffering because globalists were exploiting it—the same globalists who oppressed Kurds and Palestinians, who wanted an EU and a UN, and who believed national sovereignty was bad. This allowed him to put the fight for clean water and access to jobs and healthcare in Appalachia into the context of an international fight against globalism and its perceived task masters: the Jews. It also provided him with a one-size-fits-all solution to the problems of not only whites in America but also people all over the world: if globalism is harmful, then the people controlling globalism wish you harm. If capitalism, multiculturalism, and forced integration are ideals of globalism, then the only way to stop globalism is to retreat to your tribe. If the people who wish you harm use globalism to harm you, then your best weapon to fight them with is nationalism.

That is why Matthew believed it was fundamentally important for America to be split into ethno-states. They would, of course, trade, but there needed to be something in place to protect people from outside greed, and what would protect them was not only borders, physical and otherwise, but also a sense of cohesion among the people. To Matthew that sense could only come from ethnic and cultural unity. There was just no other bond strong enough to bind people together, and the globalists understood that, which is why they worked so diligently to desegregate and dilute the races.

"We only have each other," he said. "We're the people who lost our jobs when the government decided that coal was bad. We're the people who got hooked on painkillers that the government told us wasn't addictive. Then they throw us in jail for being addicted to the pills that the doctors fed us. When Obama said that we cling to our God and our guns, he was right, because we have literally nothing else."

THE NEXT DAY came with some bad news. Upon further vetting it had become clear that Rick Tyler perhaps wasn't the candidate that the Nationalist Front should be hitching its wagon to. They'd known all along that Tyler was a former leader within the Christian Identity movement—a white supremacist ideology that holds that whites are the true bloodline descendants of the lost tribes of Israel and that people of color are so-called pre-Adamic, created before Adam and having no souls—and that he had achieved notoriety when he put up a large billboard by the side of the highway that said, "Make America White Again." This was all well and good to the Nationalist Front. Nobody in this movement came without baggage, and although the clear white supremacist message of Christian Identity was exactly what Matthew was trying to get away from, that was, as far as he knew anyway, water under the bridge. No, the problem was of a more sinister nature. "Yeah, so we found out that he may have kidnapped some kids," Matthew told me over breakfast. They'd come across a news article from a local NBC affiliate alleging that Tyler once stole a man's wife and took off with her and her kids. Tyler, in the article, vehemently denied the allegations, and he was never charged with any wrong-doing. Still, the whole thing made Matthew iffy, and they decided to go meet with him this morning but downplay their role in his campaign. "Besides, there are rumors that he still runs some kind of family sect or something," Matthew said.

Tyler's restaurant, the Whitewater Grill, was a tidy, wood-frame diner along the highway with a low-slung red corrugated metal roof, popular with tourists heading to the Ocoee River. The main dining room was an inviting space with comfortable booths and round tables, around which Tyler's many kids scurried, re-filling waters and taking orders. Off the main dining room was a smaller space, a narrow room that just fit a single, long table that Tyler used for meetings and catered events. A middle-aged man, with graying hair and furrowed face, Tyler stood in front of the table with arms stretched out as he greeted Jeff Schoep, Matthew, and a handful of their members. He wore a gray flannel shirt and a baseball cap with the letters "WWFFD," short for "What Would the Founding Fathers Do?" to which the answer was invariably some variation of "Stick with God and stay out of this degenerate cesspool of a society that we've created for ourselves."

"Well, it's just terrible what these animals have done to our sign," he said as he shook hands and slapped backs. "I mean, if they can't argue with us, they try to shut us down. They've been doing it since time immemorial." Tyler's billboard had been taken down recently, and he was sure that somehow the Jews were behind it. "It's put a dent in our campaign, sure," he said, as people shook their heads in indignation at the unfair treatment, "but I'm going to get a bus so I can take my electrifying message on the road. Well, donations allowing, of course." Tyler's political positions were a scattershot compilation of conspiracy theory, anti-Semitism, and racism. He firmly believed that income tax was unconstitutional and that the Federal Reserve was an odious affront to democracy designed to keep Americans down. Homosexuality, according to

Tyler, was an abomination, and he believed that the official 9/11 story was a fiction forced on us by the government. Also, and most crucially, the United States needed to return to a solid white majority.

"Well, of course, the powers that be are terrified of us," he went on, implying the Jews. "Look at my main opponent," he said. "Fleischmann. Tell me that's not a Jewish name. I'm still collecting the paperwork on that one, but I will get to the bottom of it." He never explained exactly what paperwork he was collecting or what he would get to the bottom of, but it didn't matter to the people in the room. They all knew what the Jews were up to. "They probably hand out challah bread over at his campaign office," one of the guys standing around Tyler said. "Hey, I have a joke for you," the man continued. "How much does a challah cost? Six-point-six million! Challah cost. Holocaust. Get it?"

According to Tyler, Donald Trump's candidacy had loosened "social discourse," and Trump's success in the primaries had in part inspired him to run. "I'm not saying we need a Trump to field white, racially aware candidates," he said. "But, boy, has Trump made it easier."

Tyler wasn't the only far-right candidate running for office, buoyed by Trump's rise in national politics. Former KKK Grand Wizard David Duke was fundraising to get his presidential gambit off the ground, polling at a surprising 13 percent, according to a poll by the University of New Orleans' Survey Research Center.

"Honestly, I don't really think Duke is in it to win," Tyler said. "His statewide numbers don't add up at all."

Someone said that the same had been said about Trump, and look at him now. "Yeah, but Trump doesn't have Duke's baggage," Tyler said. "And also, he doesn't attack the 'you know whos.' You know his daughter is even married to one. If Trump was for real, they would kill him. They can kill whomever they want."

The Tyler children, all looking eerily similar to each other—unsettlingly so in light of the sect rumors—brought food before Tyler brought the meeting to order.

He welcomed everyone and thanked them for coming, then quickly launched into the gravity of the issues at hand and the urgency of their struggle.

"This is an uphill battle," he said with a flourish. "But we have something that our enemies don't have and never will have. It happens to be the most powerful force in the universe. And I'm speaking of the truth. The enemies can never have the truth because they are corrupt and untrue. The enemy wants nothing but the ritual murder of us, and you all know who the enemy is."

There were murmurs of agreement around the table. Someone whispered "Jews."

Tyler's speech rambled on for a good forty-five minutes, extolling the virtues of white Christians and warning about impending doom brought about by godless liberals, fertile browns, marauding blacks, and scheming Jews.

"We have to be ready to be in the trenches. When these evil minions come racing against us, we need to be able to give better than we get."

He closed the speech with details on how to donate to his campaign, and soon we were back on the road, heading to a hotel where the Nationalist Front would give a press conference announcing its new principles.

"That was weird," Matthew said. "All those kids who didn't speak but looked exactly the same creeped me out. Why can't our people just be not crazy?"

As had become the custom with these kinds of events, the NSM who had booked the venue had failed to tell management exactly what kind of group they were. As we pulled up, a frenetic receptionist did her utmost to dissuade the small gaggle of journalists who had showed up from filming the hotel's name in the same shot as the table in the corner where the NSM had placed their usual merchandise of swastika-branded trinkets. As it happened, that was all they filmed, and the Nationalist Front, a group founded on renouncing white supremacy and outright racism, launched against a backdrop of swastika-branded zippo lighters. It was safe to say it could have gone better.

"That was fucked up," said Paddy Tarleton back in Matthew's room at the hotel. After the launch earlier that day—the NF had put on an impromptu demonstration in a public park in Cleveland that had attracted exactly zero onlookers and a dozen or so cops—we were nursing some beers while the Traditionalist Workers Party took stock. "I don't know how I'm expected to be a part of this if I have to stand next to a bunch of Nazis waving swastikas."

"I know, Paddy. I'm telling you that I hear you," said Matthew. Apparently he too had been caught off guard by the NSM's display of everything they were trying to put behind them. "We have to be patient with these people. The NSM have been about the swastika for decades, and I know it fucking sucks to stand next to it, but Jeff is working on it." He felt certain that shots of the NSM swastikas would dominate the press conference coverage and that by tomorrow they would all be called Nazis in the news. "It's a setback, sure, but it's not the end of the world. They were going to call us Nazis anyway, so in a way nothing has changed."

"But Matthew, these people are actual fucking Nazis," said Paddy insistently. "They get called Nazis because that is what they fucking are, and we shouldn't be associating with these clowns."

Since joining the NF Matthew had tried to remain pragmatic. The Front provided numbers, boots on the ground. That was what was important. If they were Nazis, he could change that. But not all his guys were as confident as him. Several of the Traditionalist Workers Party members were uneasy about their alliance with the NSM and the KKK groups that came with them. Paddy wasn't the only one. Miles, Scott, and Jason all wore facemasks at shared rallies not because they didn't want their politics known but because they didn't want their pictures taken next to a guy holding a swastika. "It's fucking bullshit," Paddy continued. "And it pisses me off that you don't see it, Matt."

Matthew said he'd talk to Jeff. He wasn't the only one who'd taken heat from his members since the merger. Since announcing the new principles that renounced white supremacy and the swastika, the NSM had lost members. Not many, but because they didn't have many to begin with, it still stung. "I'll take care of it, okay?" said Matthew. "Just give it some time. Jeff stuck his neck all the way out, and he needs our support. It's not easy turning the NSM around."

The level of pushback he was receiving from his members surprised Matthew. He knew joining forces with the NSM would be controversial, but he'd never expected his guys to threaten to leave over it. He'd always imagined the TWP as a family in which decisions were made by consensus, but when he heard the displeasure his members voiced over the decision to join forces with the NSM, he wondered if he perhaps needed to become a stronger leader. If they didn't realize this was the moment to strike—this moment, when even the Republican Party, the bunch of traitors that they were, had made the choice to support nationalism by making Donald J. Trump their presidential candidate—then his party could no longer be a democracy. And if they thought the NSM were bad, wait until they saw the other groups Matthew wanted to bring under his banner.

CHAPTER 9

Hammerskins

> He who would live must fight. He who doesn't wish to fight
> in this world, where permanent struggle is the law of life, has
> not the right to exist.
>
> —Adolf Hitler, *Mein Kampf*

You could tell that John's jaw was broken by the strange way it suddenly protruded from the side of his face. He was on the ground, one hand clawing the dirt as he dragged himself out of the circle of people surrounding him while with his other hand he confusedly pawed his face as if to find out what was wrong. Standing around him were the looming figures of the Hammerskin Nation—hulking, tattooed skinheads, jeering and laughing. Although not a Hammerskin himself, John had been hanging around the group on and off for a while, certainly long enough to know better than to walk over to one of them and tell him to go fuck himself, which was what he had done only seconds before. Thick, viscous blood was pouring from his broken nose and a gash in his head, mixing with the dirt covering the rough floorboards of the porch.

"So you guys want to fight, huh?" John's words were drowned out by laughs as beer and cigarette butts rained down on him. He'd managed to drag himself onto a low bench, and the large skinhead, whose knuckles were already caked with John's blood, stood over him and pounded his shattered face. A friend of John's tried to pull the Hammerskin away, only to find himself pinned against the wall having his nose broken as John crawled across the porch, leaving a trail of blood and drool before collapsing helplessly in the dirt.

Gabe had been watching the fight from the edge of the carnage. He didn't know John well, but they had a few friends in common, and although he certainly thought John had been asking for trouble, he also didn't want to see him killed. John was slowly coming to, babbling barely audible insults through the blood. Reluctantly Gabe grabbed him by his arms and pulled him away while telling him to shut the fuck up unless he wanted the Hammerskins to beat him to death. John's friend Travis, who'd fled out a side door, pulled his Jeep around the front. Gabe dragged John's limp body across the mud and dirt before hauling him into the passenger seat of Travis's Jeep.

"Goddammed fucking idiot," he muttered to himself as the car tore out of the parking lot and down the dark highway toward Temple, a small town in western Georgia. He watched the tail-lights disappear in the darkness while everyone else went back inside. He shivered and lit a cigarette. It was past midnight and getting cold fast. He looked inside the bar for a coat that he had lost in the mayhem, but he couldn't find it and so he went back out, feeling sick to his stomach, partly from drinking and partly from the fight. He was wearing his regular blue jeans and black

Dr. Martens boots with straight, red laces—about as close to a Hammerskin uniform as you could get. Although he wasn't a full Hammerskin yet—he was only twenty-one years old—Gabe had been a skinhead since he was seventeen and a Hammerskin hang-around for the last year or so. A few years earlier, when he was a confused, angry kid in Louisville, Kentucky, who didn't really know why he hated black people, only that he did, he had seen a documentary about the Hammerskins and became enamored by the fear and respect they commanded. He knew he wanted to be a skinhead, so why not become the most terrifying skinhead he could be?

THE HAMMERSKIN NATION likes to compare itself to a tightly knit tribe. Emerging out of the skinhead scene in Dallas in the late 1980s, the organization, which now boasts chapters all over the world, has turned into the most formidable neo-Nazi organization in the country. During its almost three decades in existence its members have managed to rack up an impressive legacy of violence and crime. The history of the Hammerskin Nation is rife with extreme beatings, murder, fire bombings, intimidation, and mayhem. In 1991 in Arlington, Texas, three members of the Hammerskins killed black teenager Donald Thomas and later said that it was for no other reason than wanting to "shoot the nigger." Later that year on Christmas Eve two Hammerskins beat a black, homeless man to death in Birmingham, Alabama. Although members of the Hammerskin Nation carried out episodes like these, there is no evidence to suggest that the organization itself planned them. Still, no one has ever been kicked out of the Hammerskins for violence, and their reputation for brutality made them a highly sought after—if difficult to control—ally on the far fringes of American nationalism. Several groups, including Aryan Nations, Church of the Creator, and White Aryan Resistance, had all tried and failed to recruit the unruly skinheads to their causes. Now Matthew and Jeff had decided it was worth a shot.

Gabe, while still a member of Crew 38. He left the Hammerskins shortly after this picture was taken and started removing several of his facial tattoos.

Gabe was a member of Crew 38, a Hammerskin farm team of sorts. Much like any other gang, a prospective member had a ladder to climb before being made a full member, and the ladder to becoming a Hammerskin has many rungs. First, one needs to be a hang-around. A hang-around is almost like a stray dog hanging around a reluctant master. It means endearing yourself to a club whose members will seem almost aggressively indifferent to your very existence. This pariah status can last for years and is meant to wipe out any sense of ego and weed out anyone not willing to endure a prolonged existence as a nobody and an outsider. The next step is Crew 38, where Gabe was currently laboring. Gabe got his C-38 patch six months ago, and if he played his cards right, he could be a full Hammerskin within a couple of years.

He was soft spoken, and despite being over six feet tall and built like a fighter, he sometimes came across as shy and reserved. On his left cheek, from where his sideburn started down to the corner of his mouth, was a tattoo of a straight razor. A pair of SS bolts was tattooed next to his left eye, and runes spelling out "RAHOWA"—a common acronym in the movement meaning "racial holy war," an imminent helter skelter that many skinheads pine for—were inked on the left side of his head. Intricate lettering spelled out "HATE" over his right eye, and a pale cross graced the narrow patch of skin between his eyes. An ornate Keltic cross covered his throat, and around his neck was a tattooed noose, the rope hanging down his chest, separating two solid-black swastikas. Gabe's original plan had been to get just one swastika over his heart, but when he got home from the tattoo shop he had noticed that the swastika was facing the wrong way—counter-clockwise rather than clockwise—so he decided to get one on the other side so that the symmetry might distract from the fact that the original one was the wrong way around.

He shivered against the late October chill as he left the bar and walked along a tall, metal fence that ran east along the highway, surrounding a large field in which the Hammerskins would celebrate the annual Hammerfest the next day. His shirt, a black, skin-tight tee with a white swastika, was soaked through with John's blood. There was a gate in the fence a few hundred feet from the bar, and a steep dirt path led down onto the field, where a small stage had been erected. Gabe's backpack was resting against some speakers on the stage, and he fished out a black hoodie before rolling his bed pack out on the plywood. He could still see the lights from the bar, perched on a steep hill that had been all but swallowed by the darkness. Dull sounds came from the direction of the bar. Everything else was quiet except for the chattering of Gabe's teeth. He grabbed a baseball bat and pulled it with him under the covers. There had been some scuttlebutt about anti-fascist activists planning to sabotage Hammerfest, and Gabe had been ordered to sleep on stage to guard the equipment. As a C-38 member, Gabe's job was to do whatever the Hammerskins told him. Most of the time it meant fetching beer or ice or whatever else the fully patched members wanted. Sometimes it meant giving a beating to someone the main club wanted beaten, and sometimes it meant spending the night on a cold, lonely stage in the middle of an empty field.

He got as comfortable as the hard floor would allow, curling up in a ball inside the thin bedroll while clutching the bat. Above him in the dark he could hear the bar emptying out and the distant rumble of cars leaving down the highway. Soon Gabe was alone in the vast, dark field. He switched off a small flashlight and drifted off to sleep.

A FEW MILES AWAY, in the town of Bremen, Matthew was having trouble finding a hotel room. The receptionist at the Quality Inn & Suites, a middle-aged woman whose patience had been tested by rowdy skinheads crowding the corridors and the shocked complaints of regular guests unprepared to share their breakfast buffet with swastika-tattooed monsters, had decided that enough was enough, and although Matthew didn't exactly fit the description of a skinhead, his T-shirt with pitchforks and cog wheels and words like "traditionalist" was enough to make her err on the side of caution. "I'm sorry, sir," she said to Matthew. "There are simply no rooms available."

"But we just booked online," said Matthew. "You guys took our reservation."

"I don't know what to tell you," the receptionist said, feigning confusion. "There just isn't a single vacancy."

Matthew walked back outside to the idling car. Miles was eating some leftover pizza. Jason and Scott were inside, running the car's heater. "Discrimination," said Matthew. "Racism even." They'd spent the day driving from Matthew's place in Indiana, and Matthew had put most of his money into gas and the last of it into the hotel where they now didn't have a reservation. Miles smiled good-heartedly and licked the last crumbs of pizza from his fingers. "We'll find somewhere," he said.

An hour later they were all cramped into a double room at a Hamptons Inn across the road. Matthew had to scrape the very bottom of his credit card to be able to stay there, but it was for a worthy cause. Getting invited to Hammerfest as a speaker was a big deal. The Hammerskin Nation was defiantly antipolitical, preferring to stick to the tribelike mentality that had sustained it when so many other groups had fallen away or been vanquished by outside forces. To the degree they had a political program at all, it could be summarized by white supremacist David Lane's famous fourteen words: "We must secure the existence of our people and a future for white children." Beyond that, they didn't have nor were they particularly interested in forming a plan to carry it out. Rather than waging an all-out race war, the Hammerskins seemed happy to fight many small skirmishes, beating up whatever perceived enemy was unlucky enough to get in their way, be they interracial couples, members of the LGBTQ community, or anyone else they felt qualified as an enemy of white people in general or the Hammerskins in particular. To say the Hammerskins had a strategy is like saying that the bulls of Pamplona have a game plan; most of the time they just hit whatever's in front of them. Such as it was, it had served them well in the past but kept them firmly out of the political vanguard of the white nationalist movement.

Matthew wanted to change that, although Jeff had been skeptical. The NSM and the Hammerskins came from a similar ideology, with both groups steeped in the glorification of Adolf Hitler, but it had not brought them close. The Hammerskins openly mocked the theatrics of the NSM, and their territorial nature meant they were deeply hostile to most other groups who claimed to carry the mantle. They saw themselves as warriors, while everyone else played dress-up. Matthew's visit to the Hammerskins wasn't an official overture on behalf of the NF but more a toe in the water.

The Hammerskins' leader, Chester Doles, was a former leader of the National Alliance, once the most well-organized neo-Nazi organization in the United States, and he had told Matthew the Nation might be ready to throw its weight behind a political path. It was good news for Matthew, but Doles had also told him that he hadn't really broken the news to his members and couldn't guarantee how receptive they would be. Matthew figured he only had one shot to convince them, so he'd been working hard on his speech.

"I figure I'll try to paint a big picture," he said, sitting on one of the two twin beds in the small hotel room and clutching a large pillow like he was hugging a teddy. Miles and Scott were reclining on the other bed while Jason sat cross-legged on the floor. "Like . . . I'll say all sorts of stuff about geopolitics and Russia and Syria, and then I'll stop and say, 'Now, I know you guys have been doing this for a long time and that it feels as if we're sliding backward and that we're further away from victory than ever before, but I want to talk to you about President Duterte in the Philippines and how it affects all of us nationalists here in the US.'"

"Say sumthin' 'bout niggers!" Miles shouted in a mock southern drawl. "Matthew, they're not going to care about the Philippines," Jason said. He'd been a skinhead once and claimed to know a little about their mindsets. "Frankly, I don't even know why we're here."

As contentious as it had been within the TWP to join up with the neo-Nazis of the National Socialist Movement, Matthew's latest effort to recruit the Hammerskins was met with even more skepticism. The move was the latest in a series of hard-right tacks that had seen Matthew go from the relatively milquetoast xenophobia of Youth for Western Civilization to now speaking in front of arguably the most extreme neo-Nazi organization in the world. In Matthew's mind it was all about coalition building and "bringing the boots to the suits," but many in his group had real doubts about the efficacy of bringing skinheads onboard to their fledgling political party. "I'm not bringing anybody on," said Matthew. "I'm spreading the word, and if they want to listen, then great. These are our brothers and sisters, and we need to unite the people whose struggles are the same." I wasn't sure if Matthew really believed the Hammerskins were ready to be political or if he just couldn't turn down the opportunity to give a speech.

Miles went on in his drawl, imitating his idea of a skinhead: "Are you even one of us, you faggot sumbitch? Boys, lets round these faggots up and take 'em to the woods." They all fell into uncontrolled giggles. "It's Alice in Chains or nothing, butt pirate!" Miles howled, and Matthew gasped for breath between fits of laughter.

"So you think it's a little brainy?" Matthew said when he'd caught his breath.

"A little brainy is way too brainy," said Jason.

They agreed that Matthew was overthinking it. For all his passion about President Duterte and the nationalist nature of President Assad's struggle in Syria, Matthew decided he needed to tone down the geopolitical nature of his speech and come up with something more in tenor with the crowd. "I'll just do the old boilerplate faith, family, and folk," he said. "Who doesn't love that?"

"I honestly have no idea what to expect tomorrow," Miles said. "I mean, these people are just as likely to kick our asses than to listen to anything you have to say."

"We're guests, though," said Matthew. "That's got to count for something. It's not like we're just crashing their party out of the blue."

"I don't know," said Miles. "I heard the Hammerskins are pretty crazy."

SURPRISINGLY, SKINHEAD CULTURE has its roots not in racism or nationalism but solidarity and multiculturalism. The counterculture that would one day give birth to the Hammerskins and countless other white supremacist outfits first emerged in England in the late 1960s as a way to show kinship with the newly arrived immigrant working class coming into Britain from the West Indies. During the postwar years Britain experienced a period of economic growth, and young people, finding themselves with disposable income, gravitated toward luxury items and clothing seen in popu-lar culture. These kids, with their affinity for nice suits, expensive shoes, and Italian scooters, became known as mods, and out of them grew the counterculture that would become the skinheads. Originally known as "hard-mods," they were working-class kids of both English and immigrant backgrounds who eschewed suits for tight jeans, fine leather shoes for Dr. Martens, and carefully coiffed hairstyles for closely shaved heads.

Their choice of music was rocksteady and ska, appropriated from the rudeboy culture that had come to Britain from the West Indies in the 1960s, and early skinhead culture was explicitly multiracial. Although sometimes violent, the skinheads of the late sixties and early seventies in large part reserved their fists for supporters of rival soccer teams. This, however, would all change by the next decade. The seventies were a time of economic decline in Britain, coupled with increased immigration from Southeast Asia. Educa-tion as well as social and welfare services were brutally cut, and the country settled into a period of economic and social gloom. Against this backdrop the skinhead culture went through a radical shift away from multiracial solidarity toward violence aimed at minori-ties. "Paki bashing" and "gay bashing," the practice of randomly attacking immigrants from Southeast Asia as well as members of the LGBTQ community, became a popular pastime within certain parts of the white—and also black—skinhead culture. Although the violence was more often than not racially fueled, the skinhead movement had not yet adopted an explicit racist ideology.

The 1970s also saw the rise of two national far-right parties in Britain, the National Front and the British Movement. Both par-ties benefited greatly from the depressed economy, and both par-ties sought to recruit the large cohort of white, disaffected youths to their cause. Michael McLaughlin, the son of an IRA soldier and an avowed socialist, took over the British Movement in 1975 and framed the battle for Britain in terms the young skinheads could relate to: a primal, street-level war where they would form the first lines of attack. The skinheads, eager for a sense of direction that not only acknowledged their anger but also gave the violence it spawned prominence, happily embraced the far-right ideology. Recruitment was rapid, helped by the emergence of white power music. Particularly Ian Stuart Donaldson and his band Screwdriver became the soundtrack of the new racist movement. By the early 1980s the British Movement had been decimated by infighting, but the skinhead movement would remain strong for years, soon making its way across the Atlantic.

In 1986 an enigmatic young skinhead from Montana named Clark Martell founded Romantic Violence in the Blue Island neighborhood on the south side of Chicago. It is believed to be the first organized racist skinhead outfit in America. Clark, the sole American importer of Screwdriver and other white power bands predominantly signed with the German Rock-o-Rama label, used it to recruit kids from the poor, white areas of south Chicago. In the early 1980s Blue Island was a poor, predominantly Italian American neighborhood. Most of the kids who lived there were from working-class families hit hard by the depressed economy. Poverty stricken and surrounded by mostly black neighborhoods, Blue Island was fertile ground for Martell's dispossessed brand of white anger.

The gang later changed its name to CASH (Chicago Area Skinheads), and its members were behind a series of brutal beatings and fire bombings. In 1987 Martell and some other members of CASH broke into the house of a former member, twenty-one-year-old Amy Strickland, and pistol whipped her before writing "race traitor" on the wall and drawing a swastika in Strickland's blood.

The skinheads were an import to America, but they blossomed in the 1980s during a time of marked increase in far-right activity. Several antigovernment groups with far-right ideologies were forming around the country, especially in rural areas, where the farming crisis, the worst downturn in American agriculture since the Great Depression, had decimated countless communities and created in many of them a deep-seated anger and distrust toward the government. Coupled with the continuing decline in American manufacturing jobs and the economic recession in the early 1980s, thousands of blue-collar workers in America found themselves unemployed.

Aryan Nations was at the height of its power, claiming to have around six thousand people on its mailing list and reportedly attracting hundreds of far-right extremists to its heavily armed compound in Idaho. The Covenant, Sword, and the Arm of the Lord (CSA) had a sprawling and heavily fortified compound in southern Missouri. And The Order, or the Silent Brotherhood, performed a string of robberies and bombings across the country, culminating in a $3.6 million heist of an armored transport and the killing of liberal radio host Alan Berg in 1984 (see also Chapters 3 and 6).

Around this same time the Confederate Hammerskins was founded in Dallas, and former leader of the KKK Tom Metzger started the skinhead crew White Aryan Resistance (WAR) in California. The Hammerskins approached CASH about a merger, but CASH turned them down—among the few groups who did. Soon after their birth the Hammerskins had chapters in the American West, Northeast, and Midwest. It wasn't long before they were by far the biggest skinhead group in the world.

Although the skinheads never participated actively in the conspiratorial and militant world of the far-right patriot movement—skinheads often attended events at Aryan Nations in Idaho, but the groups never signed on in any official capacity—they were very much the product of the same sense of white dispossession. There had been many white groups, chief among them the KKK, who had fought hard against the Civil Rights Movement in the 1960s and 1970s, and their failure to curb equal rights for women and nonwhites had created a deep sense of loss. Whereas the fight in the civil rights era had been to maintain the status quo, the skinheads and other far-right groups in the 1980s operated under an assumption that their country was already lost. This made them less political than previous incarnations of white nationalism and more geared toward a cataclysmic end times. The CSA, Aryan Nations, and similar groups set their sights on carving out white enclaves in their lost country and preparing for the racial holy war that was sure to come. Others, like The Order, not content with waiting, set about starting it. But Clark Martell and Romantic Violence didn't really want a war—they just liked to fight.

Decades later their fighting had led them exactly nowhere, and the skinhead movement was flailing. Although still active in most states, by 2017 the once unquestioned might of the Hammerskin Nation was almost nonexistent, and in its place was a grab bag of unruly and unaffiliated skinhead crews whose strategic goals rarely seemed to advance past where they would go to drink when the weekend arrived. In 2002 the SPLC counted eighteen skinhead crews in America and found that most of them were under Hammerskin control. In 2006 they counted fifty-nine crews, but only six affiliated with the Hammerskins. Their downfall and that of the skinhead movement in general came down to a mix between the brutal and the downright mundane.

At its peak in the late 1990s skinhead culture was big business. The Hammerskin Nation boasted hundreds of members throughout the country, and there were countless other crews, most of them deferring to the hegemony of the Hammerskins. Their main tool for recruitment was music, and this was also the movement's main source of income. White power music was a million-dollar business and actively used its clout to recruit new skinheads for the cause. In the documentary *Hearts of Hate* about the far-right scene in Canada in the 1990s, Resistance Records founder George Burdi said, "We hear the slogan, 'White people awake, save our great race,' twice per chorus, eight times in total through an entire song and, if they play that tape five times a week and just listen to that one song, they're listening to 'White people awake, save our great race' forty times in that one week, which means a hundred and sixty times a month, and you do the math beyond that."

By the late 1990s annual gatherings such as Hammerfest attracted hundreds of attendees, but internal strife soon tore the scene to pieces. In the summer of 1999 the leaders decided that a member of the Indiana chapter of the Hammerskins should be stripped of his patch for repeatedly coming on to another member's wife. The leadership tasked five Hammerskins with removing his patch and forcing him to cover up any Hammerskin tattoos, but they got overzealous and viciously beat the offender, causing the leadership to throw them out. Eight others joined the five outcasts, renouncing their Hammerskin membership in protest, and together they formed the Outlaw Hammerskins and immediately established themselves as the mortal enemies of the Hammerskins. Their main selling point was being more violent than any others, and the Outlaws quickly spread to multiple states. Not the biggest and baddest kid in the yard anymore, the Hammerskins withered and were replaced by an undergrowth of smaller, unaffiliated crews.

Financial factors exacerbated this decimation. The peak of the skinhead movement coincided with the peak of the record industry, and the decline of the former was closely linked to the atrophy of the latter. While illegal downloads and online sharing hit the mainstream music industry like a sledgehammer, the large purveyors of hate music such as Resistance Records and the Hammerskin-affiliated label Panzerfaust felt the pain even more acutely. Their target audience was one notoriously short on disposable income, and pirating caught on like wildfire. The big white power labels were doubly inconvenienced by this, as they had recently been attacked by a slew of smaller labels determined to grab a piece of the once lucrative hate music market. While digital platforms such as iTunes later became wildly popular with fans of white power music, the distribution model no longer necessitated the clout of a large label, so the big players—and the crews they funded—foundered. In 2014 iTunes announced they would remove white power music from their service, and following the Unite the Right rally in Charlottesville in August 2017, Spotify also announced they would ban white power music from their servers.

The internet harmed the scene in other ways too. Although it has been an unparalleled recruiting tool for white nationalist groups in general, the increasingly online nature of the white nationalist movement has removed the scene's ability to self-police. Eric Woodzell, the former skinhead turned Klansman, once told me that everything went downhill when skinheads no longer needed to meet face to face to be active. "It used to be that the only way to be on the scene was to go to shows," he said. "And if you talked shit, you knew you would have your ass kicked at the shows. Now everyone can talk shit as much as they like because nobody is going to kick their ass on Facebook."

More prosaically, the skinheads increasingly found themselves defeated by age. Not only were revenues down, infighting up, recruitment languishing, and splintering rampant, but members of the first generation of skinheads were also hitting middle age. Being a skinhead is a young man's game, and some realized they no longer had the drive to drink and brawl with their friends daily, while others graduated into lives of crime or joined other gangs such as the Hell's Angels. The result was a movement bereft of its former notoriety, short on funds, and lacking in members. The Hammerskin Nation had, in the words of the SPLC, been reduced to the "Hammerskin Hamlet."

Perhaps it was time for the Hammerskins to get political, which might have been Chester Doles's thinking when he invited Matthew, now representing the Nationalist Front, to their largest annual gathering. Still, it would be a tough sell to a group that had never cared about being political.

GABE WOKE THE NEXT MORNING at dawn. His bones ached from sleeping on the hard surface. The stage, the equipment, and even Gabe's sleeping bag were covered in a soft layer of dew. He shivered and sat up, brushing the wetness from the black nylon. The campsite was oppressively quiet, and the bar on top of the hill, where last night there had been nothing but carnage, was silent. A stack of flight cases containing instruments along with two guitar amps were filed away at the back of the stage, untouched since last night. A couple of gazebo tents covered boxes of equipment resting on a piece of tarp on the grass. For all their promises of sabotage and nightly attacks, Antifa had stayed home. Not that Gabe blamed them. Attacking the Hammerskins on private property in Georgia with its lax gun laws would have been suicide. Even at night there were enough brothers sleeping in cars out on the field to fend off anyone dumb enough to try, and if anyone did, they would find themselves caught in the middle of nowhere, surrounded by guys who didn't think twice about breaking the jaw of one of their own who stepped out of line—God knows what they would do to an enemy.

"Antifa" is a catchall term for a scattered movement of radical leftists, comprising people who reject nationalism and fascism on a visceral level. Much like the far right, Antifa describes a wide variety of groups, methods, and motivations, but what binds them together is that they live to face off against racism and intolerance and that many of them would prefer to leave the cops out of it. They also believe that the litany of sins visited upon humanity by National Socialists and other white supremacists not only justifies violence against them but also advocates it as an effective tool, nicely summed up in their slogan "Smash the Fash." In that sense Antifa had been more of a unifier for the movement than Matthew could ever hope to be. As much as the various factions on the right disliked and distrusted each other, they shared a profound loathing for Antifa and would happily travel long distances to square off against them. It didn't hurt that Antifa seemed about as interested in engaging in a civilized discussion with them as they were in forming a cogent argument, so the two opposing armies had formed a happy marriage based on screaming at each other over the heads of riot police, the national guard, or whomever else was put in place to make sure the two sides never actually had to fight. Of course, there were times when actual brawls did break out—a rally in Sacramento organized by some of Matthew's guys as well as their counterparts in Oakland, the Golden State Skinheads, saw a few people from both sides end up in the hospital with stab wounds. But these were rare, and whenever they did occur they

were quickly seized upon by both sides as recruitment opportunities. Mostly the two sides pointed menacingly at each other from
their respective sides of the police barricades and dared the other
to come over to their side. It was a song and dance that both the far
right and Antifa knew well and stuck to. For now, at least.

Gabe lit a cigarette and blew a pale, blue plume into the air.
The baseball bat had been digging into his side for most of the
night, and his clothes smelled of beer and blood. A car was slowly
making its way down the dirt road Gabe had walked the night before, coasting across the grass before coming to a halt in front of
the stage. Josh and Rick, both friends of Gabe, stepped out and
greeted him. Brent, the guitarist from the band Definite Hate,
stretched his legs gingerly as he got out from the backseat. "Where
are you guys coming from?" asked Gabe.

"North Carolina," said Brent. Definite Hate was one of the evening's headliners, and when Brent's car had broken down on the
way, the Hammerskins had sent Gabe's friends—one of them a
former C-38 and the other a Hammerskin prospect—to pick him
up. They'd been driving all night and were exhausted. Definite
Hate was legendary on the skinhead scene. The band had been
around for years but only got famous in 2012 when their bassist, Wade Michael Page, walked into a Sikh temple in Wisconsin
and shot six people before putting a bullet in his own head. Since
then tributes to their fallen bandmate had been common at their
shows. All the band's members had said repeatedly that they had
had no idea what Page was planning, but the former bassist's act
of terrorism still gave the band the kind of cachet that came with
taking action rather than just talking about it. Although everyone
in the Hammerskins was careful to denounce Wade in public—or
not talk about him at all—his actions had made him a martyr in the
skinhead movement.

"Is this where we're playing?" asked Brent, pointing to the stage.

"Yeah," said Gabe. "Should be a good one. Lot of people coming."

He showed him where he could put his gear and went off to find
a beer.

As the sun slowly came up over the field, the brothers in their cars began waking up, some driving off in search of coffee and food, others having beer for breakfast. Most of the Hammerskins were still at their hotels outside Temple, but those who weren't began pitching in with setting up booths, taping off the parking area, and fiddling with the sound equipment in preparation for the first sound checks. Soon there was a steady flow of cars trickling down the dirt path onto the meadow. Some of them Gabe knew—a few of his C-38 friends from when he lived in Kentucky showed up early—but most he'd never seen before. As they arrived, the various groupings within the Hammerskins quickly found one another. The fully patched members swaggered out of their cars, clasping hands and hugging their brothers. C-38s, many of them meeting members from other parts of the country for the first time, were more timid, milling around their cars, complementing each other's T-shirts, figuring out common acquaintances, and loosening up on warm beer. A couple of Finnish guys erected a folding table along the edge of the field, covering it with stickers and CDs of various European acts. The two of them looked strikingly similar, all thick bull necks, ropey muscles, and expansive guts, covered in tattoos and matching hammers of Thor inked into their skulls. Next to them a skinny older guy with a gaunt face and gray moustache was erecting a tent for the once-powerful but now all-but-defunct Aryan Nations. The man wore loose-fitting jeans and sneakers and the powder-blue uniform shirt of the AN. On the collar was a sword and cross, emblazoned with a golden crown on a blue shield. He was carefully placing medals, photos, CDs, and books on a red tablecloth along with flyers about the AN and a sign-up sheet that would remain conspicuously empty throughout the day. He stood for a while behind his table, his body gently rising and falling on the balls of his toes, from time to time sipping from a thermos of coffee he kept behind a rack of flyers, but when no one visited he began taking short trips to neighboring booths to see what they had to offer. He had little interest in the Finns, and they had no interest in him, and for the most part the man from AN walked around by himself. It was a stark difference from the AN's heyday. No white supremacist group, perhaps with the exception of the KKK, better exemplified the rise and fall of the extreme far right in America than the Aryan Nations.

"What's with all the minivans?" Matthew asked, as his rental rolled slowly down the dirt road onto the meadow. There were dozens of cars already in the part of the field set aside for parking, and many of them were clearly family cars, schizophrenically mixing the telltale signs of suburbia—child safety seats, head-rest iPad holders—with the insignias of life on the political fringes. One car, a Honda Odyssey, sported a bumper sticker with a drawing of a small, happy family next to a sticker that read "KILL NIGGERS."

The guard at the gate had eyed them suspiciously as they explained that they were there by invitation from Dolson, eventually letting them through with a lackluster "Sieg Heil." Apparently there had been a couple of cars driving past the property taking pictures all morning, and Matthew and his guys looked nothing like the members of the Hammerskin Nation. As we drove into the field the car passed the makeshift outdoor gym, where a couple of monstrous skinheads were bench pressing in preparation for a strong-man competition to be held later that day.

"Jesus, look at these fucking guys," said Miles. "Are you sure they all know we're invited?"

"Here's hoping," said Matthew. "We should find Chester and introduce ourselves as soon as possible."

They parked the car and found Gabe, who by then had been severely burned by the morning sun. Gabe knew Matthew well from back in Kentucky, where they had lived only a few miles apart. Gabe's twin brother, Zach, identical to Gabe in every way except for the tattoos, was a member of Matthew's party. "Gabe's a really sweet guy," Matthew had told me earlier. "He can just look terrifying." Gabe's brother Zach, along with the rest of his family, was hoping Gabe would leave the skinheads for something a little less extreme, but Gabe said he was happy being in C-38. He liked the camaraderie and sense of power he got with them, even though their tendency to fight among each other was getting to him. "I have my role to play, and Matthew and my brother have theirs," he would say. "It's like if the movement is a body, then maybe Matthew is the head or the brain. The Hammerskins are the fists. A movement needs fists to make it."

He hugged Matthew and the guys and told them to get comfortable and if anyone gave them any shit to come to him. "This is quite a scene," said Matthew as he looked out over the forty or fifty skinheads crowding the field. It was rare to see such a large gathering of nationalists anywhere these days, and even rarer for nationalists to have a place like this where they could be in peace.

"I know," said Gabe. "Great, isn't it? The landlord's being an asshole, saying he wants more money or something like that, but other than that everything is perfect."

He told Matthew about the metaphor he had been thinking about where the nationalist movement was a body and he was the fists, and Matthew agreed. "I don't know if I'm the brains though," he said. "Maybe the heart." He slapped his belly. "Or the stomach."

Gabe pointed them toward a couple of folded tables next to a clutch of trees that had been set aside for the Traditionalist Workers Party, and they set about unloading the flyers, T-shirts, and banners from the car. Butch Urban of the NSM had arrived earlier that morning and was setting up next to them the usual swastika-covered NSM trinkets. While the rest of the guys finished the stand, Matthew greeted Butch and walked off to discuss the swastika and how they would need to get rid of it if the Nationalist Front was to be a success. "He gets it," Matthew said as he came back. "Butch is a smart guy."

Gabe said that they should look for Chester later because he was in the middle of a meeting with the brothers, and there was no way a C-38 like him, or anyone else who wasn't a full-blooded Hammerskin member, could go up and disturb it. While he waited, Matthew sat down to work on his speech. "Should I talk about our program for renewable energy and how wind and solar are the only possible solutions for Appalachia?" Jason said that would be a bad idea. "Fine," said Matthew, and he went back to writing, his pen forming a large and clumsy cursive on his notepad. "Immigration . . . crime . . . yada, yada, yada . . . all that stuff. It needs an arc." He put the pen down and brainstormed for a bit, throwing out phrases and ideas. "It's the best year ever. Things are happening all over the world. The war has come home. It's not just on the TV. The fight is now mainstream. Whether it's Donald Trump or European parties, we all have to talk about nationalism. The left is moving to the left and the center is being destroyed. Where are we in America? We're all fucked. America cannot be saved or salvaged. We need to work toward our independent state. Demographically we are screwed. We cannot take America back, but don't be upset. It's a great opportunity. Lessons from Europe . . . blah, blah. This is what Rockwell intended—he always wanted to go political, so we are following in his footsteps."

He looked at Miles. "What do you think?"

Miles shrugged. "I like it."

"What do you mean 'You like it'? Which part?"

"All of it."

"Does the arc make sense?"

"Yeah, sure."

"Will they get it? I don't want to be a classist prick and talk down to them."

He went back to writing, mumbling key words and phrases as he went along. "Increased, leftist violence . . . BLM is anti-white hate . . . what else?"

Miles quoted something from the movie *Mad Max* that sidetracked Matthew until they were talking about Warhammer, the fantasy role-playing game and book series.

"I hope these guys don't kill us when they realize what nerds we are," Matthew said.

There was a commotion over by the stage. A large crowd of people had gathered, and they could just make out bodies grappling in the middle. "Oh shit, it's a boot party," said Gabe, and he ran in the direction of the commotion. He was still upset about the fight the night before. A boot party is when a group of guys beats a person to the ground and then stomps him with steel-tipped boots. Dave Nichols, a burly, thick-necked former Hammerskin from Tennessee, was on the ground; the Hammerskins had descended on him as soon as he fell. The crowd cheered as they jumped on him, their massive black boots kicking him in his large belly, his back, and his head. One of his eyes was a gory mess of black blood, and it was impossible to see if it was still there or if it had somehow been kicked out of his head. Blood was gushing from multiple lacerations on his face, and still it didn't seem like the Hammerskins had any intentions of stopping. I'd heard many stories of people being stomped to death this way, and I thought for a second that this would be this poor guy's fate, but suddenly a girl who I later found out was his girlfriend threw herself over his body. It worked, and the kicking stopped. Some of them spat on the battered body as they turned around and went back to whatever they had been doing. The girl wiped the blood off the man's face and tried unsuccessfully to heave his massive body over her shoulder. By some miracle the man came to, and by an even greater miracle he was able to stagger to his feet. He left the meadow draped over the sagging shoulder of his much smaller girlfriend.

"Goddammed fucking stupid," Gabe said when he came back to where Matthew was still sitting. He and his guys had decided to hang back by the table because they knew very few of the Hammerskins and didn't want to get caught up in anything should the bloodlust prove contagious. "It's so fucking stupid. I don't get why we do this. How are we supposed to fight the niggers when all we do is fight each other? Fuck. We're supposed to be brothers, man!"

"I hear you, brother," said Matthew.

"Frankly I was surprised it took this long for a fight to break out," said Jason.

A few people came over to the TWP table as the day wore on, but none of the skinheads seemed very interested in what Matthew was selling. His brand of fascism, replete with abstruse quotes from Romanian fascists and Russian Orthodox scholars, didn't much resonate with the Hammerskins, whose ideological worldview could be summed up by the band Iron Will, who at that moment were on stage singing "Fuck niggers. Fuck Jews."

Mostly the guys just sat there, watching the skinheads swill beer and get increasingly rowdy.

As darkness fell, Doles walked onstage and took the microphone. He was a short, tightly wound plug of a man with a pedantic crew cut and the practiced military demeanor of someone who's seen many war movies. In his hand was a horn, which he raised into the air ceremoniously and filled with Miller Lite. He took a deep swig, much like the Vikings before him. "I want to welcome you all to this historic event," he roared to cheers and applause. "I recognize with great honor our Hammerskin brothers and Crew 38 that have traveled from Australia, Germany, Switzerland, all across Europe, Canada, and even South America."

"Finland!" screamed the two Fins from the table next to Matthew's.

"We are here because our ancestors are speaking to us from within," Doles continued, ignoring the Fins. "Each and every one of our ancestors are calling us to stand up and fight. I refer to this as the Call of the Blood. You have all answered that call. Thank you. We are modern-day Vikings, men. We are the alpha males of today. Living lives that are honorable, respectable, and industrialist [sic]. We are men with courage and have great pride in our European heritage. We are protectors and providers of our families. We are proud, white men."

This was what the Hammerskins had come to hear. They saw themselves as warriors, even if the rest of the world didn't, because the alternative was perhaps too painful to face. If they weren't at war, if their race wasn't threatened, and if the enemy wasn't everywhere, then what was the point of the Hammerskins? As much as any gang of thugs throughout history, the Hammerskins had created a wartime narrative in order to justify their thuggish behavior. They had invented the warrior image because the alternative was admitting that they were little more than violent bruisers who hated everyone who wasn't them. Better to be a warrior than a loser.

Doles played to this notion perfectly, weaving a seductive tapestry of end-times imagery in which everyone got to go down in a blaze of glory for his race. America was on the edge of an abyss. A storm was approaching. The wind was starting to blow. Total civil unrest was imminent. Black Americans—or Black Lives Matter—had declared war on white police officers, and although the Hammerskins were no friends of the cops, they still preferred the blues to the blacks.

According to Doles, white Americans lacked "tribal thinking," an ability that enabled people to act in the interest of their race, and it was an ability blacks had in abundance. But this was all changing. "The sense of nationalism in America hasn't been this strong for fifty years. Finally whites are standing together. Whatever you think of Trump, he has greatly contributed to the rise and return of nationalism in America."

I was fairly sure that this was the first time a politician from any of the main parties—or any politician at all, for that matter—had been mentioned favorably at a Hammerskin event, and there were even scattered cheers from the crowd. Although not quite as apocalyptic as the Hammerskins, the America Trump described from the campaign trail was unquestionably bleak, and the same sense of embattled patriotism resonated with both Trump supporters and the Hammerskins. The only difference was that in the Hammerskins' America, the Doomsday Clock was considerably closer to midnight.

"Men, we all train to stay fit. To stay combat ready at all times. Continue training. Power lifting, boxing, judo, karate, MMA, whatever . . . but train and stay fit, because the time is coming that you will be called upon to stand up and defend your family, your homes, and your loved ones."

There may well have been a time when the Hammerskins could be counted on to present some sort of fighting force, but those days were long past, and I suspected Doles knew it. The roughly one hundred attendees were a rowdy bunch but still paled in comparison to the hundreds of Hammerskins who would gather at early Hammerfests. Still, Doles persevered, playing to the martyr complex so prevalent among the Hammerskins, who all seemed to harbor some deep-seated fetish about dying in a glorious battle for the women of the white race.

"As Hammerskins we should view ourselves as a strike force," he continued. "So be responsible, men. Get your affairs in order. Get your wills in order. Our Viking ancestors would take their favorite weapon—the sword or the battle axe—and tie a lock of their lady's fine hair on it. Choose your favorite weapon—today it's probably the AR—take a lock of your wife's fine hair, take a lock of your daughter's hair, and attach it to your weapon as a symbolic reminder of why we fight. The gods have already decided our destinies, men. It's not when we die, but how we die. For us it's victory or Valhalla, so it's a win-win situation."

He raised the horn filled with tepid Miller Lite. "I would now like you to join me for a drink, as I raise the horn in honor of our late founder Joe Rowan." The skinheads lifted their various cans of beer and toasted the singer of white power band Nordic Thunder who was killed in 1994. Doles then went on to thank the strong-man competition participants and those in attendance who had supported him when he went to prison—or, as he called it, "ZOGs federal Gulag"—for weapons possession a few years ago.

"In closing, we're madder than hell and meaner than shit! Hail the Hammerskin Nation!"

In the end Matthew decided to ignore all the advice he had been given about the speech and opened up with the state of affairs in Syria where the forces of Bashar al-Assad were currently driving the rebels out of Aleppo, and from there he moved on to presidential elections in Hungary. When he got around to a recent setback suffered by Angela Merkel's CDU party in the northern states of Mecklenburg-Western Pomerania, you could practically hear the eyes of every Hammerskin in attendance glazing over. He briefly spoke about Donald Trump and the resurgence of nationalism in

America, but anyone hoping for some decent red meat was immediately rebuffed as Matthew then turned to the British referendum where a majority voted to leave the European Union. He jumped briefly back to Syria, and then, as if to dare the Hammerskins to give less of a shit, launched into a tirade about the antidrug policies of Filipino president Rodrigo Duterte.

Eventually he got around to something a little more the Hammerskins' speed as he called every white man, woman, and child to fight, stating that when white people fought, they won. The immigrants and foreigners and liberals were jackals tugging at the lion's mane, and the lion was about to wake. George Soros was pumping money into Black Lives Matter so they could attack whites on the streets, and white children in schools were taught that white people were behind every bad thing in history. "They are tearing down our monuments and they are tearing down our heritage," he went on, addressing the current controversy surrounding the Confederate flag and the removal of Confederate statues from public spaces. "They want to ethnically cleanse us from history."

He spoke about how unity was essential because the Jews hated all whites equally, no matter what group they were with. "We've talked about this before, but it's different now because our backs are against the wall."

He spoke about the need to emulate the European wave of nationalism sweeping the continent and how every group and every member had a role to fill in the movement. It was a valiant effort, but one painfully lost on the congregation. The few still hanging around the stage were talking amongst themselves, only perking up at juicy sound-bites about evil Jews or Duterte telling President Obama to go fuck himself. It was clear there wasn't much to be gained for Matthew from the Hammerskins and equally clear that he had little to offer them. The Hammerskins didn't want politics. They may have wanted war at one point, but these days they mostly wanted beer. "He should have said something about niggers," Miles whispered as Matthew talked about demographic displacement. Even if he had, it probably wouldn't have been enough. The Hammerskins were a tribe, and even if it was dying, it remained deeply skeptical about all things non-Hammerskin. Even as Matthew's politics had veered to the right in recent years, it was still politics, and the Hammerskins had no use for it.

"I'm going to bring it to an end soon," Matthew said as the last people stopped paying attention. "I promise."

CHAPTER 10

Harrisburg

> Our first rally was a huge success, even though we had
> less than a thousand people, and we went back to the
> headquarters to sing the Party song until our lungs fairly
> burst, and celebrate our entry into the speech-making
> business.
>
> —George Lincoln Rockwell, *This Time the World*

It was almost 3 a.m., and Matthew and I were sitting in an IHOP somewhere between Harrisburg, Pennsylvania, and Paoli, Indiana, when Matthew asked me why I never asked him about the Holocaust. The question caught me by surprise, not because I was unaccustomed to Matthew talking about Jews—only a few hours earlier he had ranted about how Jews were behind tens of millions of aborted white babies—but because I didn't know the answer to the question. It was on the evening before the presidential election, and I had known Matthew for a few years, watching him gain steam as a nationalist leader in America and putting together his ragtag coalition of white pride malcontents. His question made me wonder if all the time we had spent together had dulled me in some ways or softened my journalistic instincts. If you spend enough time with another person, however much you disagree with or abhor that person's opinions on certain matters, you are bound to find traits you like. And there were traits about Matthew that I honestly liked. He was always upbeat and friendly and had a way of dismissing the rest of the far right in a way that was hard to disagree with. Also, there were political issues that we agreed on. We both felt strongly for the struggle of Palestinians, and we both believed that the prevalence of money and special interests in American politics had gotten the country into trouble. Perhaps I was getting a form of Stockholm Syndrome. The more I thought about it, the more I realized that at some point along the way I had let myself get taken in by Matthew's charm and gregariousness. The folksy, friendly qualities that made him so much more dangerous than your garden-variety white supremacist had gotten under my skin, and it dawned on me that the reason I hadn't asked him about the Holocaust might be that I didn't want to hear what he had to say about it. Somewhere along the line, in the churning and virulent sea of Klan members' ramblings, neo-Nazis' aggression, and old-school white supremacists' hatred, Matthew had become an island of relative calm, someone with whom I discussed the craziness of the white supremacist movement rather than a subject whose views I dissected and scrutinized.

During my reporting I had spoken to several law enforcement officers who had infiltrated Klan and militia groups during the 1970s and 1980s, and they all said it was easy to become friendly with the people they were investigating and that keeping an eye on the ball was sometimes a challenge. Had I begun to lose sight of the ball? On this trip Matthew and I had discussed sci-fi and fantasy novels and sang along to Kenny Loggins and the Doobie Brothers. I realized that a part of me had begun to enjoy Matthew's company, and perhaps subconsciously I knew that asking him about the Holocaust—a subject about which I was fairly certain I knew what Matthew thought—would mean shattering the illusion that perhaps he was different from the others I had met during the research for this book. I chewed on a forkful of red velvet pancakes with syrup when it dawned on me that Matthew's question was a gift, bringing me back to where I needed to be. It was a wake-up call, a reminder that however friendly we had become, there was still a chasm between us that neither of us wanted to cross and certain things I could never condone. Of course, I didn't say this to him.

"I'm not sure why I haven't asked you about the Holocaust, Matt," I said. "I suppose I always planned on getting around to it, but now is as good a time as any." I put down my fork and took a sip of ice water. "So how can you defend National Socialism when it was behind the murder of 6.6 million innocents?"

With that, everything fell back into place again. It was jarring to listen to Matthew explain the mathematical impossibility of cremating millions of Jews, the lack of historical witnesses to the Holocaust, the impracticality of using Zyklone-B, and the benefits the international Jewry had seen in perpetuating the lie of the Holocaust. These were all boilerplate Holocaust-denying arguments and had been debunked ad nauseam, yet they still proved irresistible to those who wanted to give a veneer of pseudo-science to their anti-Semitism. They were feats of faux-intellectual acrobatics, nonfactual contortions designed to force a square peg into a round hole, and Matthew's refusal to acknowledge the mountain of historical evidence of the slaughter of a people reminded me that however friendly or rational he seemed, especially compared to other white nationalists, he still believed and promoted the same racist ideas.

When Matthew was done explaining how there were bound to be deaths at POW camps—which, according to him, is what the concentration camps were—but that these camps weren't any worse than what the Russians were doing at the time, he stopped and asked me what I thought about it all. I told him it was pretty much what I had expected, and with that we paid our bill and got back on the road.

We were coming from Harrisburg and another semi-inaugural rally of the Nationalist Front. Following the debacle in Cleveland, Tennessee, Jeff and Matthew had decided that they were going to weed out all the frivolous, white supremacist, or nonexistent groups from the alliance and mount one last unveiling. Unsurprisingly the Hammerskins hadn't signed on after Matthew's speech at Hammerfest, which, when Matthew thought about it, was perhaps for the best. You couldn't teach an old dog new tricks any more than you could teach a Hammerskin not to want to pummel any and every minority he comes across.

Before the rally I'd gone with Matthew and his guys to a gun store on the outskirts of town to buy some pepper spray, as Antifa had promised to attack the rally in general and Matthew in particular. As his profile grew, so did the number of death threats he was receiving, and Matthew would say that he fully expected to be killed one of these days. He'd gotten several emails and phone messages from people threatening to shoot him during public rallies, and whenever he went to give a speech Matthew would invariably tell his wife, Brooke, that he would come home victorious or carried on his shield. I wasn't quite sure if any of his guys, none of whom was particularly powerful in stature, would be able to carry Matthew's expansive frame, but the point was that Matthew claimed to be fine with risking his life for the cause and that his wife was too. Undoubtedly it was part of the far right's glorification of the Viking ethos—"Victory or Valhalla!" was a popular chant at rallies—and there were times when Matthew truly seemed to relish the idea of martyrdom. But I had also seen the hatred protestors aimed at him and was frankly surprised that none of them had taken a shot at him yet.

The trick to picking a good pepper spray, Matthew explained, was finding one that mixed ease of use with a good amount of

EVERYTHING YOU LOVE WILL BURN

spray and, of course, the right price point. Miles was rummaging around the store, looking at shiny handguns, intermittently asking Matthew if they could get a particularly imposing weapon. "We can take this out of the budget, right?" he said, pointing at a pitch-black, pump-action shotgun he had been admiring for a couple of minutes. "What budget?" said Matthew. "There is no budget."

Matthew finally settled on a black, relatively innocuous canister of pepper spray called the Disabler, which boasted that it was the preferred pepper spray of law enforcement and that it could keep an assailant on the ground for up to forty-five minutes. "Apparently Antifa has a bounty out on me," he said. "They're all broke, so I don't know how much it could possibly be. Some guy wrote on Facebook that he couldn't wait to kick my teeth in, so I liked his comment." He paid the $10 it cost for the large canister and walked out, crossing the parking lot of the strip mall and entering a DICK'S Sporting Goods, where he bought hockey tape to make the handles of the shields that they had made more comfortable to hold. The shields were constructed out of heavy plywood, then painted black and adorned with the yellow cog and pitchfork logo of the TWP. They were heavy and cumbersome, with almost zero practical use in a fight, but they looked imposing enough when the TWP marched in a phalanx with the shields raised.

Matthew wanted to be as on brand as possible, considering the spectacular failure of the Nationalist Front's last rally, where swastika-decorated trinkets and banners had overshadowed Matthew's message of postracial nationalism. This time there would be way fewer groups invited to participate, and those who had been invited had also been instructed to leave any swastikas and Klan robes at home. In that sense the rally to be held later that day on the Harrisburg capitol steps was less of a relaunch of the Nationalist Front as a launch of the Nationalist Front 2.0. This was the first event where Matthew had been firmly in control, coordinating heavily with Jeff beforehand to make sure his most Hitler-loving members would behave or, ideally, stay home. "I really don't want to look like an asshole again," he said in the car en route to the meeting point. "Last time was such a shit show." Since Cleveland many of his members had been upset about joining forces with neo-Nazis, and as much as Jeff had stuck his neck out with his members in renouncing the swastika, Matthew's neck was also in a precarious position for his overtures to white supremacists. "I just hope these guys know how to behave themselves."

Miles switched on the stereo and turned the volume up as Kenny Loggins's "Danger Zone" came on. "You know what? Fuck Screwdriver," Miles said. "Kenny Loggins is the real white power music. Only white guys ever listen to him, and he's brilliant."

Jeff was waiting in the parking lot outside a Comfort Inn as Matthew and his guys rolled up. Surrounding him was a handful of NSM members, many of them clearly old enough to qualify for Medicare. "Jeff said he was bringing numbers," Matthew said. "I didn't realize he meant cumulative age."

"We have shields, they have osteoporosis," Miles said.

Jeff walked over as they unloaded shields from the car, passing them around so everyone could get a good look at them.

A silver Ford F-150 pickup truck was idling a short distance away. It was decked out with Confederate flags and a bumper sticker with a picture of a hooded figure announcing that the KKK was "The Original Boyz in the Hood." They were the Texas Rebel Knights and had driven up from Quinlan, Texas, to support the alliance. They were presently gathered around their truck—grey haired, bearded, hulking, and scowling over at Jeff. Their presence was a bit of a problem. Obviously Jeff and Matthew were glad to have them—anyone who cared enough to show up, let alone drive all the way from Texas to show up, was welcome—it was just that the Rebels were at that moment robing up in preparation for the rally.

"They say they don't want to march if they can't wear their robes," Jeff said, glancing in their direction.

"Well, they can't," Matthew said. "We all agreed on this. It can't be like Cleveland."

"I know and I told them, but they won't listen. They said they could drop the masks, but that they needed the robes or they wouldn't march with us. Oh, and at some point before we leave here I want to gather all the speakers together and have that little talk. I don't want to be standing here hollering if folks aren't paying attention. Especially the older folks need to get this message, so I want to make sure they do." The message Jeff wanted them to get was the new guidelines on racial slurs in speeches. The event in Cleveland had been a tiny press conference, but this was the first major rally for the Nationalist Front, and Jeff and Matthew wanted to make sure none of the older guys took to screaming obscenities from the podium. This was a postracist movement now, or at least a white nationalist version of one, but they both knew that there were still a good number of members who were anything but. A couple of Jeff's most virulent neo-Nazis had left the NSM in protest after the new guidelines had been implemented, and the remaining members were ostensibly on board. Still, old habits die hard, and some of the older guard had spent years railing against "niggers and kikes." Jeff was far from convinced they could keep it bottled up in public.

"Yeah, I think that's a good idea," said Matthew. "As for the Texas Rebels, I don't really give a shit if they wear masks or not," Matthew said. "They're not wearing robes, and that's final. Let me talk to them."

He crossed the parking lot to where the Rebels were waiting. Matthew struggled to understand why Jeff kept insisting on bringing the Klan onboard, as they had pretty much proved themselves to be utter embarrassments at every turn. He suspected it was a numbers game for Jeff, who wanted large crowds more than anything else, but Matthew chafed at the notion of the KKK in a National Socialist organization. One of his favorite German propaganda posters from the war showed a metal giant with bombs for legs and fighter-jet wings rampaging through a German city.

The metal golem was decorated with Jewish flags and had a Klan hood covering its head. According to Hitler's party, the KKK, the Masons, and the Jews were all part of the same sordid cabal. Of course, these days hardly anyone in the NSM or the far right in general much cared how the Third Reich Nazis had felt about the Klan, and Matthew knew it, but it was just another reason for him to resent them being there.

One of them had pulled a gun from his glove box and was showing it to his friend, while the others were sitting on the Ford's tailgate, squinting at the low, fall sun over the hotel.

"Another day in paradise, huh, fellas?" Matthew began. The men grunted and shook his hand, but they didn't say much. I was having trouble figuring out why they were even there, as Texas was a long way away, and they hardly seemed very politically inclined. When I asked them they only shrugged and said they had heard there might be trouble from Antifa and figured they'd come up and lend a hand.

Matthew explained to the Rebels that he was all about tradition and heritage, that nobody respected the ancient ways of the Klan more, but that he was trying to build a cohesive movement, and that although they could wear their robes as much as they wanted back home, a Nationalist Front rally needed to be about unity, so they couldn't have people sticking out. "It's all about presenting a unified front," he said. "Now, I'm not trying to be a dick here," he went on, "but the thing is that this rally is going to get violent, and it will be easier for you guys to fight in more form-fitting stuff. I mean I love the tradition and the symbols, but, you know, if we're going to be looking to the man on the left or right and try to fight—I mean they're bringing weapons. They're going to try and kill us, and once lead starts to fly . . . ." Recently the specter of Antifa violence had gone up a notch when rumors of commies with firearms had taken hold. Several groups associated with Antifa had publicly stated that they would fight the far right by any means necessary, ensuring that the members of the far-right groups—most of whom seemed to relish the idea of being soldiers in a righteous battle for race anyway—came fully armed. It almost seemed as if they really believed they were heading into a gunfight.

The Rebel with the handgun waved it seductively in the air while biting his lower lip. "Two rounds from this go off, and you're gonna watch them scatter like cockroaches," he said.

"Fuck them," one of the older Klan guys said from the tailgate. They'd mulled it over for a couple of seconds and agreed that they could leave the robes in the car just this once. "We'll do what you ask this time, but that's only as a favor. Now fuck them, is what I say. Y'all say the word, and we'll wear our motherfucking robes. I don't give a fuck what they say." Jeff, who had just thanked him for agreeing to not wearing the robes and started walking back to the car, quickly returned as the older Klansman had seemingly gotten the issue confused and now believed that the Nationalist Front wanted them to wear robes but was afraid of what the public might think. "I don't give a fuck what they think. You just say the word, Jeff, and I'll robe up."

"No, no, I don't think that's necessary," Jeff said, "but thank you. Let's just all wear black T-shirts."

"Maybe we can do a photo-op or something later," Matthew said. "I want to respect your tradition, but I just want to have a good rally."

"Good idea," Jeff said. "You guys are here, and we want you to be able to represent and be happy, so maybe later on . . . at some point."

Schloer walked up and put one of his legs up on the tailgate, realizing too late that the tailgate was way too high for his pose to look anything but ridiculous. He made the best of it and pretended he had always meant to stand on one leg with his knee almost under his chin. "All due respect," he said formally, "you can fight a lot better in BDUs or street clothes, and I personally . . ." His phone began blaring the theme from the TV show *Knight Rider* from his pocket, and he used the interruption to remove his foot from the tailgate and walked off.

"All right," Matthew said after a pause. "Thanks for understanding."

"Fucking Klan," he muttered under his breath as he walked over to his car to help Miles and Jason piece together a podium.

A FEW HOURS LATER we were ordering bland chicken kung paos at a Chinese hole-in-the-wall next to the hotel. The rally had been a dud. It had started on a confusing note when the convoy arrived at the parking structure in Harrisburg and nobody volunteered to stay back to watch the cars. It seemed like everyone was expecting Antifa to be out in force and were either excited at the thought of fighting them in the streets or were less than enthusiastic about the prospect of facing them alone in a parking garage while everyone else was at the rally. Regardless of the reason, Jeff spent an awkward couple of minutes trying to get someone to volunteer while everyone stood around him and pretended not to hear what he was saying. Suddenly a demure, middle-aged man in khakis and a red windbreaker that nobody had seen before stepped forward and said he'd do it. "Umm, okay, I guess," Jeff said, a little taken aback by the stranger offering to watch their cars. "What group are you with?"

"No group," the man said. "I'm just here because I thought the rally sounded interesting."

Failing to come up with a reason why not, Jeff spread his arms and said, "Okay, guy. I guess the job is yours."

The man seemed pleased.

"If they come for the cars, just call the police. Don't do anything."

"Police. Got it. What's the number?"

"For the police? Call 911."

"911? No area code?"

Jeff looked like a man just realizing he was talking to an extraterrestrial.

"No area code. Just literally type in 911, and that will take you directly to the cops." *

The man didn't seem completely convinced but agreed to take Jeff's word for it, so we left him there, holding his phone in one hand and waving with the other as we walked down the ramp into the street.

There was no one waiting for us. No Antifa and no cops. A few cars slowed down to look at the banners, but having dropped the swastika, the NSM banners were no longer the attention grabbers they once were.

"Stay frosty," Schloer warned from the front, like a platoon leader taking his troops behind enemy lines somewhere in Vietnam. "Antifa are smart sons of bitches and could be around every corner."

One of the younger Klan guys marched alongside Matthew, eyeing every bush, corner, and parked car with suspicion. He was wearing a black NSM T-shirt, one of a stack of shirts Jeff had given the Texas Rebel Knights to wear instead of their robes. It was a solution nobody was particularly happy with. The Rebels were griping that it made them look like they were members of the NSM, and Jeff was displeased for the very same reason. It was what it was. At least they weren't wearing robes or the T-shirts they had suggested, which had a picture of several bodies hanging from trees, with the caption "Nigger Family Reunion."

"This is a heavily nigger-populated city," the younger Klan guy said, raising his eyebrows at Matthew in warning. "It may look quiet, but don't be fooled. They're here somewhere."

Matthew looked annoyed. He'd miscalculated the weather and was wearing a heavy wool coat despite it being close to 70 degrees. "Well, I've never been attacked by a black guy," he said. "I've been jumped by plenty of white guys, though. I respect black people and want to work with them."

"Yeah, I hear you. You want to work with them but you can't because they're goddammed animals. I hear you."

Matthew sped up and left the man behind. "Fucking Klan," he muttered again. By the time he realized he would be sweltering hot in his coat, he was too far from the car to go put it back, so rivulets of sweat ran down his forehead as he rushed to escape from the Klansman who only wanted to talk about "the dangerous niggers."

We got to the capitol, and the NF set up on the higher tiers. The massive domed rotunda above them and the wide, cold granite steps sweeping down toward State Street beneath them made the dozen or so nationalists seem minuscule and distant, however close one got. A phalanx of police officers had set up a cordon at the bottom of the steps, ensuring that none of the counter-protesters could reach the NF but also that no one but the NF itself would be able to hear what they were saying. Undaunted, Jeff launched into his speech, revisiting his greatest hits about how the NSM and the NF were the true patriots and that anyone who said otherwise were traitors. Multiculturalism was a failed experiment—one needed only to look around to see the proof. What was needed, Jeff said, was a white nation, a separate ethno-state for white Christians to go about their business in peace. As he spoke, an egg sailed through the sky from the other side of the barricades. It fell well short of Jeff or any of the others, but it landed with a dull crack on the riot helmet of a police officer who did his best to ignore the yolk running down his visor. Matthew and his guys stood off to the side and listened. Jason was wearing a skeleton facemask, and Miles was grinning happily in his usual red beret and the ski goggles he had bought at DICK'S Sporting Goods earlier in the day. Matthew was nodding to Jeff's speech. If he had been worried about Jeff reverting to his old neo-Nazi, übermensch, Sieg-Heiling speech, there had been no need to. Jeff's speech was conspicuously short on references to Jews, blacks and browns. Sure, it was racist, and sure, it took a dim view of anything smacking of race mixing, but at least he kept the language within the new rules of the NF. Even when he signed off with a heartfelt "Hail victory" there were only a few, scattered Sieg Heils in return. It wasn't perfect, Matthew thought, but at least it was an improvement. He made a mental note of the NSM guys who had used the old Nazi salute. They would need to be straightened out.

Matthew's speech also went well enough. He got in an obscure reference to an antifascist speech made during the Spanish Civil War that nobody but him would get and railed against George So-ros, who he accused of paying the Antifas, the bootboys of the globalist agenda, according to Matthew. He praised Duterte, As-sad, and Putin, perhaps not the most salient points he could have made in Pennsylvania, but at least no one could accuse them of being Nazis on the basis of this rally. The goal today wasn't win-ning over hearts and minds; it was proving that they could launch an alliance without tripping over their own jackboots. He ended his speech with a Hail Victory and was pleased to note that he got no Sieg Heils back.

Then the wheels came off. Because of the whole matter of get-ting the Texas Rebel Knights to forsake their robes, Jeff and Mat-thew hadn't had time to brief the other speakers of the new rules. One of the scheduled speakers was the septugenarian leader of the America First Committee, Art Jones. Jones was an old-school-style white supremacist—a sour-looking pensioner imbued with all the casual racism of a white man raised in a time when white men poured acid in public pools to keep blacks out and when it was perfectly possible to spend a white lifetime never seeing a person of another skin color unless that person was serving your food or washing your car. Being the only member of his group, the politics of the America First Committee rarely went beyond what-ever axe Jones had to grind on any particular day. Today it was mostly homosexuals and blacks.

Matthew's face was frozen in a scowl as Jones took the podium. If he disliked the Klan, he hated Art Jones. He represented not only everything Matthew despised about white supremacy but also the repeated failures of nationalism in America. Jones was a mediocre man whose notion of white supremacy was founded only on his own inflated sense of significance. He didn't love his own race so much as he hated all the others. Also, the guy wouldn't shut up.

For almost twenty minutes he spoke about the need to make America white again, railed against homosexuals using the wrong bathrooms, imagined Black Lives Matter activists hunting down white cops, ranted about Jews who controlled everything and Muslims who were at war with the West and needed to be taken out, all the while exalting Donald Trump, the only guy who had whites' backs and would clear all these miserable mongrels out as soon as he took office, which he would "no matter what the god-dammed lügenpresse said."

Jason squirmed uncomfortably next to Matthew, grateful for the mask concealing his face. "Listen to this fucking asshole," he leaned in and whispered to Matthew. "Saying we need to make America white again. Are we into deporting black and brown people now? Goddammit."

"I know," Matthew said. "But the birth of something new always takes time. Some people are just a little behind. Besides, he'll be dead soon."

Then things went completely off the rails. Steven Howard, the ropey, short Grand Wizard of the North Mississippi White Knights, kicked off his speech with a loud, "All you faggots and niggers out there are cowards!" Clearly he hadn't gotten the new guidelines. There was a TV production crew trailing Howard and his guys for a documentary series that would run on A&E, and there had been rumors in the movement that they were being paid well for their time. It would eventually surface that the rumors were true and that the production company had provided the Knights with elaborate direction and fabricated scenes. The show was immediately canceled.

"What the fuck?" Matthew said as Howard's words landed. "Who is this guy, and why is he talking?" He exchanged glances with Jeff, but short of grabbing the microphone from Howard's hands or cutting the power—making them all look like idiots—there was nothing they could do.

"Hey, you black people," Howard went on in a winding Mississippi drawl that was so pronounced it would probably be offensive to most Mississippians. "If it wasn't for the white man fighting, you'd still be in the fields picking cotton!"

Matthew threw his arms out in resignation. This is what the press would write about tomorrow. All people would know was that there was a Nationalist Front rally where they spoke about keeping blacks in the fields. It was Cleveland all over again, only this time it was much bigger and much more public. This wasn't some backroom in a hotel. There were dozens of people watching. And TV crews. If it weren't for the fact that it undermined all the work he and Jeff had done, it might even be funny.

"To be fair, if it wasn't for the white man, the blacks probably wouldn't have been picking cotton in the first place."

Matthew sat down with Jason and Miles, not wanting to be seen standing next to Howard, who at this point was incoherently flinging slurs at a crowd he claimed consisted of nothing but commies and faggots.

It didn't stop after Howard. He had opened the flood gates, and when it was time for the Texas Rebel Knights to speak, they had clearly decided to ignore whatever direction Jeff and Matthew had given them earlier.

"And all you black asses out there," their leader, Lonnie Coats, yelled into the microphone, "Screw you, assholes! The Muslims and Hillary want to kill all you faggots, and you can all kiss my big, white ass!"

"SOMEBODY SAID 'FAGGOT' from the podium?" Jeff asked, shocked. After the rally, which had dissolved as the various Klan groups competed to see who could be the most offensive from the podium, everyone had rendezvoused by the hotel where we had first met. Matthew and Jeff both looked grim and decided they should withdraw to a restaurant to discuss what had just happened. As far as message control, the rally had been a disaster, and the events of the day had made the challenges of gathering the far right under one umbrella abundantly clear. Jeff had told me earlier that he saw his party and Matthew's as the political and intellectual lodestars of the NF and that the rest of the groups were there to provide support and numbers. But if that was the case, I wondered why Jeff kept giving them speaking slots at their rallies. "We have to respect them, even if we don't agree with how they do things," he said. To me this represented the crux of the challenges I saw in the Nationalist Front's future: the far right was a fractious place, and if you only brought in the groups who saw things like you did, you would end up with a pretty small alliance. But if you invited almost everyone, as Jeff and Matthew had preferred to do until now, you ended up with an alliance that was all over the place.

I'd asked Matthew why he kept trying to bring other groups into the fold rather than going outside to try to grow the pie, but as he had told me many times, he wanted to do both. The various groups already belonging to the far right were low-hanging fruit, and Matthew believed he could grow the alliance through members who already belonged to the movement and at the same time woo Americans who felt disaffected and betrayed by the major parties. He didn't seem to understand that his relative moderation compared to the other far-right groups was his major selling point and that getting in deeper with the KKK and skinheads might alienate many of those who might otherwise be receptive to his politics. In a way he was doing exactly what he had criticized the NSM for doing all this time. Jeff had always told me that the public would get over their use of the swastika when they realized the power of their politics, and Matthew was now saying the same thing: the public would get over the fact that the Nationalist Alliance included white supremacists. I had a hard time believing that Matthew didn't see the similarities and wondered if he had perhaps been daunted by the challenges in attracting people from outside the movement, so he decided to play it safe and block recruit from other groups.

As long as the far right had existed in America there had been the schism between the so-called boots and suits. The boots were people like Matthew and Jeff, happiest when they got to throw rallies and march with their comrades, not afraid to get their hands dirty and used to being on the bottom of the political food chain. The suits, meanwhile, were the more moderate, monied, and slightly more palatable class—what the media, by then, had begun to call the *alt-right*. They were the conservatives who flirted with the far right like Ann Coulter as well as the far-right members who flirted with conservatism like Richard Spencer and, more consequentially, Steve Bannon, who for years had run the self-proclaimed "mouthpiece of the alt-right" and was now Donald Trump's campaign chief. The two factions rarely met, and as a boot, Matthew was struggling against the limits of his station. He needed the suits to grow his pie, but, ironically, the ingredients in the pie he currently had were his biggest obstacle to growing it further. The alt-right was in vogue, and if anyone had been keeping score, the suits were currently far outperforming the boots in terms of fame and consequence, but it wanted nothing to do with skinheads and Klansmen. To people like Richard Spencer, the KKK and the neo-Nazis were obscene and outdated, and unless Matthew could convince Spencer and his comrades that there was value within his ranks, then his alliance, although certainly an unprecedented achievement, would still be largely irrelevant. Even as an alliance, it was still the same old groups who bickered and fought, and it was difficult to see what had really changed. Jeff and Matthew both recognized that there had been a shift in the country and that nationalism and xenophobia were becoming acceptable among wider swathes of the population, but at the moment they were failing to capitalize because they were courting the wrong crowd. Matthew had repeatedly told me that he believed the days of the KKK were over, and he had ridiculed and mocked the skinheads and neo-Nazis, yet he was still insisting on dragging them with him into the future.

After the failed Harrisburg rally I began to suspect that the reason Matthew was still courting them had something to do with his ego. Becoming a leader of a movement that takes nationalism mainstream was a tall order, and Matthew must have known that the odds were stacked firmly against him. At the moment he was a big fish in a very, very small pond, and I wondered if he perhaps, consciously or subconsciously, preferred it that way. To me it seemed like the only other reason why he chose to associate with the dregs of the white supremacist movement was that he just wasn't very smart, and I knew him well enough to know that wasn't true. Say what you will about his politics, but Matthew Heimbach wasn't an idiot.

"Try, like, eight times," Matthew responded to Jeff's question. "Steven called everyone a faggot, so did Lonnie and even Art."

"Shoot. Really? Yeah, I've been getting complaints," Jeff said.

"Yeah, it was pretty awful. Well, I guess it could have been worse, compared to how they've been before, but still . . ."

"I was thinking that maybe we should have just yanked the microphone, you know, tell him to get off the stage, but that would have made us look bad."

"You know one way to solve this could be if we set up a Nationalist Front speakers bureau," Matthew said. "That way we can control what is being said. We can read over the speeches beforehand."

"But I did that with Lonnie's speech," Jeff said. "There was hardly a word of what he said in the speech he showed me. He just went off book." Jeff had also gotten in a quick briefing before the speeches and told Lonnie that there were certain words that would not be accepted. The examples Jeff had used had been "fuck" and "motherfucker," and he had felt that those examples should have adequately impressed upon Lonnie that there would be no cussing. He had, however, neglected to specifically ban "faggot," "nigger," "queer," "bitch," "kike," and "black bastards," all of which Lonnie had ended up using in abundance.

"Well, that's why we need a speakers bureau. We need approved speakers. Just because some Tom, Dick, or Jane brings two or three guys to the Nationalist Front doesn't mean they should get the microphone."

"I hear you, but how can we do that without offending people, though? How can we tell an Imperial Wizard that he's not allowed to speak?"

"If the group has a speaker with a proven track record of being on message, then there's no problem. We just have to get better at message control. I mean, maybe we need to arrange some kind of political grassroots training for these groups."

Matthew had been trained at the Leadership Institute, a DC think tank that had hatched some of the country's leading young conservative firebrands like James O'Keefe as well as the established elites. Senate Majority Leader Mitch McConnell had received training there, as well as tax hater Grover Norquist. As Matthew liked to say, "They're probably not very happy that they trained me, but I sure am." His training had given him an abiding fondness for the nuts and bolts of political organizing, and he would spend hours poring over press releases and speeches before he was happy with them. He was still easily sidetracked and often misjudged his audience, as illustrated by his speech about the Filipino president to the Hammerskins, but his training gave him confidence. Matthew's faith in his own ability to make the KKK care as much was almost admirable.

"What's more, if we professionalize, we'll also weed out the people we don't want, because a Klansman who just wants to get behind a microphone and say 'fucking niggers' quite frankly isn't going to bother putting in the work to write a proper press release."

Jeff still wasn't completely convinced. He knew how frail egos were in the movement and how set people were in their ways. As much as he liked and respected Lonnie, he was also fairly certain there was no way the old Imperial Wizard was going to let his speeches get vetted or agree not to speak at rallies. Matthew suggested that they do private events parallel to public rallies and allow the more uncontrollable members of the NF to speak there and not in front of press at the main event, sort of like an oratorical kiddie pool where they could practice.

"We're only as strong as our weakest link," Matthew said. "You guys pulled off a very successful event today, but we all know that the only thing that is going to be replayed is Steven Howard screaming, 'You Hillary Clinton–loving faggots should come down to Mississippi! We'll beat your nigger-loving asses.' So it sucks a little bit in the short term, but in the long term our hard work will just be blown to pieces if we allow these weak links. We have people in our organizations that have sacrificed for this. Jason moved to a trailer in rural Indiana for this, and to have their sacrifices invalidated is more disrespectful than telling some Klan leader that he has to clean his shit up or he can't talk."

The divergence of their philosophies wasn't surprising. Jeff had been in the movement for a long time, and for as long as he had been active he had belonged on the extreme end of the spectrum. He had been a National Socialist, and he had been a neo-Nazi, and as such, he hadn't been afforded the luxury of picking his friends and allies. Matthew, however, had been on a rightward trajectory and could still remember a time when he was maybe not welcomed but certainly not shunned in polite political society. He believed he knew what it took to build a winning coalition, and as a relative neophyte on the scene, he felt he had a fair understanding of how things worked in the outside world and why things didn't work in the world of the far, far right. Jeff, Matthew was convinced, would get it too. He just needed Matthew to prod him in the right direction.

"More than anything it is disrespectful to you, Jeff," he said. "You organized this thing, you kept the speakers safe, and for them to just turn around and say whatever the hell they want, that makes me mad. It's this anarchy that has ruled in the movement for the longest time. We're fascists, for god's sake. We should be all about order. If they can't follow our simple orders, then they're not in it for the right reasons."

Jeff nodded. He'd come to trust Matthew and respect him as someone who knew how to get things done, and the flaws he was pointing out had been gnawing at Jeff for years. He just hadn't had the right partner to do anything about them.

"We're in a historic position to bring nationalism in America out from the shadows," Matthew said. "But we can't do that if people keep going off the reservation. God bless those Klan guys, but 'Fetch the robes'? Are you fucking serious?"

They decided that the Nationalist Front would come up with a pamphlet for speakers and a shirt that would be given to all member groups. The shirt would be black with a small NF logo on one shoulder and the logo of the respective group on the other. It was not decided who would pay for them, but they agreed the first step was getting the various groups to send logos to Jason immediately. Collaboration and discipline would be more important than ever, as everyone there expected to soon be living in a country ruled by President Hillary Clinton. They all agreed that being white in America was about to become a whole lot harder.

CHAPTER 11

The Suits

The white man is now on trial. Hate laws are against him. No
hate laws can be applied to a nonwhite. That makes the white
man a third-class citizen, in my mind.

—Richard Girnt Butler

Donald Trump's electoral victory brought out an inherent problem with the nationalist movement in America. The resurgence
of white nationalism in the United States had grown out of dissat-
isfaction with the current state of affairs. It was a deeply opposi-
tional force, one that argued that the whole system would need to
be thrown out and rewrought if the country was to ever get back
on track. Now, to their own surprise, the election they had so vo-
ciferously alleged was rigged against them had swung their way,

and they found themselves in the wholly unexpected position of having won. Now what?

Shortly after the 2016 general election I drove down to DC to meet Richard Spencer. Spencer coined the term *alt-right* back in 2008 and, during the run-up to the election, had become the embodiment of the new wave of nationalism that the rest of the country was only just waking up to. If Matthew was part of the boots faction of the nationalist movement, Spencer was the apotheosis of a suit. He was affluent, well educated, and well spoken. He had a degree from the University of Virginia, a master's degree from the University of Chicago, and an unfinished doctorate from Duke. He wore tweed, drank tea, and mixed an air of affected intellectualism with the smug arrogance of every evil fraternity kid from 1980s college movies. He and Matthew had never met, but Matthew had written him off as a cocktail-sipping asshole who was afraid to get his hands dirty; I suspected that Spencer likewise had little love or understanding for Matthew. Spencer's nationalism felt much more like an intellectual exercise performed for his own amusement than any form of deep-seated conviction. He would casually throw out some outrageous statement and then sit back and enjoy the carnage. His politics revolved around what he called *identitarianism*, which he explained as identifying first and foremost as a white man of European descent. It was a bastardization of identity politics that assumed that whites—and white males in particular—had similar political interests based on being white and male alone, but he'd managed to create a following for himself through it. He once tweeted that "all women want to be taken by a strong man" and was an early proponent of Donald Trump. Somehow he and a cadre of other nationalists had been able to mount a virtual army from disgruntled internet dwellers, misogynists, racists, and self-proclaimed firebrands that, in their own minds at least, had given Trump the presidency.

There were, of course, many reasons for Trump's victory, only one of which was the mobilizing of the alt-right Twitterverse, but in the days immediately following the election of Donald Trump, when the world was flailing for an answer to what the hell had happened, Richard Spencer and the alt-right seemed as good an answer as any. This, of course, was giving Spencer too much credit and Trump too little. Even though race was still very much an issue, the alt-right's reach was limited. In the month before the election Richard Spencer, by far the most well-known member of the alt-right, only had roughly eighteen thousand followers on Twitter. Certainly a muscular number, but hardly enough to sway a presidential election.

I'd spoken with Richard a few times over the phone during the campaign, and he seemed to have been growing increasingly en-amored of Trump as his scattershot campaign threw a grab bag of conspiracies, misogyny, xenophobia, and baffling stupidity against a wall to see what would stick. Throughout our conversations he displayed first a jaded lack of enthusiasm, which gave way to cau-tious hope and eventual full-throated support for Trump. His sup-port, however, was less based on Trump's actual political stances, which Spencer himself would admit were all over the place, and more with what he believed Trump represented about US society. Not only was the country waking up to the importance of race; it was also shedding the exhausting shackles of political correctness. More than any political issue, the alt-right treasured their right to be infinitely offensive, preferably toward women or minorities, always under the banner of free speech, and with Trump as their candidate, the malcontents of the world had someone champion-ing their right to be abusive.

I met Spencer in a noisy restaurant in the DC suburbs, where he lived on and off and maintained a barebones headquarters for his think tank, the prosaically named National Policy Institute (NPI). NPI's main function was to throw an annual conference for the other suits of the movements and to publish the *Radix Journal*, a quasi-intellectual blog and journal in which Spencer and oth-ers pontificated on Jews, political correctness, women, and other things that concern them. He sat under a flat-screen TV mounted on the wall and watched with a look of bemusement as his own face flickered across the screen intercut with shots of young, white men with arms outstretched in salute and concerned-looking cable news panelists.

The NPI conference was just over and had ended with shouts of "Hail Trump!" The whole thing had been caught on video and had prompted, after much prodding and pulling, Donald Trump to denounce the alt-right while still denying he had done anything to energize them. Spencer wasn't so much disappointed at the denouncement as he was happy that Trump had given them a shot at the limelight in the first place. As he saw it, Trump may not have created the alt-right, and the alt-right may not have handed Trump the election, but the two were deeply intertwined ideologically. And with Trump in the White House and Stephen Bannon, the former CEO of alt-right mouthpiece *Breitbart News*, as a close adviser, the alt-right now had a seat at the table.

Spencer sipped his tea and watched the spectacle with a shit-eating grin. "It's nuts, right? I mean it's nuts," he said, grinning as if the outrage he had caused was an actual and delicious flavor he could savor. "A year ago nobody knew who I was, and today I'm turning down interviews all over the place."

Spencer was the gift that kept on giving to journalists desperate to put a face on the alt-right. He was articulate, happy to talk, could be trusted to say offensive things, and also, seemingly to the surprise of everyone, didn't look like a monster. Josh Harkinson, writing for *Mother Jones*, in a moment of breathlessness, described him as "An articulate and well-dressed former football player with prom-king good looks and a 'fashy' (as in fascism) haircut." The articles often focused on Spencer's education and distinctly unextreme demeanor as something that set him apart from traditional white supremacy in America, ignoring the fact that American nationalism had always had "intellectual" factions and that it is quite possible to be a white supremacist and smart at the same time. Also, Spencer was hardly the first educated man to advocate wildly racist ideas. Even within his sphere there were men who had been peddling their shtick of pseudo-scientific nativism for decades.

Richard Taylor, who had inspired both Spencer and Matthew, debuted his publication *American Renaissance* in November of 1990, and many had been doing it for even longer. The novelty with Richard Spencer, apart from having had the good fortune of coming up with the term *alt-right*, was that he understood the power of the internet to build and mobilize a following. Where former incarnations of the far right had been reliant on rallies, concerts, and compounds to recruit and mobilize, Spencer and his minions needed only their smartphones and an endless appetite for disruption and offensive behavior. Matthew had a leg in each camp. He was savvy enough when it came to proselytizing on social media but much more comfortable taking his show on the road.

Still, what Twitter giveth, Twitter also taketh away, which is why Spencer had been in an indignant outrage when we spoke a couple of days before. He'd been kicked off Twitter for inciting hatred, which was like giving a speeding ticket to a Formula 1 driver, and now he had lost his most important way of communicating with the world.

"I've been beheaded," he said dramatically. "Exterminated. Gagged. Honestly the whole thing is a witch hunt. It's deeply undemocratic, but they're crazy if they think they can silence me. I'm getting more attention than ever."

The alt-right had become marvelously adept at playing the victim when something they said invariably got them in trouble, a strategy that served them well, allowing them to act persecuted and adding to the narrative that white men are the real victims in an unfair world.

We watched for a while as CNN showed a loop of pictures of Spencer and his followers saluting Trump. A few people in the restaurant recognized him, some glaring openly and others trying to conceal their staring. Spencer raised his teacup and smiled at all of them.

"This whole neo-Nazis in DC thing is so stupid," he said. "Everyone is blowing it completely out of proportion. It was a moment of enthusiasm. We got carried away, and someone jokingly shouted,

'Hail Trump,' and people latched onto it. It wasn't a political state-ment. It was a joke. Trolling, even." This had been the alt-right's typical response to any outrage and one lifted from the schoolyard bully playbook: "Come on. It was all a joke. Stop being so sensitive."

"You people are going to call us neo-Nazis anyway, so I guess a few people thought it would be fun to throw it back in the media's faces. This was just a prank. Overenthusiasm." Spencer acted like the magnanimous father of unruly children. Whenever his follow-ers said or did something outrageous, he would roll out this char-acter to great effect. "I can't vouch for all the things these people say, but they're my people, so I'm not going to condemn them for it either. The right needs this kind of rambunctious outrageousness, just like it needs the opposite."

Spencer saw himself very much like the opposite. He enjoyed lobbing rhetorical bombs as much as any other troll, but he saw his role as providing the intellectual vanguard of the movement, staking out a course for others to follow. "These are the foot sol-diers," he said of his thousands of Twitter followers. "My job is to be the intellectual lodestar that provides direction. The movement needs both. It needs the Dionysian passion of the masses on the one hand and the Apollonian vision of the future on the other."

Spencer was fond of statements like these, ones that highlighted his classical education and underlined his image as a man of let-ters. He claimed that his main inspiration was Friedrich Nietzsche and the classical French thinkers and would say things like, "The white race has a drive that is almost Faustian in nature."

By "Faustian in nature" he meant that the white race has a drive to invent and to improve that other races lack. In his ethnocentric worldview the white race is behind every important technical ad-vancement in the history of humanity, and his intellectual ballast is an impressive collection of cherry-picked facts that support his opinions.

He believes we are living in end times, not in an apocalypti-cal way but in a paradigmatic one. He told me that the America that emerged after World War II, a country in which equality and togetherness were cherished ideals, is coming to an end and that Trump is the first horseman of this apocalypse. "We're seeing the end of white America," he said, echoing the thousands of nationalists before him who had lamented the progress made by other races. "But more importantly perhaps, we're seeing the end of unconscious white America. We're witnessing the collapse of the heady liberalism of color blindness and the rise of an explicit racial consciousness on the part of white people. We're not completely there yet—people in Michigan who voted for Trump didn't do it because they support the alt-right—but unconsciously many whites are voting for their race."

Spencer believes that for everyone else but whites, race is their first form of identification. A black man first and foremost identifies as a black man, whereas whites have been told over and over that this is wrong and racist, so their first form of identification comes in the form of political allegiances—"I'm a conservative/liberal/libertarian"—or geographic connection—"I'm a New Yorker!" This, according to Spencer, is a fundamental problem with whites. "We're just too stupid and cucked to think in these terms," he said. "In some ways African Americans are a lot smarter than us. They get it."

I never knew if he really believed that African Americans could be smarter than whites, just as I never truly knew if Matthew believed that other races could be as good as, if not better, than whites. Perhaps they had learned a lesson from previous incarnations of nationalists that white supremacy wasn't going to win hearts and minds, or perhaps they really had evolved into a more magnanimous form of nationalists. Could it be they were serious when they said, "White pride, not white power?"

Matthew told me several times that he respects and sympathizes with the poverty of African Americans and Latinos in Chicago. The way the United States incarcerates black people in staggeringly higher numbers than it does whites disgusts him. He laid down flowers outside the Emanuel African Methodist Church in Charleston after Dylann Roof's shooting spree. Spencer said similar things. "White suffering isn't worse than black suffering. It's just not the same."

There was, of course, nothing wrong with being proud of one's race, and there were whites who suffered in America, but white pride became problematic when it failed to realize that there was an affirmative quality to "Black pride and black power." There was a need for black power and pride because the African American community had been disempowered, disenfranchised, and shackled—both figuratively and literally—for generations. Affirmative action—a policy deeply hated and ridiculed by white nationalists who felt like they too had been passed over for opportunities to better themselves—had been put in place because it was the only way we as a society could ensure that minorities got access to education and the work force, and despite waning support—Chief Justice John Roberts once wrote in a majority opinion from 2007 concerning admittance by race to certain magnet schools that "the way to stop discrimination on the basis of race is to stop discriminating on the basis of race"—it was still our best weapon against the legacy of Jim Crow.

The problem with white pride is the same as with All Lives Matter. It implies that there isn't a gap between races, that the long history of state-sanctioned white supremacy in America hadn't created a radically uneven playing field. Saying "white pride" is offensive not because there is anything inherently wrong with being white but because it demonstrates a profound lack of respect for the struggles that minorities had fought and are still fighting. There is massive suffering in poor and predominantly white parts of the country, but using this as proof that the struggles of whites are the same as those of African Americans is like saying that global warming is a fallacy because it's snowing outside.

"This is when we need to go to work," Spencer continued as the news coverage finally ended. The general of an army composed of mostly nameless avatars on Twitter, Spencer felt the challenges of turning a counter-culture into a viable political movement even more acutely than Matthew, whose followers, although fewer than

Spencer's, were real-life people willing to march i
realize that the alt-right to this day has been m
the internet is what has gotten us this far. Thirty ,
movement wouldn't have been possible. Matthew Heimba
be fighting in the streets while I sip martinis, but I'm fine wιτ
that. We need to build an intellectual footprint too, and that can't
happen in the streets."

Still, Spencer was keenly aware of the limitations of the internet
when it came to capitalizing on the momentum they had gained,
and he worried about the movement being aborted by private
companies banning the alt-right from online platforms. Facebook
and Twitter were both tinkering with new rules governing hate
speech, as was Reddit, the home of nihilistic, alt-right spawning
pool 4Chan. In the paranoid echo chambers of the far-right forums, the Jews who controlled the media, ever walking a tightrope
between making money on their products and controlling their
users, were beginning to clamp down on freedom of speech. This
was ostensibly to prevent terrorism, but the alt-right suspected
more nefarious reasons afoot.

"Sure, it sounds paranoid," Spencer said. "But one can easily
imagine private companies removing us from their servers. We
could of course have our own servers, but it would make our
work infinitely more difficult. We can get kicked off social media
platforms, but you can take it even further: Would Google censor search results?" In fact, in April of 2017, Google did announce
a change in the way its core search engine works in an attempt
to curb hate speech and the spread of extremism and fake news.
Similarly, the European Union began work on a law that would
force social media platforms to address hate speech on their sites.
Spencer would continue to enjoy his growing popularity on Twitter at least until the writing of this book, but it didn't change the
fact that Twitter could at any moment have him rubbed out, and
he knew it.

"It's clear that we've been able to build a movement of online
people, many of whom are anonymous," he said. "But at some

ɔint all that energy needs to spill out into the real world for it to
have any practical use. We need to meet politicians and host con-
ferences. The alt-right would never succeed as a party. We're influencers, and we need to take that seriously and professionalize."

At the time it wasn't exactly clear what he meant by "profes-
sionalizing." He was living in Whitefish, Montana, but had ambitions of building a new and bigger headquarters for NPI in DC,
where he would use his newfound notoriety to coax the volatile
alt-right from the digital and into the physical world.

Meanwhile Matthew existed very much in the space between the
virtual and the real world. He was working as a picker for Amazon,
spending twelve hours a day in almost total darkness, receiving
people's orders on a screen, then scurrying through the shelves
to find them—once he fetched twelve identical, plus-sized, sexy
Cinderella costumes for one customer. He'd been forced to put the
work with the Nationalist Front on the back burner, as his summer of rallies and marches had put a strain on his already over-
worked credit card, so he needed to bring in some extra cash. Also,
Brooke was pregnant again, expecting their second child in June.

He called me in late December with some strange news. Richard
Spencer had called Matthew to ask him if he might be interested in
helping him run for Congress. Ryan Zinke, the sole representative
of Montana, had been tagged to join Trump's cabinet, and Spencer
believed he could do well in the exceptionally libertarian-minded
and right-wing-friendly political environment of Montana. "He
really called out of the blue," Matthew said. "I guess he realizes
that I know how to talk to real people. It could be a big deal for us."

It was too late for Spencer to get on the ballot as anything other
than an independent in the special election, so he needed signatures, which would mean crisscrossing the state and talking
to rural voters to get them on board. Endless driving and talking
to workers and farmers were what Matthew did best. "It'll put a
crimp in my work with the Nationalist Front," Matthew said. "But
it would be worth it." He didn't say as much, but if there was any
truth to it, then Spencer and Matthew working together would be

a major development in the insulated world of the alt-right. Their relationship was a perfect metaphor for the schism between boots and suits dividing the far right, and if they could somehow work together, they would both be able to take their respective visions of the far right further: Matthew would achieve a new level of respectability with the alt-right white collars, and Spencer would gain some credibility with those who saw him as an aloof dandy.

I called Spencer and asked about it after I spoke with Matthew, and although he was cagey about the specifics, he told me that he and Matthew had indeed been talking about working together and that they would meet for a sit-down on Inauguration Day in DC.

IMPLAUSIBLY, MATTHEW HAD BROUGHT his Angry Birds pajamas to the inauguration and was wearing them while nursing a cup of tepid coffee in the dingy downstairs restaurant of a Best Western in Manassas outside DC. His thick, bristly hair stuck out at odd angles, and his eyes were bleary and tired after driving for most of the previous day. Sitting next to him by the table were Miles Smythe and Scott Hess. Across from them were Robbie Weiss, a small and wiry southerner, and his fiancée, Katherine. Jeff and some of his guys from the NSM had wanted to be there too, but money was tight. Miles was chatting endlessly about how excited he was to see the capital and troll anti-Trump demonstrators and that he might even troll Trump supporters, for that matter. Miles had a quality about him that made him seem above the mundane machinations of the real world, or at least removed from them. When we'd been at Hammerfest together it had become clear that he'd never used an ATM card before when he revealed he had no idea what a PIN code was. He supported Trump with the aloof enthusiasm of someone who wanted to set fire to something just to see what happened but also didn't really care one way or the other whether it burned. He didn't really mind Hillary and didn't really like Trump that much but seemed to have gone with the candidate who would piss the most people off. Trump was a ridiculous spectacle, and Miles was an avowed fan of ridiculous spectacles. He was also one of Matthew's most loyal friends.

Behind them a TV tuned to *Fox News* was blaring the latest about the inauguration. Aerial footage showed crowds milling around DC and queuing up outside checkpoints leading onto the Mall. The next day Trump would claim, incorrectly, that the crowds at his inauguration were the biggest in history. The coverage switched to footage taken the night before from outside the National Press Club, where members of Trump's online coalition of alt-righters, trolls, and racists had arranged an inaugural ball called the DeploraBall. The footage showed protestors outside throwing rocks and eggs at the attendees.

"What a shit show," Matthew said. Although one of the country's preeminent nationalist leaders, he hadn't been invited to the party, and during the last couple of weeks, as the circle of activists arranging it publicly imploded over the so-called JQ—the Jewish Question—it had become increasingly uncertain whether the ball would go ahead at all. "It's so ridiculous," Matthew said. "[Twitter user] Baked Alaska, who was one of the main guys behind the DeploraBall, tweeted some stuff about the Jews running the media, and apparently some of the other guys took offense. All hell broke loose, and everyone who was seen as anti-Jew got booted."

The Jewish Question had created a schism in the movement between the alt-right and the "alt-lite." The latter was a term coined by the hardline alt-righters like Richard Spencer, the blogger Brad Griffin, and others to describe the paleo-conservatives, libertarians, and dilettantes who had piggy backed onto the alt-right and were now trying to change it by expelling everyone on the "wrong" side of the JQ. Griffin, in a post on his blog *Occidental Dissent*, described it this way:

> By the Alt-Lite, I am referring to Breitbart, the Milo [Yiannopoulos] phenomenon, Paul Joseph Watson and Infowars, [Mike] Cernovich and a few other people. A few years ago, none of these people were around. They certainly weren't nationalists. They saw that

our movement was steadily gaining ground and opportunistically hopped on the bandwagon. We've always known this would be a problem once our movement began to hit a critical mass.

In addition to the recent bickering over the JQ, in the days before the inauguration one of the most influential actors in the alt-right—blogger, podcaster, and virulent anti-Semite Mike Enoch—was revealed to be Mike Peinovich, a NYC-based software developer who is married to a Jewish woman. His blog, *The Right Stuff*, collapsed, and his audience of close to one hundred thousand regular readers scattered. Although these infractions might seem minor to anyone outside the far right, in the movement they were tectonic incidents, obsessively discussed and dissected.

"Honestly, sometimes I can't believe how dumb our movement can be," Matthew said of the Mike Enoch affair. "We have to get serious about things if we want to move forward. This anonymous, online bullshit can't go on. We need to get our shit together."

The prospect of meeting Spencer excited Matthew. He maintained that he still believed Spencer was a martini-drinking asshole, but when he said it now it was in a more backslapping, locker-room-talk kind of way, whereas before he seemed almost spurned when talking about the suits. Although Matthew was in his own right a respected leader in the movement, Richard Spencer was undeniably the brighter star—and certainly got more attention from the media—so I suspected that Matthew was flattered to be asked. There was a casual plan to meet up with Spencer somewhere later, and we agreed to call him during the day to figure out the particulars. Matthew and I had both texted him that morning but hadn't heard anything back yet.

Matthew took a last sip of his coffee and stood up. It was almost 9:30 A.M., and we should have been in DC hours ago.

The train was strangely empty for Inauguration Day, and we had a car to ourselves as we discussed how long we thought Trump would stay in office. Matthew, who was quick to say that he had never been a staunch Trump supporter in the first place,

Matthew Heimbach and Miles Smythe riding the train into Washington, DC, for Inauguration Day. TWP members Robbie Weiss and Katherine Weiss are in the foreground.

had become increasingly skeptical as Trump's nepotism and mercenary self-interest became apparent, yet he still felt confident that when Trump was removed from power—and we all agreed that Trump would most likely be removed from power—it would be because the Jews and liberals had ousted him and not because of his own ineptitude.

Matthew had changed out of his pajamas into a collared T-shirt and cargo pants under a heavy, gray coat. Miles wore his usual red beret, decorated with a Trump button, while Scott, who claimed to be immune to the cold, wore only a short-sleeved shirt and a pair of oversized Aviator sunglasses.

"So are you going to be able to get us all into this fancy inaugural lunch today?" Miles said.

Matthew gave him an exasperated look, and I asked what he was talking about. "Goddammit, Miles, we weren't supposed to tell Vegas."

"Tell me what?" In all the years I'd known him there had been very few things that Matthew had told me off the record, and I'd sometimes gotten the feeling that he had been getting too chummy with me, often forgetting I am a journalist and telling me things I perhaps wouldn't tell a journalist if I were in his shoes. Matthew called me over to his seat and told Miles to go sit somewhere else for a minute, then he looked conspiratorially over one shoulder before leaning in closer and saying in a hushed voice, "So I've been invited to give a talk at the Capitol Hill Club today. It's very hush-hush, but I guess you were bound to find out anyway."

Apparently a GOP operative who had been close to Governor George Wallace had contacted Matthew and invited him to speak at the Capitol Hill Club, a storied and influential club for leading Republicans and located directly across from the Capitol. "It's an amazing opportunity," he said. "It's a real chance to get our point across to the GOP. They know that we represent the real white working class." He wouldn't tell me exactly who he would be speaking to, only that they were some real "players in the party."

"I need to pee," Scott said as they stepped out of the Metro station and into the crowd. L'Enfant Plaza was one of just two Metro stations close to the Mall and parade route that would be open that day, so most of the people coming into town came through here. All around were vendors selling hats, flags, buttons, towels, T-shirts, and anything else that would fit a Trump logo.

"You're kidding, right?" said Matthew. "You need to pee now? There is literally nowhere to pee here. Hold it in."

Scott said he couldn't and that he would go back into the Metro station to find a bathroom. Matthew and Miles, who didn't feel like waiting around, walked into the crowd while Katherine and Robbie hung back to wait for Scott.

A little further up the street a small group of protestors shouting about water preservation had set up a demonstration in an intersection. Matthew and Miles stood off to the side and watched as the demonstrators chanted.

"Look at these fools," Matthew said. "You need force to back up your talk, and do these people have that? No. They need the force of the capitalist state to protect them from us."

A black SUV with police plates drove up and stopped in front of the demonstrators. An officer leaned out the window and asked them to step aside so they could pass. "Don't stop, officer," shouted Matthew as the SUV slowly made its way through the throng. "Fucking run them over!"

He looked in dismay at a group of demonstrators who had brought drums that they were playing. "Stand up, fight back, bongo your way to revolution," he scoffed. He and Miles walked along the perimeter of the protests, mocking and shouting insults. At one point they started singing to the tune of "Santa Claus Is Coming to Town":

> *You better watch out, you better not cry.*
> *You better not pout, I'm telling you why.*
> *Right-wing death squads coming to town.*

The whole scene filled Matthew with visceral disgust. He despised the anti-Trumpers for being liberals pining for a candidate who was actively gunning for white working men and women, but he was dismissive of Trump voters because, as close as they were to voting according to their race, they had still been hoodwinked into voting for a mainstream political party and, thus, remained firmly within the system they wanted to throw out. He walked the streets of DC as someone who had passed into the matrix and now watched in benevolent amusement everyone else still struggling within the lie of Republicans vs. Democrats.

We walked west along Independence Avenue, trying, with no luck, to find someplace to cross the Mall. Scott, Robbie, and Katherine walked behind, with Matthew and Miles up front. Matthew seemed to have no interest in talking or playing politics, giving just polite responses to reporters who recognized him. "Trump was never our guy," he told a camera crew. "We support what he's trying to do about immigration, but we're not Trump supporters. Still, we wish him well."

To another crew he said, "I don't trust Trump to do right by us at all, and the left are galvanized like never before, but we're ready. This last year saw over a billion anti-Semitic impressions per month online. We won the meme war. Ours is a youth movement. It's against political correctness, democracy, and equality, and it's building."

Matthew still hadn't heard anything from Spencer, so he texted him again.

Scott saw protestors and enemies everywhere he looked and walked the streets of DC like he had somehow been directly involved in Trump's victory.

He wasn't alone. All over DC Trump supporters seemed much more interested in gloating than celebrating. Like the candidate himself, they knew their victory had been historically narrow, but unlike Trump they seemed to feel that the hair's breadth of their victory made it all the sweeter. It wasn't so much that they had won but that they had taken something from the enemy and the enemy felt bad about it. Everyone's favorite joke was a meme about enjoying a cup full of liberal tears. They may have won, but they were still bitter and angry and determined to be assholes about it.

Scott shouted, "Oy vey" to a couple of Jewish kids, and as they passed a small group of people holding "Dump Trump" signs he said, "I can't wait for Trump to give us the go-ahead to start beating the shit out of you people," not quite loud enough for them to hear him but loud enough for it to seem like he had wanted them to.

"Take it easy, Scott," Matthew said. "No incitement. I don't want to fight over something we started." On Twelfth Street we came across a group of horses being prepared for the parade. "Hey, Matt," Robbie shouted, "I better not see any protestors punching a horse. If I see anyone punching a horse, they're done."

"Okay," said Matthew. There were no reports of horse punching that day.

EVERYTHING YOU LOVE WILL BURN

"This feels like the beginning," he said as they turned back toward L'Enfant Plaza, realizing that crossing the Mall would be impossible. "Does this feel like the beginning to you guys?" There had been rumors of Antifa attacks around the city, and if Trump was being attacked by commies, he must be doing something right. Matthew relished the thought of the power of the state turning against the filthy left-wing agitators. He believed that the arc of history curved toward nationalism and a strong state, that the decades of globalization and secularization had been leading up to either a spectacular implosion or a major rightward course correction. He was ready for both.

I asked him what he thought the GOP wanted him to talk to them about. "I think they're realizing that they need to think differently when it comes to Appalachia," Matthew said. "They know that we know how to speak to white voters who are poor, and I think—hoping at least—that they want to pick our brains about how to hold on to those voters."

Matthew seemed to believe that he held some kind of unique sway over whites in Appalachia and that the GOP wanted a piece of it. I wasn't convinced that the Republican Party didn't have their own ways of reaching the rural and disaffected areas of the country, but I had to admit that it was strange that party members would invite a well-known white nationalist into their most sacred club on Inauguration Day unless they needed him for something.

Back at L'Enfant Plaza they came across another protest. A small group of young people had gathered on the corner. One of them was shouting at the crowds as they walked past. "Do you really want a president that grabs pussy?" he asked.

"Rather that than someone who grabs babies right out of the womb," Matthew said. If he had learned one thing in his years of screaming matches and debates, it was "never let anyone get you on the defensive." The other person clearly knew the same thing and immediately hit back with "Yeah, what about someone who's so corrupt he won't even release his taxes?"

Matthew, Miles, and Scotty in Washington, DC, on Inauguration Day.

The interaction soon descended into screaming. Matthew tried to explain to the guy that all he wanted was a world where communities could decide their own fates, while the protestor responded that perhaps not everyone wanted to live in ethnically homogenous societies. Meanwhile Scott was telling a female protestor that when they came to power he would have her put in a concentration camp but that he would call it a "fun camp" and that she would be forced to make toys. The altercation only lasted a few minutes before the demonstrators moved on. "Hey Matthew, did you hear what I said to that liberal piece of shit? Fun camp. Did you hear that, Matthew?"

Matthew said he heard.

We took the Metro to Capitol South, where Matthew's Republican contact, who wished to remain anonymous, invited everyone to dinner before the meeting. The man was older, perhaps in his late sixties, with the restless, opportunistic air of a huckster. Over burritos at a noisy Mexican restaurant overlooking the Congressional Library he described being there when Governor

Wallace got shot and how the murder was probably connected to the Deep State and that we should all watch how the Deep State would probably try something against Trump too. He claimed to have been a friend of Barry Goldwater and to have spent his career in the wings of the GOP party, seemingly trying to bring back the racist heydays of the Dixiecrat era.

"Today is a big day," he said. "Make no mistake about it. This is the time to mobilize. The left are bringing two hundred thousand people to DC tomorrow, and we need to be able to do the same. We need to bring thousands of people into the movement."

Matthew's source said that the movement needed money, the GOP needed the movement, and today would be the first step in bringing the nationalists and the GOP together. "A few years ago the GOP wouldn't be able to even sit in the same room as you, but things have changed, and now we need each other. This is a big day."

He threw a hundred-dollar bill on the table and took Matthew with him to the Capitol Club, where he said many people were excited to meet him.

Miles, Scott, Robbie, and Katherine waited for a couple of hours, finishing the cocktails Matthew's friend had bought them, and walked around the Capitol as the crowds began to head home. Then they sat on the curb outside the Capitol Club and watched as Republicans in khakis and blazers and suits arrived and went through the doors. They tried to get in, but Matthew's contact had said it was for Matthew only, promising them "next time." A middle-aged woman in a large, flowing dress with green and blue flowers came through, holding a young, blonde girl by the hand. The woman was wearing a Trump hat with the words "Make America Great Again" written across the front.

I wondered what Matthew had to say to this crowd and whether the Republicans could possibly understand him. I wondered, too, why this well-dressed group of elite Republicans needed Matthew— if Matthew's contact was to be believed. The GOP were certainly no strangers to race-baiting, having hinged much of their southern electoral strategy in the sixties, seventies, and early eighties on the implicit racism of the so-called "southern strategy," in which they used loaded terms rather than explicit racism to win the votes of those still skeptical about desegregation and civil rights. Lee Atwater, legendary GOP strategist and campaign consultant, explained,

> You start out in 1954 by saying, "Nigger, nigger, nigger." By 1968 you can't say "nigger"—that hurts you, backfires. So you say stuff like, uh, forced busing, states' rights, and all that stuff, and you're getting so abstract. Now, you're talking about cutting taxes, and all these things you're talking about are totally economic things and a byproduct of them is, blacks get hurt worse than whites. . . . "We want to cut this," is much more abstract than even the busing thing, uh, and a hell of a lot more abstract than "Nigger, nigger."

FINALLY MATTHEW CAME BACK. He was elated. The meeting had gone well. In a room full of GOP strategists and state legislators he had been introduced as "the next president of the United States," and things had only improved from there. He said that he made no attempt to hide who he was, his politics, or his affiliations and that no one seemed to have a problem with it. He said he'd spoken at length about the white working class, their problems, and how to strengthen the GOP's hold over them. When he finished, he had been given resounding applause.

The group got back on the Metro toward Virginia. "It's crazy," Matthew said on the train. "Remember how only a year ago we were sitting in a pizza restaurant in Kentucky, hardly ten members in our party? Today, a year later, I'm giving a speech in the most important Republican club to a group of Republican operatives. Things are happening. I can feel it."

"I always believed it," said Miles. "We're president now."

We called Spencer a few more times but got no reply. Matthew, still excited about how the GOP had embraced him, was suddenly less interested in helping Spencer.

"That guy's a douche," he said. "We don't need him. After today we'll have much better allies than Spencer."

Miles was tinkering on his phone. "Whoa," he said suddenly. "Hey guys, something happened to Spencer!"

Everyone crowded around the phone and watched a video play on the small screen. Spencer was being interviewed when someone off camera asked him about his lapel pin. Just as he finished explaining how Pepe the Frog had become a symbol of the alt-right, a masked figure burst onto the screen and punched Spencer hard in the face.

"Holy shit!" Matthew said. "Did that just happen?"

We watched as the assailant ran off while Spencer clutched his jaw and straightened his hair.

"That's crazy," Matthew said. They all seemed to get a tiny amount of joy from watching the guy who had snubbed them all day and who, by the looks of it, had never been in a fight in his life, meet the realities of Antifa.

"I mean Spencer is kind of a dick, but damn, no one deserves getting sucker punched like that. Play it again, Miles."

CHAPTER 12

The College Boys

The Constitution was written by white men alone. Therefore, it was intended for whites alone.

—National Socialist Movement website, undated

The first hundred days of Donald Trump's presidency came and went with no cataclysmic, world-ending events but rather an unending chain of scandals, screw-ups, and indignities. Trump took office amid a flurry of executive orders, lawsuits, and allegations of foul play, and his agenda floundered in the face of the realities of governing and the infighting among his band of political outsiders. Some hardline nationalists, including Matthew, voiced their disgust and indignation as Trump failed to uphold even the most basic of campaign promises, but most on the far right were happy to pin his failures on Democrats and the media.

Matthew quit his job at Amazon and moved to Tennessee, where he made deliveries for a company sympathetic to the cause run by Captain Culpepper in the NSM. Brooke, pregnant with their second child, and little Nicholas would stay in Paoli until Matthew had enough money for a down payment on an apartment in Tennessee. Meanwhile he had work to do. He and Jeff had settled on a campground in Kentucky for their upcoming rally, and Matthew was busy making overtures to groups that might be interested in joining them. He was talking to his old friends in the League of the South, a secessionist group, as well as others, like the white nationalist group Identity Evropa. It was starting to feel like a coalition of groups, a coming together of people whose views on the nuts and bolts of nationalism might differ but who nonetheless shared a profound belief in the urgency of the cause.

Spencer, who had decided against running for congress, found that being punched in the face twice—he was punched again later on Inauguration Day—was the best career move he could have made. Being bloodied by Antifa gave him the respect of the elements in the movement who up until then had found him too soft. He began remaking himself into a leader and a rabble-rouser, giving speeches with his shirt sleeves rolled up and railing against the barbarians he had fought in the streets.

Dan Elmquist and Doll Baby, whose son, Odin, was born in early 2016, left the Virgil Griffin White Knights and relaunched the Nordic Order. Dan wanted his to be an organization like the Klan had been in the old days, completely rejecting the modernism of politics and any softening of their agenda. "I don't want anything to do with all this talking," he told me. "I think it's time for the Klan to go back to doing what we do best: we need to be a militant organization that people fear." At that moment it was all hypothetical though, as the members of Dan's new group had a tendency to leave and form Klan groups of their own. It was a betrayal that Dan constantly griped about, and he would often call me and grumble about "Klan justice coming their way." Shortly after Dan and Doll Baby's wedding a police officer shot Gary Delp. On the evening of October 24, 2015, Delp's house caught fire. As his old, wooden house burned around him, Delp at first refused to leave. Finally he emerged on his stoop wearing nothing but underwear and holding a pistol. He charged toward the cops who had arrived on the scene with the fire department, and they shot him. Delp survived, but being shot inevitably takes a toll on an old body, and he was never the same after. Dan worried about him a lot until he passed away in the summer of 2017.

As it turned out, Trump's election wasn't the apotheosis of the nationalist movement in America, but there were signs that his presidency had impacted the mood of the country. The SPLC reported that the number of anti-Muslim hate groups had tripled from 34 in 2015 to 101 in 2016. According to the FBI's hate crime statistics, attacks against Muslims were up 67 percent in 2015 compared to the year before, and hate crimes in general were up 6 percent. Although there was no way to prove that Trump's ascendance caused this uptick, Trump supporters and "deplorables" all over the country were self-deputizing in the name of Trump. He may not have delivered on his campaign promises, but to many the very fact that he was president was a sign that America belonged to whites.

The far right and Antifa settled into a comfortable routine of demonstrations and counter-demonstrations, setting up a war of convenience that both sides used to recruit new members. The alt-right used the opportunity to claim the implausible mantle of championing free speech. This was, of course, a highly dubious claim, as the free speech they advocated only included their right to be "honest" about Jews, blacks, and other minorities, but it was a relatively simple case to make in the face of screaming, masked, and armed antifascist protestors. What's more, some elements of the alt-right—such as Ann Coulter and Milo Yiannopoulos, who had made many of its causes their own—booked high-profile speaking engagements at prominent universities only to see their events cancelled in the face of public outcry. These cancellations not only solidified the far right's belief in its own persecution but also made the argument that the speakers were indeed victims of censorship, whose First Amendment rights were being trampled, more palatable to those who would otherwise reject the content of their messages, such as moderate conservatives and even moderate liberals.

Despite Matthew's years of bridge-building efforts and outreach, it was Antifa who did more than anyone else to bring the far right together. They had been a regular feature at countless far-right rallies in the past, but Donald Trump' election energized the radical left and brought a host of new members to their ranks. The amped-up presence of Antifa at rallies as well as the sense that the left was attacking not only them but also a president who for the first time spoke up for white people galvanized the members of the far right, many of whom increasingly felt that the skirmishes with Antifa were the precursors of larger battles to come between left and right. As difficult as it was for the various factions of the right to agree on much, their shared loathing of Antifa seemed adequate to build some sort of coalition on. Even groups who shared little ideologically with the alt-right—such as the Oath Keepers, a group of former law enforcement and military personnel who dedicated themselves to make sure that the Constitution, at least their interpretation of it, was upheld—started showing up to far-right rallies in order to "provide protection to the First Amendment."

"Right now it seems that organizing to neutralize the Antifas is a big attraction, and I hope it continues," Brad Griffin, the blogger who runs the popular alt-right Twitter feed and blog *Occidental Dissent*, told me. "Once it hits critical mass, more people will come to real-world events. It won't stay corked up online in the long term. It isn't as fun."

IN LATE APRIL Richard Spencer announced that he would be giving a talk at the campus of Auburn University in Alabama, and it immediately and quite predictably set off a flurry of threats and counter-threats. The Antifa website itsgoingdown.org breathlessly announced, "Racist 'Alt-Right' leader Richard Spencer and his goons had decided on a show of force in the South, threatening to overrun the campus of Alabama's Auburn University with white power combatants armed with 'safety gear.'" In response, a group calling itself a "White Student Union at Auburn" and that until recently had been going under the impressively serpentine acronym WAREAGLE—Whites of the Alt-Right Educating Auburn Gentiles for Liberation and Empowerment—took it upon themselves to plaster Auburn with earnest warnings of the dangers of the antifascists. "We don't mind if you disagree with us, we just want you to be safe," the flier said with maternal concern. The night before had seen a big brawl between nationalists and Antifa at Berkeley, and everyone was expecting a rematch, which is why the university informed Richard Spencer that he would not be welcome at their campus after all, to which Spencer replied that he would come anyway because Auburn is a public school and First Amendment Laws applied. He would just hold his speech outside—in front of God, Antifa, and everyone.

Simultaneously he and Cameron Padgett, the soft-spoken Georgian who had rented the venue and invited Spencer, quickly sued. They enlisted the services of Sam Dickson, an attorney with ties to several far-right causes, including the KKK, who argued that public safety concerns weren't enough to override the First Amendment. The judge agreed, and Spencer would again be allowed into the actual university building to speak.

Matthew called me a couple of days prior and said that Mike Enoch, the disgraced agitator behind the website TheRightStuff.biz, the podcast the Daily Shoah, and now Spencer's top lieutenant, had contacted him on behalf of Spencer and asked if he would bring some guys down for protection. Matthew hadn't heard from Spencer since the inauguration snub but still seemed happy to be asked and promised to bring a handful of Traditionalist Workers down. I arrived before anyone else, and Matthew asked me to get the lay of the land because it would be their job to hold off Antifa in a public space, and they would prefer that space to be easily defended. I told him I really wasn't comfortable picking the battleground for the latest alt-right/Antifa skirmish but did let him know that the cops were out in force already, so they would probably be fine regardless of where they were.

Auburn University is situated on a picturesque campus, and the only indication that it isn't a northeastern liberal arts school is its students' distinct conservative bent. Even so, Richard Spencer's brand of nationalism is too much for most of the student body, and on the morning of the speech many of them were gearing up to protest, drawing up signs of "Love Trumps Hate" and "No Fascists at Auburn."

I stopped at a coffee shop just off the main drag, populated with earnest-looking students working at an impressive stack of signs. I asked a young woman about what she knew about Spencer. She described him as a Nazi who got punched in the face once. I asked her if she thought there would be violence today, and she said she'd heard rumors that people were coming in to fight but that most kids at Auburn just wanted to voice their displeasure. "I wouldn't mind punching that asshole in the face myself," she said, "but I'd just as soon let him talk and then get out of town."

I walked back up toward campus along South College Street and spotted a couple of black-clad kids pulling PVC pipes out of bags. Antifa were here, but so far no sign of Spencer or Matthew.

A small group of guys were lounging in the shade of a leafy tree on the quad, conspicuous in their uniforms of tanned khakis, crisp white polo shirts, and the fact that they were equipped much like a destitute lawn hockey team who had been forced to settle for whatever protective gear they could scrounge up at Goodwill. Some wore BMX helmets, others had lacrosse helmets, and others had to make do with surgical facemasks. They were uniformed only in the sense that they all looked completely ridiculous in similar manners. One had opted for a T-shirt rather than a polo and had written the words "Commie Filth" on the back. Having miscalculated the width of the T-shirt, the T-shirt read "COMMIE FI," with the rest of the phrase bunched up illegibly on his right shoulder. Still, he displayed it proudly as he waved around a cross on a stick. "We're just concerned dudes," one of them, who, like the rest, introduced himself as Chad in what they probably believed was a clever spin on the hacktivist mantra "We Are Legion." The alt-right is Chad, apparently. "We don't want commies to start any trouble on campus," Chad continued, "and we want to make sure that Spencer gets his First Amendment rights. That guy's a goddammed hero."

This was another new face of the alt-right under Donald Trump. Freed from the burden of political correctness, white frat boys could now explain to the world how white frat boys were the true victims of feminism, affirmative action, and other forms of anti-white persecution and could, with a straight face, stand up in public and rejoice in someone finally fighting for their rights as white, affluent college guys. I thought of the phrase, "With friends like these, who needs enemies" and wondered how rich white guys complaining of unfair treatment could be anything but a millstone around the alt-right's neck. In a way I understood the complaints of Matthew's constituency (if not Matthew himself). They were white, but they were also poor, undereducated, underrepresented, and living in a part of the country where economic opportunities were almost nonexistent. The warriors of WAREAGLE were young men in their early twenties and students at a fine university where the cost of attendance ranged from $30,000 to $50,000 per year. This isn't to say that a college education automatically buys you happiness or secures you economic stability, but they were hardly systematically oppressed.

This was all part of the ongoing alt-right identity crisis that had been unfolding since the inauguration. If the election of Donald Trump had emboldened racists such as the boys of WAREAGLE to come out of the woodwork, then did that mean they were alt-right now? They certainly weren't ordinary Republicans, and they weren't Nazis, but they also didn't have the ideological baggage of many of the original alt-right members who had spent years, even decades shaping their politics. Would the alt-right umbrella be able to accommodate the recent flood of liberated racists, or would whatever cohesion they had built collapse? In the face of such a deluge of giddy white priders, would the far right become completely diluted, or would they manage to establish a coherent political strategy and capitalize on the moment? Both Matthew and Spencer saw the current opening of the floodgates as an opportunity, though they acknowledged that they needed to mold these babes in the woods into focused nationalists.

Simultaneously the alt-right was going through a painful and very public breakup in which they weren't sure if they were the dumpee or the dumper. The members of the alt-right felt they had played a large part in making Donald Trump president, and now he wasn't taking their calls anymore.

"It certainly feels like a parting of ways," Richard Spencer had told me a few days before the speech at Auburn. "A lot of us feel disillusioned and even burned by Trump. In a sense we thought that the alt-right could be Trump's brain, but now he has Ivanka and Jared and Paul Ryan for that. Basically people who aren't me. You can't really prepare yourself for what it feels like."

Like most breakups, the relationship had been troubled for a while. Many in the alt-right were disappointed in Trump's rapid embrace of conservative dogma, focusing on healthcare and tax cuts rather than getting to work on building his wall—by himself with a hammer in the desert if he had to. Yet the final straw came when Trump launched missiles at Syria following President Bashar al-Assad's chemical weapons attack against civilians in early April. Not only was Trump breaking his promise to not engage in any new wars; he was also pissing off Putin, whom many members of the far right admired, as well as attacking the man they saw as the only nationalist leader fighting terrorists in a godless part of the world. In short, Trump was doing exactly what they had warned their followers that Hillary Clinton would do if she were elected. Matthew was calling for Trump's impeachment on Facebook. Richard Spencer said he condemned the attack, and Paul Watson, a writer for the conspiracy-oriented InfoWars.com, tweeted that Trump was "just another deep state/Neo-Con puppet," announcing that he was "officially OFF the Trump train."

What's more, at the very beginning of Trump's term he unveiled a budget that would disproportionately hurt many of the working-class people who voted for him. Among other things, it would eliminate the Appalachian Regional Commission as well as slash farm aid. I asked Matthew if he was disappointed in his guy. After first underscoring the fact that Trump was never "his guy," Matthew explained how he basically didn't care about anything Trump said or did so long as he built a wall and kept the country out of war. Now that he had bombed Syria and seemed to be vacillating on whether he really wanted to build a border wall, the alt-right was scrambling to reclaim the antiwar, closed-borders mantle.

"His domestic policies have been just one lame shit burger after another," Spencer told me when I asked him about Trump the president versus Trump the candidate. "He's become a normal president, and we can't trust him anymore. Still, it presents us with an opening. We can be the vanguard we always wanted to be, and vanguards are powerful."

A COUPLE OF HOURS before the speech was scheduled to begin, Matthew arrived in his rental car along with Robbie, Katherine, Scott, Gabe, Jason, and Tony Horvater. Tony was Matthew's friend from Cincinnati who had once planned to run for city council as a TWP candidate. The campaign had never manifested itself, but Tony was still a trusted party member, albeit one who had deep misgivings about Matthew's increasing association with the most extreme right-wing groups. All of them except Tony were dressed in black, with the new polo shirts of the Nationalist Front and matching black bandannas wrapped around their necks while holding black shields emblazoned with the TWP logo. Robbie and Scott

Gabe helps Scotty with his helmet at Auburn University.

sported helmets, and Gabe wore a black cap and had covered his hands in work gloves with the knuckles wrapped in hard plastic.

I was surprised to see Gabe again. He'd recently decided to leave the Hammerskins and moved back to Louisville to be closer to his family. Since Hammerfest he'd become increasingly disgusted at the Hammerskins' willingness to fight each other instead of the enemy, and he began withdrawing from his brothers in C-38. At a regional meeting in North Carolina a couple of months after Hammerfest a large Hammerskin decided to test Gabe's commitment and jumped him. Afraid that the fight might spin out of control and end with more of the brothers joining in if he fought back, Gabe had taken a few punches without resisting. He wanted to prove he was strong and could take a beating, but he'd also seen how these fights had descended into boot parties for no apparent reason and didn't want to end up dead on the clubhouse floor.

After it was all over the Hammerskin who had attacked him pulled him aside and asked why he hadn't fought back. Fighting was such an integral part of being a Hammerskin that Gabe's reluctance to fight back was either a sign of weakness or an indication that something was wrong. "Why do you even want to be a Hammerskin if you don't want to fight?" the guy asked. Gabe said that he wanted to be a warrior but that he wanted to fight *for* his race, not fight his race. "Dude, your race doesn't give a shit about you," the Hammerskin had said, laughing in his face.

"That's when everything came together for me," Gabe told me later. "I wasn't a warrior, and I wasn't doing anything for my race. I was an attack dog for the Hammerskins. Nothing more. They didn't even respect me. All I was good for was smashing whoever disrespected them at bars." He realized that Hammerskins were nothing but bullies and thugs and that he wasn't interested in being either. He handed in his patch, and with that, he was out. He'd known Matthew for years, and his twin brother, Zach, was a TWP member, so it felt natural for Gabe to join.

Matthew and his guys marched over to the group of Chads, where a small collection of curious onlookers had gathered.

"What is it that you want?" a young woman asked the Chad with the "COMMIE FILTH" T-shirt.

"I want Jesus, and I don't want commie filth," Chad said. "What's so hard to understand about that?"

The police had erected barricades around Foy Hall—which an enterprising Chad had renamed "Goy Hall" in a not-so-clever allusion to non-Jews—where Spencer would give his speech. Nobody was allowed on the other side of the barricade, and Matthew worried that it would leave them open to attacks from the rear. "Those sons of bitches sold us out," he muttered about the cops as he cast uneasy glances behind him.

A screaming match ensued between a protestor and one of the Chads. "You're supporting rape!" she shouted into his lacrosse helmet. "What you're saying is that you're basically supporting rape!"

The Chad in the helmet, not to be outdone, accused her of loving Sharia law.

Antifa showed up, but only briefly. They all wore some sort of armor and facemasks, and the police, citing a law against concealing faces in public, made them unmask, prompting them to leave with promises to come back later.

"I don't know why you're a libertarian. Libertarianism is dead, man," one of the Chads was saying to a student in the crowd. "There is no center anymore. Just be a nationalist already."

The woman and the Chad in the lacrosse helmet were still arguing, now surrounded by people filming the scene on their cell phones. In the war between the left and the right, no weapon was more powerful than the meme, and only a few hours later the showdown would be posted online with captions that claimed it proved whatever the poster wanted it to prove. "How can you say that?" the girl implored. "America is the land of the free!" Chad shook his head, seemingly unable to fathom how someone could be that naïve. "America is the rape and AIDS capital of the world," he said.

A young kid in a hockey helmet and an American flag draped around his shoulders explained to me that America needed to get rid of all welfare because "if you look back at the 1920s there was no welfare and all the blacks had jobs."

Eventually the barricades opened. A brawl broke out on the quad between one of Matthew's guys and a protestor. The protestor, a looming guy with spiky hair, swung at Matthew's friend but missed and got punched in the face. They both got arrested, and both sides cheered at their great victory.

We all filed into a large hall. The Chads took up the first couple of rows, while the next five or six were occupied by a mixed bag of Spencer/Trump sympathizers identified by various stickers, buttons, hats, and T-shirts. The back half of the spacious auditorium was filled with curious onlookers and protestors.

Matthew and his guys took seats along the aisle, ready to leap into harm's way in the event that someone tried to storm the stage. Nobody had seen Spencer yet, and Matthew hadn't heard from him. Mike Enoch, a squat, scruffy-looking man with a five o'clock shadow and baggy pants, walked over to say hello and tell them he appreciated that they came and that Spencer appreciated it too.

Matthew and Scotty during Richard Spencer's speech at Auburn University.

"Happy to help," Matthew said as Enoch went back to the podium in anticipation of Spencer.

"Just as an FYI," Matthew told Scott, who was occupying the chair in front of him. "If anyone tries anything, just deck them with your shields. Also, if we're going to chant, remember that our chants come in threes. No tapering off after two." He turned to me. "Did you hear I'm suing Trump?"

Trump's attack on Syria had particularly disgusted Matthew. As a proud Russian Orthodox, he was enraged by the betrayal. He was also a codefendant along with Trump in a lawsuit brought by a Black Lives Matter activist who alleged that he had shoved her at a Trump rally and that Trump had incited the violence (see Chapter 8 for more details). Now Matthew wanted nothing to do with his codefendant. "Trump should be impeached," he said. "It just proves that if you want anything done, you have to do it yourself."

Spencer took the stage with a buoyant "Oh yeah!" It was a new persona he was trying out. Part motivational speaker, part snake oil salesman. Rather than being just part of the intellectual lodestar of the alt-right, the breakup with Trump was pushing him to become a more traditional leader, one who went out and rallied the troops rather than spent all his time pontificating in front of a computer.

"The movement needs an enigmatic, badass leader," he told me later. "Sometimes my role needs to be a bit of the entertainer."

He wore a blue suit and theatrically took his jacket off and, with a metaphorical flair lost on no one, rolled up his sleeves: time to get to work.

He slinked across the stage, a seductive swing of the hips under a budding paunch, switching it up from earnest to serious to incredulous when he talked about something absurd like sexual identity. "I'm a woman this week. Now I'm a tranny, now I'm gay. Buy this, buy that. This is what's known as the end of history."

He lamented how consumerism had replaced identity in society and that the result was a gaping hole in each and every white person where the notion of white identity had once dwelled. He cursed the black cloud of guilt hanging over white men—guilt for the Holocaust, slavery, colonialism, Jim Crow, misogyny—holding them down and "preventing them from being heroes and reentering history!"

The Chads ate it up. These were small and confused boys, and Spencer cut through their confusion and allowed them to place the blame for whatever failings they had squarely on everyone else.

Spencer's speech was part revisionist history lesson, part lecture in political science, with convenient facts cherry picked and inconvenient ones discarded.

"There is something explicitly white in challenging someone to a fair fight," he mused. Someone in the back shouted, "Tell that to the colonies," but Spencer didn't seem to hear him. "Even if whites were inferior in every way, I would still fight for them."

"He's coming around," Matthew whispered. The point Spencer was making is one Matthew has been making for years, saying that no race is better or worse than another; it's just that the white race happens to be his race.

"Thank goodness we're not inferior, though," Spencer said with a grin. "We're fucking awesome."

The Richard Spencer Show went on for close to an hour, after which he opened the floor to questions, which he then proceeded not to answer.

"You challenged a lot of perspectives tonight," an undergraduate said, "but you only cited feelings and emotions. You stood up there tonight and said, 'The world is a worse place, and don't you feel that way, white people?' But literacy rates are the highest they've ever been"—"Who cares," Spencer interjected—"the number of people who die in war is the lowest it's ever been, infant mortality is the lowest it's ever been, women who die in childbirth is the lowest it's ever been . . ." The Chads started shouting, fed up with his fact-based nonsense. Facts were the problem because they explained nothing about how they felt. What good were numbers that showed that the world was moving forward when white men in particular felt like they were losing ground? Who cared about child mortality and childbirth casualties and literacy rates? What mattered was that the Chads in the front rows felt small and didn't like it.

Spencer gave a dismissive wave of the hand. "Look, I don't know how to begin here," he said. "This idea that I should throw facts at you all or quote things—I just find it a little bit lame, to be honest. I'm going to speak truthfully. And in terms of facts, suicide rates among whites are at epidemic levels, along with drug use, joblessness, sleeping more, spending their lives on Netflix. The idea that history is linear and just keeps getting better is just kind of nonsense." He was correct on the former—a study by researchers Anne Case and Angus Deaton from 2015 found that reduced labor force participation, reduced marriage rates, and increases in reports of poor health and poor mental health had led to a rise in both the death rates and drug use of middle-aged white Americans—but there was little use in comparing the Netflix habits of current Americans to past generations. "We could throw facts at each other all day long, but at the end of the day a fact only has meaning because of the perspective looking on it. There is no fact that you can cite that will destroy identity or make it irrelevant. Facts are lame. Let's talk about stuff that matters."

This was, of course, the crux of the alt-right philosophy and, as many have argued, could even explain the election of Donald Trump. It was a fact that minorities had gained increased representation in positions of power in governments, universities, corporations, and the media. According to the Pew Research Center, political representation for African Americans, based on representation in Congress, has steadily increased, and a report from Career Builder in 2015 noted that the number of women, African Americans, and Hispanics in the workforce had gone up, although the same report also acknowledged that the number of women in high-paying jobs has declined. In addition, women graduated from college in higher numbers than men. These were all facts, but it was also a fact that they angered and confused the Chads.

There was a barrage of questions. Those in any way critical—and they were in the majority—were either booed and heckled by Chads and Mike Enoch or batted away by Spencer: "You can ask your question, but you're kind of boring me, to be honest." A young woman had her question drowned out by jeers about her outfit as the Chads rose in their seats. "You should be ashamed of yourself, sweetheart!" someone yelled.

"You got no fashion sense, honey!"

The event ended, and Enoch, along with a couple of stern guys in army fatigues, ushered Spencer out the door and vanished. Matthew, perhaps hoping to exchange a word or two with him, was left standing in the throng as the audience exited the auditorium. "We have to keep our ranks!" he shouted behind him as they were jostled out the double doors and into the balmy Alabama evening.

The protestors were waiting, descending on the small band of fascists as they walked toward their car. Scott, Robbie, and Katherine had their combat helmets on, and Gabe was forging ahead and then returning in long, loping steps, almost urging the protestors to attack him. Matthew was up front, a strained yet persistent smile on his lips as he waved to the angry protestors. Then there was a kerfuffle behind him. For some reason everyone was coalescing a few yards back, protestors converging on something Matthew couldn't see. He looked around and counted his guys. Katherine, Robbie, Tony, and Jason were right behind him. Scott was at his side, peeking grimly over the edge of his shield. "Fuck, they've got Gabe," Matthew said. "Guys, they got Gabe!" They all turned, and Matthew ran straight into the crowd, shield at his side, pushing people out of the way. Scott followed at his heels, his helmet pushed up so he could see properly and using his shield to clear a path while somewhat inexplicably screaming "Sieg Heil!" at the top of his lungs.

Nothing had happened to Gabe, who had been off to the side the whole time, and it wasn't entirely clear what had caused the commotion. They regrouped and resumed walking. The crowd followed. Then they were walking faster, and then the crowd was walking faster. Then someone in the crowd started running, and then Matthew started running, and then they were being chased or giving chase and nobody was quite sure what was happening. Protestors, running and screaming but somehow never attacking them, surrounded Matthew and his friends. They were being overtaken, swallowed up by the crowd, and Matthew decided that rather than being picked off one by one, they would make a stand. If they were going to take a beating, they might as well do it together. They stopped and turned, crouching behind shields as the throng descended on them and then . . . nothing. They knelt there, expecting fists and kicks, and watched in surprise as the protestors split and ran around them, continuing their wild chase after who knows what. It lasted a few seconds, and then it was over. The last stragglers passed them, and Matthew watched as they ran off, rounding the corner on South College Street and stampeding down East Magnolia Avenue. "Well, that was strange," he said as he dusted the dirt off his knees and got to his feet.

Tony was missing but called later and said he had been cornered and was hiding out in a church a little further up the road.

There were protestors patrolling the street outside, so Matthew asked if I would go pick him up, as I wasn't one of them and would presumably be able to pass through unmolested. I parked outside and waited as Tony snuck out and jumped into the passenger seat. "I've never been happier to see a commie," he said as we drove off. I wondered if I was crossing some ethical line going to help him, but I had no desire to see Tony, who was moderate in his politics compared to the rest of the TWP, get beaten. If it had been someone I was less inclined to have in my car for the twenty-minute drive back to the hotel, it might have been a different story.

Tony had been and remained deeply skeptical of Matthew's alliance with the NSM and his overtures toward the Klan and skinheads. He was firmly convinced that they needed to be political and that Matthew's continued association with Nazis was hurting them. "Matthew wants followers," he said. "It's flattering to him that these people want to join him, but I think it's clouding his vision. He needs to see that these fucking people only hurt our cause and that he can be a leader of Nazis and he can be a leader of nationalists, but he can't be both."

The argument inevitably fell on deaf ears, as Matthew continued to insist that avowed nationalists like the NSM, who were used to marching in the streets, could be turned into an asset when he got them under control. Tony and many other TWP members could only watch in mounting frustration as their leader's political fate became increasingly intertwined with the most remote fringes of the far right.

"That's why I was so happy we came to this," Tony said. "Guys like Spencer and Mike Enoch are the future of the movement, and I think they are realizing that they need Matthew as much as Matthew needs them. We need to get this part of the movement together if we're going to stand a chance."

Supposedly Spencer would be at a friendly bar in town and was interested in talking, so we all headed there. Scott was feeling sheepish after everyone had heard his Sieg Heil battle cries and tried to explain that it was a form of trolling that could give him the advantage in a fight. When we got to the bar Spencer was nowhere to be seen, and neither was Mike Enoch. Christopher Cantwell, the jocular host of *Radical Agenda*, a popular internet-based radio show, was there and seemed happy to see Matthew. "It's good that you guys are finally getting together," he said of Matthew, Spencer, and Enoch. "Now we got something."

At 4 a.m. the next day I was at Hartsfield-Jackson Airport outside Atlanta to fly back to New York. Slouching uncomfortably in a seat by the gate was a sleeping Mike Enoch. He woke up as I sat down next to him. He hadn't heard about the chase and the weird fights from last night and was surprised that Matthew and his guys hadn't just snuck out the back with him and Spencer.

"It's really cool that Matthew showed up, though," he said. "That guy has balls and can be counted on. I think we should do more together." The next weekend Matthew and Jeff were putting on a big Nationalist Front rally in Pikeville. "I might show up," Enoch said. "Matthew certainly has my support from now on."

I told Matthew about it a couple of days later, and he seemed genuinely excited about what Enoch said. Praise from Enoch was tantamount to praise from Spencer, and I sensed that Matthew still wanted Spencer's admiration, even though he'd come far on his own and despite the repeated snubs. After the inaugural hiccup Matthew had told me repeatedly that he didn't need Spencer, but when Spencer asked him to come to Auburn, Matthew didn't hesitate. Now he had Enoch's support, whatever that meant. It was clear Spencer brought a whole different crowd than Matthew, and I wondered if the two factions would ever be able to work together—and if they did, what they might accomplish.

CHAPTER 13

Hail Heimbach

The revolution has always been in the hands of the young.
The young always inherit the revolution.

—Huey P. Newton, cofounder of the Black Panther Party

A week after the Auburn rally I was driving through the steep and claustrophobic hills of eastern Kentucky on the outskirts of the town of Pikeville. I was looking for a disused coalfield somewhere in the hollows where the NF event Matthew had organized was taking place. I'd been driving for an hour and a half on a trip that should have taken me thirty minutes. The GPS had lost all sense of direction, sending me in maze-like circles and down dead-end roads. It was getting dark, I was running low on gas, and I had somehow passed the same derelict, shuttered gas station three times.

This was supposed to be my last rally with the NF, after which I would go back to New York and finish my book. It didn't turn out that way, but the Pikeville rally was promised to be a big event, a culmination of Matthew's work, so it felt like as good a place as any to wrap up my research. I'd spent the last few weeks thinking about where the movement was and where it was heading, and as Trump seemed to slowly morph into a more traditional politician policy-wise—on everything else he was still pretty much all over the map—I wondered if the far right had hit a ceiling. Granted, they had gotten more adept at bringing attention to themselves, but their support for Trump's candidacy had so far not translated into any political victories. Truthfully, I felt as close to understanding nationalism in America as I was to finding Matthew's coalfield rally. The movement had come far and, at the same time, gone nowhere at all. Yes, Trump was a nationalist borne into office on the wings of far-right sentiment, but so what? What had it gotten the far-right groups who helped elect him? As far as I could tell the only palpable nationalistic outcome of Trump's presidency so far had been a perceived license for racists to be open with their bigotry. Matthew and Spencer were both trying to ride the same wave Trump had into some kind of brave new world, but if it was difficult to imagine their utopian ethno-states ever coming into existence, it was equally difficult to imagine their brands of alt-right nationalism joining mainstream politics. So the question, as asked by Spencer, Matthew, and pretty much everyone else in the alt-right after the election, remained: What now?

They both talked about big things happening, but I had yet to see a single rally draw more than fifty or so people. It illustrated the challenge Spencer had described when I met him in DC after the election. No one argued that the far right wasn't a hefty presence online, but even their most successful real-world manifestations rarely broke a hundred people. But did it matter? If the online hive mind of the alt-right had helped produce Donald Trump, then it was of little consequence how many people they managed to gather together in a field. Perhaps the modern incarnation of the white nationalist movement in America was destined to be an influencer of whatever populist demagogue came after Trump.

As for the people in the far-right movement, I felt I could say a few things with confidence. Some were angry, some were scared, some were confused, and some were trolls. Some were warm and caring; others were petty and filled with homicidal loathing. Some were what I thought they would all be: narrow-minded and hateful; others were thoughtful and considered. Some disgusted me, whereas others I honestly liked. They all felt like they were losing out, and I always thought that if they would only lift their gaze a little, they would see that they were not alone.

The long-abandoned coalfield had been no one's first choice for a location, and when the event was conceived, the plan was to hold it at Jenny Willey State Park near downtown Pikeville, where locals could saunter in and out, take part in the festivities, and see for themselves that the NF was no more a hate group than the local 4H. But the opposition had been swift and harsh, and the city of Pikeville, worried that their town would become a battleground for Nazis facing off against antifascists, looked for ways to cancel the whole thing. NSM had handled the actual booking of the space and, as was their wont, disguised it as a "family reunion." The trick had a proven track record, to the chagrin of many unsuspecting hotel managers, but when Floyd County sussed them out and realized it was a public event, it gave the city officials the out they were looking for: they slapped an event agreement on the nationalists. Built into the agreement was an insurance requirement stating that the NF would need to spend close to $10,000 they didn't have on a policy. Faced with the embarrassment of having to cancel a much-publicized event, Matthew went looking for options and eventually found a sympathetic soul with a piece of flat land in the hollows. They would hold the meet-and-greet and the workshops there and then drive in a convoy into Pikeville for the actual rally. It wasn't ideal, but at least being on private land might offer some protection against Antifa, who had already announced they would do their best to shut the event down. City officials banned the use of masks in the hope of dissuading as many as possible from coming. The University of Pikeville announced that it would shut its doors for the day and urged its students to leave town if they could; several businesses promised to stay closed. Even Senate Majority Leader Mitch McConnell weighed in, releasing a statement that said, "Based on what I've read about this group, it does not in any way reflect the values of the Eastern Kentucky I know. I wholeheartedly oppose its mission." Other than a massive police presence, the NF would be met by tumbleweeds.

I felt bad about the whole thing because holding the rally in Pikeville had—wholly inadvertently, I might add—been my idea. After the event in Harrisburg six months prior I'd sat down with Jeff and Matthew for an interview, and at some point we had discussed Appalachia. I told them about a reporting trip I had gone on to Pikeville, explaining that it was a nice little town in a depressed area that was working to pull itself out of an economic slump caused by the downturn in coal mining and that it was an interesting mix of urban and rural. As it turned out, it was exactly what Matthew and Jeff had been looking for.

Although Pikeville itself was slowly pulling itself out of poverty, the surrounding Pike County remained mired in hardship. Unemployment held at close to 9 percent, more than twice the national average, and there was no reason to think it would change anytime soon. In the election Trump had carried the county by 80 percent. If there ever was a perfect county to test Matthew's version of nationalism, this was it.

I spotted a couple of bikers with Confederate flags on their vests and decided to follow them in the hopes they were also going to the event. Soon they turned onto an unmarked dirt road that wound its way into the steep, forested hills, kicking up dust as they maneuvered their heavy bikes over boulders and sinkholes. A small house stood at the bottom of the hill, and the three locals sitting on the porch shouted to go slower as we passed; apparently the dust from our vehicles seeped into their house and got everywhere.

EVERYTHING YOU LOVE WILL BURN

The road snaked higher through the woods for a mile or so until the coppice opened to a large expanse, surrounded by clutches of trees and mounds of rock debris left behind from when the place was mined. A vast vista of mountains could be seen in the distance as well as a commanding view of the dirt path leading from the main road—anyone coming up would be spotted well before reaching the top.

The flat had been seeded by grass in that particular way that coalfields were typically reclaimed: thin, eerily uniform tufts of grass unconvincingly sprouting from the dirt like hair plugs. A handful of cars crowded the entrance to the field; beyond that, someone had lit a large bonfire, filling the dusk with ochre light that flickered onto a large, rectangular gazebo tent erected on the far side of the clearing. It had been furnished with two long tables and black folding chairs, and behind it were a power generator and a couple of smaller gazebos where various trinkets were sold.

A surprisingly large number of people crowded the field. There must have been almost a hundred people, making it, by a good margin, the largest white nationalist gathering I'd attended. A Porta-Potty had been set up toward the far side, and around it was a makeshift parking lot with a dozen or so cars and a handful of tents. Matthew stood in the center of a small crowd and waved me over. "Isn't this something?" he said as he gestured out toward the field and the crowd. He was beaming. "I can't tell you how good this feels. Finally!"

I spotted Jeff, Butch Urban, Harry Hughes, Schloer, and Gunner from the NSM surrounding a table along the perimeter where they hawked what I assumed were their usual wares. This time, though, there was hardly a swastika to be seen, and I wondered if there was a room somewhere filled with all the NSM's unsold Nazi memorabilia. "It's not bad, is it?" Jeff said. "It took some work, but I think it's starting to happen. A lot of these people I've never even seen before, so we must be attracting new people." As I looked around I saw none of the groups I'd seen at earlier NSM gatherings, and it struck me how thoroughly Matthew must have made them clean house.

Gunner had brought a friend to the event, an earnest-looking blonde woman in her early thirties. He'd recently gotten fired from his job at the IRS when his politics were exposed, and he was in the process of suing them for unlawful termination. "Apparently it's illegal to take pride in your race," he said with disgust. "This is why we need a White Lives Matter," his friend added. "But people misunderstand us on purpose. See, when we say, 'White lives matter,' we don't mean that white lives matter more than others—We just want white lives to matter as much as other lives."

I told her that what she just said was the exact meaning behind Black Lives Matter, that there was an implied "also" behind "Black lives matter."

She nodded. "Yes, why do only black lives matter?"

"I wasn't saying that," I said. "I said that the idea behind Black Lives Matter is that black lives should matter as much as other lives. And right now they don't."

"I know," she said. "Why should their lives matter more than a white person's?"

I left her and Gunner by their car and went to get some chicken.

In addition to TWP and NSM, the groups attending were the Right Stuff, the Dirty White Boys, the League of the South, the Council of Conservative Citizens, and White Lives Matter as well as a host of other individual players and smaller groups. For all their previous debacles, Matthew and the NF had managed to pull together a wide swath of far-right groups. Auburn had been a bonding experience for many of them and demonstrated a need for everyone to stand together to defend each other. A couple of days before, Matthew had told me how interest in his Pikeville event had skyrocketed after the skirmish in Auburn and that groups he'd had little to do with before, such as Identity Evropa, had shown up solely because of it. Christopher Cantwell was there after promising the week before that he would show, as was Brad Griffin from *Occidental Dissent*. "Last year I would never have come to this event," he said, nursing a can of Coke. Brad was somewhere between alt-right and alt-lite, and although he was an old friend of Matthew's, he had little patience for the more extreme elements of the right, such as the NSM. "And it isn't just me. An event like this could never have happened a year ago. We would all have just stayed on our individual islands talking shit about each other." In Griffin's eyes what changed wasn't the election of Trump or the many overtures from Matthew. "Everything changed when Antifa punched Spencer," he said. "When they punched Spencer they punched all of us. We now have a common enemy. Most of these people are here to hear what Matthew has to say, but I guarantee you that a lot of them are here because Antifa have said that they will be too."

It was a common sentiment, and by far most of the conversations I heard that night were about the horde of Antifa supposedly gathering somewhere in town. In the days leading up to the event the far-right forums had been bubbling over with gleeful machismo as members reminded each other that Kentucky was an open-carry state with Stand Your Ground laws. "Sounds like a fun time! STAND YOUR GROUND!" one *Daily Stormer* commenter said. "Communist hippies want to riot in a place where 200,000 Bible-loving, armed to the teeth Militia hill people live, and attack them. That's gonna work out Soooooooo well," said another.

To that end there was no shortage of weapons on the coalfield. Matthew carried his usual 9mm Smith & Wesson in his belt. Scott had an old, worn assault rifle of some kind that he carried in a strap on his back. Katherine sported a hot-pink 22, and her fiancé, Robbie, either fearing the worst or happy for an excuse to arm himself, had thoroughly kitted himself out with a jet-black AR-15, a 9mm strapped to his tactical vest, and a riot helmet. He and Scott looked slightly encumbered, attempting to shift their weapons to their backs as they ate chicken from paper plates. Scott had assigned himself guard duty and walked back and forth from the tent to the top of the dirt road, checking in with newcomers and exploring rumors of Antifa attacks. Gabe was there too. He seemed happy and comfortable as he strolled the field. He was growing his hair out and had started laser treatment to remove some of his more extreme tattoos. The "HATE" over his right eye was gone, and he was in the process of having the SS bolts on his left cheek removed. Where once two sharp shapes had been was now discolored, swollen flesh. "It hurts so fucking much more to take them off than on," he said. "You have no idea."

Captain Culpepper of the NSM came over to where Matthew was standing. There would be some speeches shortly, and Culpepper was trying to come up with an order of events. "Hey, Matthew, um, Art Jones says he would like to speak. I said I would discuss it with you." Jones was the curmudgeonly head and the sole member of the America First Committee whose speech at Harrisburg had come close to undoing everything the NF stood for. Matthew threw a glance over to the tent where Jones, tall and emaciated, stood in the glare of the fluorescent lights with an arm raised in an awkward salute.

"No. No fucking way. Not that fucking guy," Matthew said angrily. "I don't care what you tell him. Tell him there's no room on the schedule or something. He can't talk."

Culpepper returned to Jones and said something in a hushed voice, a hand resting on the old man's shoulders as he shook his head. Jones nodded and didn't look over at Matthew. "That guy is the fucking worst," Matthew said. "He's fucking butt cancer."

Schloer sauntered over, his body language insistently formal as ever, as if he were inspecting troops. His demeanor was awkward—stern and regimented in a way that suggested insecurity rather than authority. Matthew and his guys called him "The Tater Gator" behind his back because of a time he'd angrily insisted that they had eaten all the potato salad before he'd had a chance to taste it. "How are things with the Muslims in Norway, commie?" he asked in a joking manner that I suspected made us both equally uncomfortable. I'd always felt like he preferred when I wasn't around, and he'd certainly never joked around with me before.

"You guys getting raped left and right and through all hours of the day?" I laughed politely at his awful joke.

Jeff welcomed everyone to the gathering and made sure to mention that it was, in fact, the annual national gathering of the NSM. There couldn't have been more than a handful of NSM members in attendance, and most of the other groups were Matthew's conscripts.

After Jeff, Matthew also welcomed everyone and congratulated them on gathering on the anniversary of Benito Mussolini's death or, as Matthew called it, his "martyrdom." There would be plenty of time for speeches tomorrow, he said, so he would keep it short, and he did. After he was done speaking, he'd finished a beer and cracked another when a shaky voice came on the speakers; Art Jones, despite Culpepper, had snuck up and taken the podium. "What the fuck?" Matthew said, loud enough for the first couple of rows to hear him. "Son of a bitch. Why didn't anybody stop him?" But nobody had, and it was, of course, too late now. Nationalism was all about respecting what came before, even if what came before was an aging supremacist who'd overstayed his welcome in the movement. Jones came armed with a staggering array of numbers and statistics, and over the next forty-five minutes he went through them all. "Sixty-five percent of voters will support a party that fights for their interests." "Fifteen percent this and seventy-two percent that." As he'd done in his speech in Harrisburg, he cursed the two-party system and the Jew party system and the Queer party system until he had thoroughly lost even the most polite and attentive audience member. Even his wife, who sat docilely by his side throughout, looked catatonic. By the end Matthew was so bored that he wasn't even angry anymore.

A rumor started to spread around the coalfield that an attack was imminent. Someone had heard from someone else that the guys living in the shack at the bottom of the hill had seen cars drive up the dirt road with their lights turned off—it could only mean that Antifa had found out where they were and were about to launch an assault. Scott and Robbie went into bunker mode, grabbing their rifles and squatting down in the ditch on either side of the road where it emerged from the woods. They sat there in pitch darkness, glaring down the barrel of their guns into the void, searching in the inky-black woods for signs of marauding communists coming to sucker punch them. Paddy, Matthew's friend and favorite folk singer, was pacing nervously close to the bushes by the gazebo tent. "This isn't what I fucking signed on for, man," he said. "I just wanted to write music, and now Matthew has me dying up in the fucking hills of Kentucky with a bunch of fucking Nazis. Fuck."

No attack came, and eventually Scott and Robbie clambered out of their ditches. The commies had been defeated in the sense that they hadn't attacked. There was a clear assumption that the enemy knew where they were and wanted desperately to attack them, so the only possible reason they didn't was because they knew they couldn't win. Thus, in the warped logic of the nationalists' war games, the absence of an attack was a solid win. With that knowledge, they all went to bed.

THE NEXT MORNING I drove through Pikeville on my way back up to the coalfield. A couple of cops were busying themselves erecting a barricade on the main street, and I asked if they had seen or heard anything. They shrugged. They'd also heard the rumors of out-of-towners descending on Pikeville, but so far everything had been quiet. No shops were open, and the streets were empty. Even Antifa were nowhere to be seen.

At the coalfield the day was just getting started. By nine o'clock it was already sweltering, despite summer still being a month away. Flies were competing over a box of jam donuts on the buffet table, and a handful of attendees sat lethargically on folding chairs, watching as Matthew strode back and forth in the middle of the field, teaching some of the guys to march. He shouted orders and instructions in a loud voice, even though there were only five guys marching. "Keep formation!" he said. "Never break formation!" The men were only mildly interested and looked sufficiently confident in their ability to put one foot in front of the other, so Matthew soon told them to get out of the sun.

As much as a rally, Matthew had envisioned the weekend as a team-building exercise where the far right would bond, commune, and learn a thing or two. There was a lot of new blood on the field, and as someone who'd seen his fair share of Antifa clashes, Matthew wanted them to understand the importance of military discipline—unless it was too hot, of course. In addition to his impromptu marching class, he had planned a course in theology and a lesson in gas mask etiquette. Throughout the morning he walked the field, shaking hands and clapping shoulders. Jeff was there too, but he kept to his own guys, huddling around the cars as Matthew glad-handed. Although this was technically Jeff's event, it was clear that Matthew was in charge. Jeff had founded the NF and invited Matthew along, but Matthew had been in the driver's seat ever since. I understood why Jeff had wanted to involve Matthew in the alliance—Jeff had block recruited before, and although he vehemently denied it, he clearly had been counting boots in the NSM and realized he needed more—but I wasn't sure why Matthew felt like he needed *them*, especially given his recent overtures to Richard Spencer's camp. Whatever the reason, the NF was his vehicle now, and apart from the NSM and a couple of other early member organizations like Art Jones's shambolic one-man show, he had stripped away everything that Jeff had come up with, right down to the name of the organization. Matthew was magnanimous about it, or perhaps he was smart enough to realize that the image he'd crafted of himself as a selfless and reluctant leader was more valuable than the outcome of a power struggle with Jeff, especially if he was controlling the workings of the organization anyway. He made sure to thank Jeff at every turn, giving him credit for the foresight and initiative it took to build the Nationalist Front, all the while building it in his own image. If Jeff was aware, he wasn't letting on.

"I want to talk a little bit about how we are ruining ourselves," Matthew said later in front of a small audience inside the gazebo.

This was Matthew's theological lecture, and he wasn't holding back. "Porno is overwhelmingly Jewish. It pimps out white men and woman. It perverts the beauty of having kids. This is how they break us, and this is how they bring about our demise. But if we are strong and moral, the Jews will have nothing on us. That is why the Jew hates you—because you are a people who can break their hold over this world."

Matthew's religion somewhat separated him from other elements among the far-right, but with his religion came a strict traditional view on gender roles and cultural norms that dovetailed nicely with the rest of the alt-right's mostly reactionary view of society. Spencer's politics were avowedly nonreligious, although it did embrace Christianity as a central element of white heritage. He accepted that feminism had led to progress for women's liberation, but he also once told me that he wished that women would keep out of higher education. Although many of the white nationalists weren't religious at all, some of their views on women were downright biblical. In a blog post on the alt-right site CounterCurrents .com, the site's editor Greg Johnson once wrote, "The position I favor on abortion in a White Nationalist society is that some abortions should be forbidden, others should be mandatory, but under no circumstances should it simply be a matter of a woman's choice. I am pro abortion, not pro choice."

The circumstances under which Johnson believed abortion should be mandatory were: severe fetal defects, if childbirth endangers the life of the mother, and, of course, if the fetus in question is of mixed race. In Johnson's words: "If a woman gets pregnant on vacation in Jamaica, an abortion should be mandatory if she wishes to return to white society." But, as Johnson admitted, "this is just utopian daydreaming."

The audience tolerated Heimbach's Russian Orthodox diatribes because they knew as well as he did that it was his event. Matthew's time had come. Mike Enoch told me the week before that he had been watching Matthew for a long time, eyeing him up as he schlepped across the country—marching, speaking, sometimes fighting, and never taking a break. Even if you disagreed with Matthew—and plenty did—no one could argue that he hadn't worked hard to prove himself. Also, many in the audience had come for the prospect of being part of something bigger. Those who had been in the movement for a while knew how rare a true alliance was, and this one, at least for the moment, seemed like the real deal.

"There can be no infighting," Matthew said. "No compromise for this revolution. We need a whole new system built by our blood, sweat, and tears. Let there be no misunderstanding: This is a revolutionary movement. We are not American nationalists; we are white nationalists. The American Empire has left us behind. It has deserted the principles upon which it was built, and there comes a time when a building is too derelict to save. This is where we are. This is where we are going."

As Matthew spoke, rivulets of sweat ran from under the brim of his black cap, dripping from the tips of his bushy beard. It was his stump speech about revolutionary glory and perhaps martyrdom, and he'd told some variation of it many times. Most of the men there had read the dystopian daydreams of William Luther Pierce in *The Turner Diaries* or, if they didn't read, watched and rewatched *Red Dawn*, in which a small band of American patriots led by Patrick Swayze take on and defeat the Russian forces occupying America. They dreamed of being Spartans or the brave fighters of Vienna who broke the Ottoman invasion in 1683. The coming revolution would take away all doubt and make the world simple, and this is what they craved the most. I suspected they needed to know that there was an enemy who hated them and wanted them dead, because the opposite—that there was no grand, evil scheme against them, merely that the world was a massive, complex organism that perhaps had little use for them—was too terrifying to bear. It reminded me of the Elie Wiesel quote: "The opposite of love is not hate, it's indifference." Hatred they could deal with, indifference was horrifying. So rather than being insignificant ciphers in a vast and demeaning world, they became feared partisans in an existential struggle.

To ram the point home, Matthew ended his speech with a favored quote by José Antonio Primo de Rivera, founder of the Spanish Phalanx, the Spanish fascist party. "Revolution is the work of a resolute minority. Hail Victory!"

Then a short barrel of a man from American Vanguard taught everyone how to wear a gas mask, ending every lesson with ". . . or you're gonna be sucking gas."

"This unity thing is a hell of a drug," Matthew said as he watched his comrades mill around the buffet table, eating donuts already melted in the hot morning sun. Mike Enoch had showed up earlier, and Matthew was excited to see him because he was a conduit to Spencer and a stratum of the far right that Matthew had been unable to reach thus far. Enoch's presence there didn't mean that therightstuff.biz would sign onto the Nationalist Front in any sense, but the alt-right, much like high school, was all about who you were seen with, so his presence was a definite endorsement. "Me and Spencer are colleagues now," Matthew said. "I'll still call him out on his bullshit, and lord knows there's a lot of it, but I think he realizes that we're pulling toward the same goal. This really is years of work finally coming together. I mean, you were there for most of it. Tell me this isn't special." I had to admit that, as far as far-right gatherings went, this was a success. It still didn't measure up to the Aryan Congresses of the 1990s or the Nordic Fests at IKA in the early 2000s, where hundreds gathered, but this was a different era, and bringing together 120 or so relatively politically minded white nationalists in the middle of nowhere was undoubtedly a feat. "The beauty here is that there is no space to have your own opinion. Normally in white nationalist groups it's all 'come as you are as long as you show up'—they just want numbers. But we've laid down our positions on everything, and those not onboard can stay away. I can control all of this."

A walkie-talkie Velcroed to Robbie's chest crackled, and news came through that three Antifas had been spotted in the center of Pikeville.

The chatter went back and forth on the radio. All the voices were excited about the prospect of meeting the enemy, and bravado was running high.

"That's it? Three goddammed Antifa," one said.

"They are going to get run over," said another.

"If the cops grab them, I'm going to get myself arrested too so I can find them in jail and fuck them to death," said a third.

A couple of antifascist rallies had been scheduled and then canceled as both the nationalists and Antifa ratcheted up their rhetoric. The nationalists were always going to be armed, but Antifa had also advised its members that concealed-carry licenses from other states applied in Kentucky and that those who had concealed weapons should feel free to bring them.

Robbie and Scott were checking and rechecking their ammo and the firing mechanisms on their rifles. They kept the safeties on, but each had a round in the chamber, just in case they needed to act fast. There seemed little need for it on our remote coalfield, but perhaps they knew something I didn't.

"I wish there was a better place to poop than those Porta-Potties," Jason said, eying the green box suspiciously just as a large man came out after having been in there for a long time.

"The struggle is real, my man," Matthew said.

As Jason reluctantly headed for the green box, Matthew fished his phone out of his pocket and called Brooke, who was home in Indiana, seven months pregnant with a boy to be named Patrick. "Nothing's happened yet, honey," he said as he walked a tiny circle in the grass. "I just wanted to call to say that I love you and I love Nick and I love Pat and I love Rosie the Rat." Rosie was a pet the family had recently gotten. "Say a prayer for me, and I'll try not to get shot."

We got lost on the way into Pikeville, then we briefly found our way and then got lost again. As we left the coalfield we were all in one convoy, with Captain Culpepper up front and Matthew riding with me, Jason, and Tony Horvater somewhere in the middle. Soon we were two convoys, neither sure of where the other was, and then we were three until we were a host of one- and two-car convoys confusedly driving around a maze of hollows. We stopped, turned, stopped again, and turned again. Culpepper was on the radio asking where we were and asking where he was, and nobody could give him a satisfactory answer to either question. Matthew and Jason had both run out of tobacco and weren't handling withdrawal well. Matthew was grumpy because Jason didn't bring enough batteries to film the speeches, and Jason was grumpy because Matthew hadn't told him to bring extra batteries. We'd been driving for almost an hour, and the GPS, in the rare moments it sputtered to life to reveal where we were, told us we were forty-six minutes away. "How is that possible?" Matthew asked. "When we started out, we were forty minutes away, and that was an hour ago."

Parts of the convoy had made it to Pikeville and were sending dispatches via walkie-talkie back to those of us still lost. The Oath Keepers had showed up, and someone said they looked goofy but were armed to the teeth. "Someone's walking along the side of the road with a knife," a voice said. "I don't know if he's Antifa. He does have a man bun, though."

Finally we made it, and thirty-three cars gathered in the parking lot of a Pikeville Carl's Jr. so that everyone could use the bathroom before the event. The town itself was a ghost town, and Carl's was the only place open. Hughes told everyone to check their guns and ammo, and the parking lot erupted in a cacophony of clicks and grinds as bolts were pulled back, magazines slammed in, and safeties snapped on and off. It seemed like everyone had brought guns, and I wondered if somewhere across town in another parking lot Antifa were gearing up in the same way. There were pistols, AR-15s, shotguns, revolvers, flak jackets, helmets, backpacks filled with spare ammo, vests weighed down with full magazines, CamelBaks for water, gas masks, spare gas masks, backup gas masks in case the spare gas masks failed, first aid kits, backup guns in boots and on vests, knives of absolutely every variation, brass knuckles, ankle holsters filled with pepper spray canisters—there was even a homemade axe that looked like it was lifted straight from *The Lord of the Rings*. They were overprepared for anything short of a full-scale invasion of a foreign country.

A girl in her early twenties with a swastika on her T-shirt looked around at the town as her boyfriend tried to force two 9mm pistols into a vest pocket designed for only one. "This is a nice town," she said. "You know, if they're so poor and miserable, we should teach these people to raise rabbits. Rabbits are like dogs. They're really good company."

"They eat rabbits here, babe," the boyfriend said as he gave up on carrying both pistols in his vest and stuffed one in his pocket, where it immediately threatened to fall out.

"In that case, no. They shouldn't have rabbits."

For all their preparedness when it came to weaponry, they had forgotten the generator, and it was discussed at some length whether they should just stand there without speeches to make their presence known. Gabe was teaching some rookies the difference between a German salute and a Roman salute. "A roman salute is with a lower arm and your thumb tucked under your palm," he said, demonstrating. "The German kind, arguably the more imposing of the two, has the arm raised higher, and the thumb straight along the fingers. You know, I heard that Hitler himself did a Persian salute, which is a little more like a hello." Gabe tucked his elbow to his side and raised his lower arm straight up with a flat hand.

Someone finally got their hands on a generator, and the speeches started. As always, they were largely a waste of time. Fifty or so Antifa protestors had arrived and screamed from across the street, drowning out everything else. The nationalists told them to come over to fight like real men, which, of course, they couldn't because there were police everywhere. The pantomime of it all was getting a little old. Jeff spoke first and did his standard spiel about coming together and fighting for the white race. The nationalists seemed happy with the speech and joined in for a chorus of "Hail Victory"

Gabe, Robbie, and Scotty at the Nationalist Front rally in Pikeville, Kentucky.

when he was finished. There were even a few "Sieg Heils" from overzealous NSM members. Old habits die hard.

Matthew's speech was fairly boilerplate too. I'd heard it dozens of times. The call to action, the fellow nationalists around the world, the faith, family, and folk mantra.

He wound the whole thing up with a "Hail Victory," but the nationalists behind him started their own chant, singing "Hail Heimbach" over and over. The chant went on for minutes, and Matthew turned to his followers with a sheepish grin, bowing awkwardly at times but letting the adulation wash over him like a warm shower. Jeff didn't join the chant and stared straight ahead. Matthew awshucks'ed for another minute or so until the chanting ended and was replaced by backslapping and applause. If there had ever been any doubt as to who was running the largest coalition of white nationalist groups in America, there was none now.

IN THE CAR on the way back Matthew was beaming. "That was pretty special," he said. "I mean . . . yeah, that whole Hail Heimbach thing . . . it was silly, but, yeah . . . it was pretty special."

"You earned it," said Tony. He despised the NSM and was happy to watch Matthew take charge. "Those fucking guys need to fold. They can't go on like this." The night before he had told me how Matthew had ended up paying for all the food both days, even though it was, on paper at least, the NSM's event.

"That's fine," Matthew said. "I don't mind. But honestly, how many guys did they even bring to this thing? Like, five?"

"They haven't built this," Tony said. "They've fucked it up several times, but they haven't built it up. You did that."

Matthew knew he was right. He had done all the legwork. Jeff had started the Nationalist Front—although it had been the Aryan Nationalist Alliance at the time—but Matthew renamed it, wrote most of the principles, and weeded out the groups that never would have gotten onboard with what he was trying to build. What's more, Matthew credited Jeff at every turn, despite the fact that everyone knew Matthew was the one who built it. Just that morning a Klan group from Alabama had come up for the rally because they had been following Matthew's work for years. He's the one who went to Auburn to defend Richard Spencer—the NSM was nowhere to be seen. He was in talks with the League of the South (LOS) about bringing them on board. In the years following its foundation in 1994, LOS had been the most important neo-Confederate, secessionist group in America, with membership at close to 10,000. Since then it had fallen on hard times, and although their leader, Michael Hill, claimed to have 25,000 members, the actual number was probably closer to 250. Regardless, joining forces with LOS was important because they had contacts and credibility all over the South, and it was Matthew who had made that connection happen. No one else. And Tony was right: every time there was a fuck-up it had come from the NSM. They'd even almost cost them the Pikeville event because of that stupid family reunion booking that anyone could have seen was fake. Who knew what they would screw up next?

"Jeff's a great guy," Matthew said in a conciliatory manner. "He's a solid leader, and some of his guys are good. I'd follow Culpepper anywhere. But his troops are just so goddammed dumb. It's the only word for it. They're just too dumb to get what we're doing here." He called Brooke and told her about the event. "They ended it all with a 'Hail Heimbach,'" he said into the receiver. "It was pretty great actually. No, no, my head is the same size. I love you too."

Back at the coalfield the party was in full swing. We'd gotten lost again and were late coming back. Mike Enoch was giving a speech about white privilege, saying that there was no privilege from where he was sitting. He was followed by a guy with a guitar and wearing wraparound sunglasses, even though it was dark, and a shirt he'd opened to the bellybutton. He explained that he'd written a song about the struggles of white people. "Shit's getting real out there, baby," he said with a Dirty Harry–esque squint behind the glasses. "It's a war, and that's why this song is called 'The Battle.'" He started playing a fumbling bluesy chord progression while his voice searched up and down the spectrum for the right tone. He settled on a pitch that wasn't quite there but close enough.

"So sick of white genocide," he sang atonally. "Our children, our children's children are counting on us. I'm a white working man, and work is what I do. I work every day, every week, maybe two. I always pay my taxes, always pay my bills."

It was hardly Dylan, but it went over well enough with the crowd, who seemed to find nothing odd about someone writing a blues song about whites having it hard.

A short kid in his early twenties called Max took the microphone and immediately started screaming about liberals "building transgender bathrooms on our graves." "There was no Holocaust! At least not yet!" He went on and on, skipping from topic to topic but always coming back to the detestable Jew. "We need to act as an exterminating vessel of holy rage to defend ourselves."

Everyone thanked Matthew, who beamed proudly in the front of the room throughout. Vanguard America had built a massive axe, a replica Italian fasces, where the handle was wrapped in a bundle of sticks to symbolize strength in unity, which they presented to him with a "Hail Heimbach!" while the entire coalfield joined in.

I thought back to when I'd first met him, drunk on a pickup truck with some skinheads somewhere in North Carolina. I wasn't sure whether he had changed or if America had, but whatever had happened, he was now somewhat of a leader of men. I still had no real idea what he wanted or what his end goal was, but I was sure he wasn't happy to just be a cog in the machine anymore. I thought about something his old professor Kurt Borkman had mentioned. He believed that Matthew wanted to become a martyr, and as I watched Matthew lift the axe he had been given over his head like a Viking, I thought Borkman might be right. Realistically, what other acceptable outcome could there be? All his heroes were martyred, and Matthew was smart enough to know that political victory most likely wasn't in the cards for him or any of the others in the movement. He could be a leader in a movement whose leaders were either killed, imprisoned, or turned into Art Jones, and although I could easily see Matthew become the latter, he would probably much prefer martyrdom.

The bonfire was dying, and the landlord, who had no affiliation with the movement, stood by the embers and played a sad song on a trumpet. Cars were filing down the dirt road, kicking up dust that would infuriate the neighbors. Matthew was driving a rental back to Tennessee and was slowly backing out of the parking lot when he called me over.

"What did you think?" he asked me again.

"It was good," I said. "A lot of people."

"How many people do you think the NSM brought?"

I said I wasn't sure. "Maybe a handful?"

"That's what I thought too. What should I do with those guys?"

"I don't know," I answered. Later I would find it curious that he'd asked my advice about NF business and even more curious that I hadn't thought it was strange at the time. Matthew seemed preoccupied with his cofounder's group. "I'm sure if you talk to Jeff, he'll have his guys fall in line," I suggested. "They've come a long way already."

Matthew thought for a while. "That's the thing," he said finally. "I don't want to talk to Jeff. I want him to bend the knee."

And with that he drove off.

The Hard Right

Young fool. Only now at the end do you understand.

—Emperor Palpatine, *Star Wars Episode VI: The Return of the Jedi*

Of course, Pikeville wasn't my last event, and I don't know why I assumed it would be. Writing a book about something that is ongoing is a surreal affair because one needs to decide at some point when the story in the book ends, whereas in real life it continues, unaffected by narrative concerns.

There is always a next rally. Always something bigger and more consequential. In this story it was Charlottesville.

Pikeville changed almost nothing. For all the talk, press, online bluster, police presence, shops closing, plane tickets bought and miles traveled by people to get there, it had zero effect on any-

Members of the "hard right" getting ready to march to the Unite the Right rally in Charlottesville, Virginia. Shields are decorated with the alt-right flag.

thing. The Nationalist Front gained one new group, the Exalted White Knights out of Alabama, who promised they weren't white supremacists and claimed they were as committed to politics as Matthew was. People had fun, though, and it was decided that the far right should do these kinds of events more often. Other than that, things went back to normal. Matthew went back home and set about relocating his family to Tennessee. Early in May his second son, Patrick Heimbach, was born.

Charlottesville would build on the solidarity created in Pikeville. It was given the hashtag-friendly name Unite the Right and was to be a grand and much-overdue coming together of the leaders of the alt- and far right. The lineup of speakers was unquestionably impressive, living up to the name of the rally. Richard Spencer would be there, as would David Duke, Matthew, and Mike Enoch. Also scheduled to speak were David Hill, founder of the League of the South, and alt-right internet luminary Anthime Gionet, aka

Baked Alaska, who announced on his Twitter feed on the eve of the rally on August 11,

Tomorrow we make history at #UniteTheRight.

Matthew had top billing. His name was on the poster along with the other prominent leaders of the far right. He had arrived.

I hadn't planned on going. I'd been to more than my fair share of these things, and I wanted to be done with it. But throughout the summer of 2017, as the rally drew nearer, Matthew began telling me that Antifa promised to bring thousands to Charlottesville. According to him, they were flying in from New York, Chicago, and Oakland as well as busing in from Philadelphia and Pittsburgh. At the same time, the number of threats against him had been increasing. In the end a mix of curiosity, fear of missing out, and force of habit drew me to Charlottesville. I'd been going to these things for so long that it seemed strange not to.

I hadn't seen Matthew and the rest of the TWP members since Pikeville, but once I arrived at Charlottesville, it felt immediately like something had changed. The night before the rally a few of the members kicked me out of a party at their house. I'd brought another journalist who they immediately suspected was a Jewish spy, and Scott, Matthew's gormless henchman, fetched a bacon pizza and asked her to eat it in what he believed was a clever ruse to ferret out Jewish infiltrators. There was an edge to the crowd I hadn't seen before. There were more guns than I was used to and much more bravado. As soon as I got there Matthew Parrot told me I had to leave. "Nazi Joe is here, and he'd be fucking pissed we invited a journalist. He's going to come up and start something. You guys better get out." As menacing a name as it was, I soon found out that "Nazi Joe" was an alias the TWP used for Eric Striker, undoubtedly another alias. Striker was a short, skinny kid with a big head and cartoonish features who liked to rant against Jews on the website the *Daily Stormer*. He was about as daunting as a very small dog, but his animosity spread among the usually bookish TWP crowd and, in some way I couldn't quite put my finger on, altered the tenor of my relationship with the group. Matthew wasn't there, but Striker said he spoke for him when he said I could stay but "the kike had to go." I was taken aback by the aggression. It felt more like a skinhead gathering than a TWP party.

The next day provided further hints that Matthew was hardening, slipping further to the right.

A couple dozen TWP members in matching uniforms and construction helmets (a not-so-subtle nod to the TWP's pro-worker bent) gathered early in the morning in a parking structure a couple of blocks from the park where the rally would take place. In their hands were riot shields, flags, and clubs. They were the tip of the spear, primed in case Antifa was there. Then came the LOS, NSM, and a few other groups. All told, there must have been close to a hundred people—all marching behind Matthew. He wore his new uniform, a snug, black shirt that stretched over his paunch, a black armband emblazoned with the silver logo of the TWP, and a black tie stuffed into the buttons of his shirt. Unlike his men, he didn't carry a shield or a club, and his helmet was a military-style combat helmet rather than a construction hat. One of the guys from the LOS was telling the group to use the clubs against the abdomen, not the head. The head was assault, the abdomen was not. I wasn't completely convinced he knew what he was talking about, but to be fair, he also said to not strike unless the enemy struck first, which I guess made it all more legal. "We're not the alt-right and we're not the far right," he roared with his club in the air. "We're the hard right!" A pickup rolled up, and as if to underscore his point, Chester Doles, Peaches, and a couple of other guys from the Confederate Hammerskins jumped out.

I was surprised to see them, but not as surprised as Gabe, who had not left the Hammerskins on good terms. "Did you know about this?" I asked Matthew.

"Of course," he said. "Me and Chester have been talking. They want to go political." This was either a lie or Matthew was delusional. Thinking the Hammerskins could become a political group was like believing a pack of hungry wolves could perform community theater; it was an entertaining thought, but clearly the wolves would just eat the audience and everyone else. I looked at Matthew's crowd again. Spencer wasn't there. He, Mike Enoch, and the members of American Vanguard, Identity Evropa, and everyone else who belonged to what had become known as "white nationalism 2.0"—simply another term for the suits of the movement—were meeting elsewhere. This was a 1.0 crowd, and I was struck by the realization that Matthew, who had once spent a freezing March day outside the Conservative Political Action Conference happily arguing with conservatives, was now a completely different person from the one I met years ago. The transition had been gradual, and perhaps I had been too close to see it. Much like you don't notice yourself aging, I had failed to see Matthew's politics harden over time. Now, in the stark glare of the parking lot fluorescents, surrounded by what could only be described as troops, shaking hands with the Hammerskins, marching with the old guard of the movement, his transformation was obvious. Matthew was no longer "the affable, new face of organized hate" but rather someone who believed he was at war.

THE RALLY IN CHARLOTTESVILLE was terrible and inevitable. After years of egging each other on, after threats, small and not so small clashes, after countless boasts of the glory of fighting for one's race or the justness of smashing the fascist hordes, Antifa and the far right finally got their battle. It was ugly, violent, and tragic, and when it was over it had torn the far right completely apart.

The TWP partied that night as if someone hadn't just died at a rally they had taken part in. They told themselves that they had been attacked and that Heather Heyer, to the degree they mentioned her at all, was an enemy combatant who had died in battle. The next day Matthew put out a bland statement blaming the left for inciting violence. I remembered how, during the inauguration, he had screamed at a car driving through a throng of demonstrators to "Fucking run them over!" I was convinced at the time it was hyperbole, but seeing now how little he cared that a life had been lost, I wondered if I had misjudged his capacity for cruelty and violence. As long as I'd known him, Matthew had used the phrase "They are literally killing us!" with great pathos as he described the alleged attacks against whites by the elites and Jews. Now that a person had died, he refused to even name her. Matthew Parrot wrote on Facebook that as far as he was concerned, James Alex Fields, the driver of the car that rammed into counter-protestors and killed Heather Heyer, was an honorary member of TWP for life. Jason Kessler, until then the relatively unknown organizer of the event, tweeted out an article from the *Daily Stormer* that in graphic terms called Heyer a communist and implied that she was, by extension, responsible for the Gulag and all other atrocities performed in the name of communism.

In the days and weeks that followed, a schism appeared between those who took a hard-nosed approach to the events at Charlottesville and those who didn't. Richard Spencer disavowed Kessler after his tweet and expressed regret that Heyer had died; he was then immediately labeled a coward and a sell-out by those who believed Heyer was an enemy combatant. American Vanguard, the group to which Fields allegedly belonged, claimed he was not one of theirs, maintaining that Fields was just a guy who happened to dress like them and got his hands on one of their shields. Matthew believed the murder in Charlottesville would break American Vanguard. "They don't have the maturity as a group or the infrastructure to be able to absorb something like this," he told me over the phone. "They'll vanish soon enough."

Unite the Right exposed a weakness in the white nationalist movement in America. Despite the fact that race is a clear issue in American life—a majority of Americans, most of them white, favor keeping Confederate monuments in public spaces—the aftermath of Charlottesville showed merely sharing a devotion to "white heritage" isn't enough to sustain a movement, especially one that experiences such scrutiny and outrage in its infancy. Despite its name, the Unite the Right groups were never truly united in anything but being white and angry. According to many who took part in arranging the event, the speakers list included twelve names, all from different factions, suggesting that it wasn't so much an event for the various groups to come together as it was *the* place for aspiring leaders on the far right to be seen. The bickering, disavowals, and counter-disavowals in the wake of Charlottesville are a reminder that, for all the attention it received and hysteria it created, the far-right movement in America still had no idea what it was doing. This isn't to say that the groups and their members, on their own and together, aren't capable of violence, harassment, and even acts of terror, merely that corralling their efforts into a focused political movement would be akin to herding a flock of particularly hateful and racist cats.

"I think everyone is shell-shocked right now," the far-right blogger Brad Griffin told me. "I don't think this is near as big a deal as some people are making it out to be. This tempest will calm down. The news cycle will roll on. We should hold a big event on private property in the fall. After that we should resume activism as a tactic."

After Charlottesville Matthew didn't want to do any more rallies. "There's no point to them," he said. "We never get to speak anyway." He was moving still more of his guys to his property in Tennessee. One of his members had donated $40,000 that he was going to spend on a lumber machine so he could build what he called an "Amish-like community" on his property. He still wanted to build his white homeland but had seemingly abandoned all plans of working with Spencer and the suits. "Charlottesville proved that people are going to call you a Nazi regardless. There's no center anymore. There's no moderation. If you want to be in the movement, you better be prepared to put on the helmet and the armband and get into the streets."

As he saw it, Charlottesville had been an unmitigated success. He'd found out who his friends were and who his enemies were. Spencer, he believed, was a flash in the pan. His approach was doomed to either fizzle out or to be taken over by the GOP. Identity Evropa were cowards who had fled the fight. The Hammerskins held more promise—they hadn't agreed to join the NF, but Matthew was talking to Chester regularly, and they were already discussing how they could work together. "The focus going forward needs to be community organizing," he said. "We need to show people that we care."

Still, I found it hard to believe he was that naïve. He'd come a long way since I first met him, but he'd also not moved an inch. No one could argue that he hadn't created an alliance of disparate far-right groups. He had curated an organization that somehow housed neo-Nazis, KKK, alt-right, and other racists, but it begged the question: To what end? His friends from his former life, the one that included Youth for Western Civilization, had moved on, some to influential positions within conservative circles. But Matthew, for all his eloquence and affability, was now an avowed National Socialist, a dedicated anti-Semite, and the de facto leader of some of the most radical white supremacists in the nation. He still maintained that his end goal was a true party for the white working man and that he still didn't consider other races inferior in any way, but at the same time he was rubbing elbows with the most alienating crowd conceivable. Although his plan was to work locally and convince everyday Americans that fascism was their friend, somehow he'd convinced himself that he could do it with the help of Klansmen and tattooed skinheads. Where he once had ridiculed Jeff Schoep for being delusional enough to believe that the American public might somehow get behind a party sporting the swastika, Matthew now believed that the public would somehow come to trust the friendly neighborhood Hammerskins, "kill niggers" tattoos and all.

Ultimately, I believe that the far right in America, at least the incarnation I spent years covering, is destined to fail. Not because America is inherently good and that the forces of justice and progress are always stronger than those of intolerance and hatred, but because white supremacy is doing just fine without the far right. The country has spent decades perfecting an ostensibly nonracial form of white supremacy, and it is serving with remarkable efficiency. Private prisons, mandatory sentencing, seemingly unchecked police power, gerrymandering, increasingly limited access to healthcare and abortion—these are all tendrils in an ingenious web designed to keep people poor and powerless. Yes, white people were caught in that web too, but when it comes to those experiencing poverty, African Americans, Native Americans, and Latinos vastly outnumber whites. The people Matthew was ostensibly fighting for—the broken, beaten, and forgotten whites of Appalachia and the Rust Belt—weren't victims in a war against white people but rather collateral damage in a war against poor people and minorities. I believe Matthew was right when he said that the elites and politicians hate his people, but they don't hate them because they're white; they hate them because they're poor.

In an essay posted on his blog *Occidental Dissent*, Brad Griffin described how one of the failures of nationalism 1.0 was that it had been too extreme. According to Griffin, it attracted an audience of edge cases: naturally disagreeable people incapable of finding common ground. "Their message and presentation was stupid, vicious, crazy or ugly. It was easier for the opposition to brand these people with stereotypes and marginalize them." He didn't say as much, but he was describing the groups that Matthew was surrounding himself with.

According to him, nationalism 2.0 was different because society was fundamentally different. First and foremost, he attributed this to the rise of social media and Donald Trump. "Donald Trump was the rock that White America finally threw through the glass window of the status quo," he wrote. Political correctness was falling by the wayside, and the new nationalist movement would be there to articulate a new vision of society.

The only problem with Griffin's line of thinking was that the leaders of the alt-right as well as the movement's members had been unable to come up with a vision aside from trolling the vast swaths of the population who fell into one of the groups the alt-right had a problem with—feminists, liberals, LGBTQs, African Americans, Latinos, Jews—and bellyaching that whites were being replaced. It wasn't a policy platform so much as a series of gripes and offensive jokes. Their claim that Americans were tired of political correctness—a dead horse that Trump had flogged with gusto since the very beginning of his campaign—was largely unfounded beyond the echo chambers of the internet. The alt-right's first attempt at real-world activism, the debacle in Charlottesville, had decimated them. It couldn't have gone worse. They hadn't been heard, only seen, and the sight of white nationalists marching in the hundreds on American streets had largely frightened and disgusted Americans. The aftermath revealed that there were far more people willing to take to the streets to protest the nationalists than people willing to stand with them. In light of the tragedy in Charlottesville, Griffin's ideas about how the far right would forge ahead—"shifting into the real world now . . . will create stronger bonds as people get to know each other and work together in real life. It will be a fun, positive atmosphere that the disaffected will want to join and participate in"—seemed laughably naïve.

In the end, Matthew both succeeded and failed at the same time. He built the large alliance on the right that he'd always dreamed of, but it was a darker, angrier, and more extreme version than what he had pitched me all those years ago. If his plan had been to use his alliance to win the hearts and minds of those who weren't yet "red-pilled," then his goal seemed farther away than ever. There was a reason the NSM had been around since the sixties with almost nothing to show for it: because despite all the latent racism in America and the explicit and implicit white supremacy built into the fabric of our society, National Socialism would always be a fringe outlier. By succeeding, Matthew had made the same mistakes that all the coalition builders before him had made. The NF would never be a political force in America. If Matthew played his cards right, he might become the next George Lincoln

Rockwell, William Luther Pierce, or Richard Butler. But his steady path further and further to the right guaranteed only one thing: Matthew Heimbach would always be an extremist.

ACKNOWLEDGMENTS

Out of all the people who contributed in so many ways to this book, I sometimes feel like I had the smallest hand in its creation.

First and foremost I would like to thank my amazing family, whose endless patience allowed me to spend so many days and nights traveling while reporting for this book. I asked a lot from them, and there would have been no book without them. Thank you.

Thank you also to my parents and my brother for everything.

I owe a huge debt to my agent, Richard Morris, who worked tirelessly—and without pay, I should add—shaping what was at one point a loose collection of articles into something that might one day be a book.

Many thanks are due to my wonderful editor, Katy O'Donnell, who has been eternally patient, insightful, and understanding and whose steady hands made this book a reality. In the same breath I should also thank everyone at Nation Books for all their support and kindness. Thank you to Alessandra Bastagli for believing in this book in the first place and for your guidance and support ever since; to Brooke Parsons for teaching me how to talk about this thing in a way that makes it sound like I know what I'm talking about; to Miguel Cervantes for guiding me through the baffling waters of digital marketing, and to Christine Marra and Josephine Mariea Moore for cleaning up my grammatical mess. It must have been no small feat.

Also, thank you to Nation Books in general, for letting me be part of an incredible group of writers and book lovers.

I would also like to thank Michael Shapiro at Columbia University's School of Journalism. His boundless enthusiasm, inspiration, and feedback have been the foundation of every piece of journalism I've written, none more so than this book.

Thank you to my fellow travelers Anthony Karen and Johnny Milano, who kept me sane during countless rallies and gatherings. A special thanks to Anthony for saving me that time Antifa threw a brick at my face. In their defense, I was bald and standing next to a bunch of National Socialists. Easy mistake.

Finally, thank you to the journalists and researchers who came before me and without whose invaluable work and insights this book would never have been possible, and thank you to everyone who let me interview them on background and whose names could not be included in this book.

NOTES

INTRODUCTION. ELECTION DAY 2016

2   **parka and Angry Birds pajama pants:** Joe Helm, "This White Nationalist Who Shoved a Trump Protester May Be the Next David Duke," *Washington Post*, April 12, 2016, www.washingtonpost.com/local/this -white-nationalist-who-shoved-a-trump-protester-may-be-the-next -david-duke/2016/04/12/7e71f750-f2cf-11e5-89c3-a647fcce95e0_story .html.

2   **predicted, "then Clinton would win.":** *Morning Edition*, NPR, November 7, 2016, www.npr.org/programs/morning-edition/2016/11/07/500970882/ morning-edition-for-november-7-2016.

3   **children before taking his own life:** Associated Press, "Second Child Dies After Paoli Shooting," *Times-Mail*, February 12, 2015, www.tmnews .com/news/local/second-child-dies-after-paoli-shooting/article_1e9d9914 -b2f8-11e4-a55b-93744e18a0fd.html.

3   **They are killing us, literally killing us.":** Annie Ropeik, "Paoli Factory Closure Latest Loss for Declining Wood Industry," *Indiana Public Media*, October 17, 2016, http://indianapublicmedia.org/news/paoli-factory -closure-latest-loss-declining-wood-industry-107197.

4   **some eight hundred thousand jobs:** Trevor Houser, Jason Bordoff, and Peter Masters, "Can Coal Make a Comeback?" Columbia University, Center on Global Energy Policy, April 2017, http://energypolicy.columbia.edu/ sites/default/files/energy/Center_on_Global_Energy_Policy_Can_Coal_ Make_Comeback_April_2017.pdf.

4   **mines wasn't even a tenth of that:** Christopher Ingraham, "The Entire Coal Industry Employs Less People than Arby's," *Washington Post*, March 31, 2017, www.washingtonpost.com/news/wonk/wp/2017/03/31/8 -surprisingly-small-industries-that-employ-more-people-than-coal.

4   **because of rampant drug overdoses:** Margaret Talbot, "The Addicts Next Door," *New Yorker*, June 5 and 12, 2017, www.newyorker.com/ magazine/2017/06/05/the-addicts-next-door.

6   **switched coats, and then voted again:** Philip Bump, "Trump Says He Will Only Lose Pennsylvania if There's Widespread Voter Fraud. That's Very Wrong," *Washington Post*, October 1, 2016, www.washingtonpost .com/news/the-fix/wp/2016/08/12/donald-trump-says-hell-only-lose -pennsylvania-where-hes-down-9-points-is-if-cheating-goes-on.

CHAPTER 1. THE BATTLE OF TRENTON

18 **than unmarked cars and stakeouts:** Wayne Manis, retired FBI agent, interview with author, February 2017.

19 **while exercising their constitutional rights:** "Planned New-Nazi March Sparks Violence," CNN.com, October 15, 2005, www.cnn.com/2005/US/10 /15/nazi.march/index.html.

19 **right to march through Skokie, Illinois:** *National Socialist Party of America v. Village of Skokie,* 432 US 43 (1977).

19 **defend groups that protest with firearms:** "U.S. Rights Group Rethinks Defending Hate Groups Protesting with Guns," Reuters, August 17, 2017, www.reuters.com/article/us-virginia-protests-aclu-idUSKCN1AY06L.

25 **Anti-Racist Action had attacked the NSM:** Adam Tait III, "Neo-Nazi Rally Leads to Brawl in Pemberton Borough," *Central Record South Jersey,* April 21, 2011, www.southjerseylocalnews.com/community_news/neo -nazi-rally-leads-to-brawl-in-pemberton-borough/article_d086b676 -dba6-52ef-9e0a-1125e03103af.html.

CHAPTER 2. THE LITTLE FÜHRER

34 **that he was a federal informant:** Nate Thayer, "How a Disgraced KKK Leader Became a Key FBI Operative in a Bizarre Radioactive Ray Gun Case," *Vice Magazine,* August 21, 2105, www.vice.com/en_us/article/3bj5x5/ kkk-leader-fbi-ray-gun-821.

34 **Barker gave the Klan a black eye:** Ibid.

37 **600 percent between 2012 and 2016:** J. M. Berger, "Nazis vs. ISIS on Twitter: A Comparative Study of White Nationalist and ISIS Online Social Media Networks," GW Program on Extremism, September 2016, https:// cchs.gwu.edu/sites/cchs.gwu.edu/files/downloads/Nazis%20v.%20ISIS%20 Final_0.pdf.

39 **nicknamed him "The Little Führer,":** Ryan Lenz and Keegan Hankes, "The Little Führer," *Intelligence Report,* Southern Poverty Law Center, February 25, 2014, www.splcenter.org/fighting-hate/intelligence-report/2014/ little-führer.

CHAPTER 3. THE DEFENDER OF
WESTERN CIVILIZATION

50 **with hundreds of small red flowers:** Matthew Heimbach, interview with author, March 22, 2017.

56 **Founding Fathers fought and lived and died.":** Patrick J. Buchanan, "The New Patriotism," October 25, 1999, www2.gwu.edu/~action/buchref .html.

56 **unwilling to "drain this political swamp":** "Transcript of Pat Buchanan's Acceptance Speech," *ABC News,* August 12, 2000, http://abcnews.go.com/ Politics/story?id=123160&page=1.

57 **Donald Trump into the White House:** Richard Kreitner, "December 9, 1958: The John Birch Society Is Founded," *The Nation,* December 9, 2015,

www.thenation.com/article/december-9-1958-the-john-birch-society-is
-founded; Robert Welch, *The Politician* (Appleton, WI: Robert Welch University Press, 2002), www.robertwelchuniversity.org/Politician-Final2
.pdf; Daniel Bell, *The Radical Right* (New Brunswick, NJ: Transaction Publishers, 2008).

58 **the perpetuation of the white race:** Patrick J. Buchanan, *The Death of the West: How Dying Populations and Immigrant Invasions Imperil Our Country and Civilization* (New York: St. Martin's Griffin, 2002).

59 **union for white students was offensive:** Poolesville High School and Montgomery County Public Schools did not respond to author's requests for comment.

63 **no serious scholarship supports this:** Thomas Dalton, "The Great Holocaust Mystery," *Inconvenient History* 6, no. 3 (2014), https://inconvenient history.com/6/3/3331.

64 **the Gentile populations of the world:** Jayne Gardener, "The Abortion Industry Is Led by Extremist Jews," DavidDuke.com, March 22, 2008, http://davidduke.com/the-abortion-industry-is-led-by-extremist-jews; "The Jewish Supremacist Hypocrites Behind the Radical Feminists 'Femen,'" DavidDuke.com, December 9, 2014, http://davidduke.com/ jewish-supremacist-hypocrites-behind-radical-feminists-femen.

64 **at undermining white, European culture:** David Duke, *Jewish Supremacism: My Awakening to the Jewish Question* (Mandeville, LA: Free Speech Press, 2007).

65 **deliberate anti-white discrimination at Towson:** Jeremy Bauer-Wolf, "White-Pride Organization Proposed at Towson University," *Baltimore Sun*, September 7, 2012, http://articles.baltimoresun.com/2012-09-07/ news/bs-md-co-white-student-union-20120907_1_white-student-union -white-identity-matthew-heimbach.

66 **the campus grounds looking for evildoers:** "TU Crime Trends, 1995–2014," Towson University, Public Safety, www.towson.edu/publicsafety/ documents/tuccrimetrends1995-2014-28pdf.pdf.

CHAPTER 4. KIGGY

71 **bigger and to no longer "feel invisible.":** British Council, "The European Study of Youth Mobilisation," British Council Active Citizens Programme, March 2011, https://research-repository.st-andrews.ac.uk/bitstream/ handle/10023/1838/British_Council_ESYM_Report_March_2011_.pdf ?sequence=1.

74 **Shiloh and that they lived in Hell:** David M. Chalmers, *Hooded Americanism: The History of the Ku Klux Klan* (Durham, NC: Duke University Press, 1965).

75 **descended into terror and brutality:** "Organization and Principles of the Ku Klux Klan, 1868," University at Albany, SUNY, accessed July 31, 2017, www.albany.edu/faculty/gz580/His316/kkk.html.

75 **their seats to the Klan's endorsement:** Chalmers, *Hooded Americanism*.

75 **in an unprecedented show of force:** Joshua Rothman, "When Bigotry Paraded Through the Streets," *Atlantic*, December 4, 2016, www.theatlantic .com/politics/archive/2016/12/second-klan/509468.

CHAPTER 5. THE NSM TURNS FORTY

104 **wanted to please his aloof father:** William H. Schmaltz, *For Race and Nation: George Lincoln Rockwell and the American Nazi Party* (Stillwater, MN: River's Bend Press, 2013).

104 **left-wing and communist propaganda.":** George Rockwell, *This Time the World* (Kindle Edition), 35.

104 **a "sophisticated and smart people.":** Ibid., 25.

105 **even by sending him to Brown.":** Ibid., 52.

106 **never sees: the world of the Jews.":** Ibid., 117.

106 **short-sightedness and racial degeneration.":** Ibid., 130.

106 **treason against their nations or humanity.":** Hans Toch, *The Social Psychology of Social Movements* (New York: Routledge, 2014), 24.

107 **the article—victims that I invented!":** "Interview: George Lincoln Rockwell," *Playboy*, April 1966, http://newspaperdeathwatch.com/wp-content/uploads/2011/04/Alex_Haley_interviews_George_Lincoln_Rockwell.pdf.

107 **duration of the hour they were there:** A. M. Rosenthal and Arthur Gelb, *One More Victim: The Life and Death of a Jewish Nazi* (New York: New American Library, 1967).

108 **time in my life, the Jewish question.":** Dr. William L. Pierce, "The Radicalizing of an American," *National Vanguard*, no. 61 (1978), http://williamlutherpierce.flawlesslogic.com/the-radicalizing-of-an-american.

109 **idealism in the face of public outrage:** Rosemary Pennington, "On George Lincoln Rockwell," *National Vanguard*, September 13, 2015, http://nationalvanguard.org/2015/09/on-george-lincoln-rockwell.

109 **leader with "the guts of Malcolm X.":** "Interview: George Lincoln Rockwell," *Playboy*.

109 **dying in a swirl of laundry detergent:** Fred P. Graham, "Rockwell, U.S. Nazi, Slain; Ex-Aide is Held as Sniper," *New York Times*, August 26, 1967, 1, 14.

110 **German solution but an American one:** Leonard Zeskind, *Blood and Politics: The History of the White Nationalist Movement from the Margins to the Mainstream* (New York: Farrar, Straus and Giroux, 2009).

110 **fraction of one percent will respond.":** "Prospectus for a National Front," The Legacy of Dr. William Pierce, August 21, 1970, http://williamlutherpierce.flawlesslogic.com/prospectus-for-a-national-front.

113 **with only a few modernizing flourishes:** "25 Points of American National Socialism," National Socialist Movement, www.nsm88.org/25points/25pointsengl.html, accessed July 26, 2017; "Program of the National Socialist German Workers' Party," The Avalon Project, Yale Law School, Lillian Goldman Law Library, http://avalon.law.yale.edu/imt/nsdappro.asp, accessed July 26, 2017.

113 **$10 to a failed campaign in Tennessee:** "88 PAC: Contributions to Federal Candidates, 2006 Cycle," OpenSecrets.org, www.opensecrets.org/pacs/pacgot.php?cmte=C00410571&cycle=2006.

114 **no other groups could claim to be bigger:** "National Socialist Movement," Southern Poverty Law Center, www.splcenter.org/fighting-hate/extremist-files/group/national-socialist-movement, accessed August 10, 2017.

CHAPTER 6. THE SOLDIERS OF THE EARL TURNER

116 **United States and we won't shoot you.":** Richard A. Serrano, "Witness: Nichols Wanted Government Overthrown," *Los Angeles Times*, November 6, 1997, http://articles.latimes.com/1997/nov/06/news/mn-50864.

117 **with the global eradication of all Jews:** Andrew Macdonald, *The Turner Diaries* (Fort Lee, NJ: Barricade Books, 1996).

117 **death threats against prominent politicians:** Federal Bureau of Investigation, "William Luther Pierce," https://archive.org/details/WilliamL.Pierce.

117 **nature of the radical right in America:** Zeskind, *Blood and Politics,* 20.

117 **theory than on hardheaded political thinking:** "Prospectus for a National Front," Legacy of Dr. William Pierce.

118 **Alabama governor George Wallace:** Debbie Elliott, "Wallace in the Schoolhouse Door: Marking the 40th Anniversary of Alabama's Civil Rights Standoff," *Morning Edition*, NPR, June 11, 2003, www.npr.org/2003/06/11/1294680/wallace-in-the-schoolhouse-door.

118 **weak-willed members in droves:** Dr. William L. Pierce, "From Attack! to National Vanguard," National Alliance Bulletin, February–March 1978, republished by Rosemary Pennington, *National Vanguard*, March 15, 2015, https://nationalvanguard.org/2015/03/from-attack-to-national-vanguard.

120 **you're too damn dumb to bother with.":** Daniel Levitas, *The Terrorist Next Door: The Militia Movement and the Radical Right* (St. Martin's Press, Kindle Edition), 77–79; "FCC Probes Supremist [sic] Broadcasts," Levitas, *Terrorist Next Door,* 90–91.

120 **law enforcement officer in the country:** Ibid., 218.

121 **payment for their manifesto, *The Blue Book*:** Kevin Flynn, *The Silent Brotherhood: The Chilling Inside Story of America's Violent, Anti-Government Militia Movement* (Signet, 1989, Kindle Edition).

121 **so than the collection of income tax:** Ibid.

123 **cutting his own throat," Simpson railed:** William Gayle Simpson, *Which Way Western Man* (Hillsboro, WV: National Vanguard Books, 1978).

123 **is but for what his ancestors were:** Ibid., 603.

123 **Aryan homeland in the Pacific Northwest:** Evelyn A. Schlatter, *Aryan Cowboys: White Supremacists and the Search for a New Frontier, 1970–2000* (Austin: University of Texas Press, 2006).

125 **a total of 190 years in prison:** "2 White Racists Convicted in Killing of Radio Host," *New York Times,* November 18, 1987, www.nytimes.com/1987/11/18/us/2-white-racists-convicted-in-killing-of-radio-host.html.

126 **terrorist attacks against Americans:** *Presidential Decision Directive 39,* PDD/NSC 39, United States, White House Office, June 21, 1995, www.hsdl.org/?view&did=462942.

127 **insurgent fighter and independent:** Travis Morris, *Dark Ideas: How Neo-Nazi and Violent Jihadi Ideologues Shaped Modern Terrorism* (Lanham, MD: Lexington Books, 2017).

127 **this is exactly what is desired:** Louis Beam, "Leaderless Resistance," *Seditionist* 12, February 1992, www-personal.umich.edu/~satran/Ford%2006/Wk%202-1%20Terrorism%20Networks%20leaderless-resistance.pdf.

128 **"We're starting the Turner Diaries early.":** James Gunter, "Affidavit of Probable Cause," State of Texas, County of Jasper, June 9, 1998, archived by

the Smoking Gun, www.thesmokinggun.com/file/texas-dragging-death-0, accessed August 6, 2017.

128 **The Order with a specific movement:** J. M Berger, "Alt History: How a Self-Published, Racist Novel Changed White Nationalism and Inspired Decades of Violence," *Atlantic,* September 16, 2016, www.the atlantic.com/politics/archive/2016/09/how-the-turner-diaries-changed -white-nationalism/500039.

CHAPTER 7. NATIONAL KILL-A-WHITE-PERSON DAY

133 **against those who tried to kill them:** "Farrakhan Calls for 10,000 FEARLESS Who Are ABOUT THAT LIFE!!!!," Ahmad770, YouTube, August 3, 2015, www.youtube.com/watch?v=ImaPsvNBTgY.

146 **black, gay, and Jewish people to join:** Jenny Awford, "The Ku Klux Klan Opens Its Door to Jews, Homosexuals and Black People in Bizarre Recruitment Drive," *Daily Mail,* November 10, 2014, www.dailymail.co.uk/ news/article-2828425/The-Ku-Klux-Klan-opens-door-Jews-black-people -homosexuals-new-recruits-wear-white-robes-hats.html.

147 **was killed, allegedly by his own wife:** Eric Killelea, "KKK Leader Allegedly Killed by Wife and Stepson: What We Know," *Rolling Stone,* February 15, 2017, www.rollingstone.com/culture/kkk-leader-allegedly-killed -by-family-what-we-know-w466965.

150 **favored "keeping the Negro in his place.":** Chalmers, *Hooded Americanism.*

150 **"a classy order of the highest class.":** Michael Newton, *White Robes and Burning Crosses: A History of the Ku Klux Klan from 1866* (Jefferson, NC: McFarland & Company, 2014).

CHAPTER 8. THE ANA

159 **to accomplish real political power:** Helena Smith, "Golden Dawn Ditches Boots for Suits in European Election Makeover," *Guardian,* May 23, 2014, www.theguardian.com/world/2014/may/23/golden-dawn -greece-european-election.

159 **13 percent of the vote in their election:** Office for Democratic Institutions and Human Rights, "Hungary: Parliamentary Elections, 6 April 2014," OSCE, Warsaw, July 11, 2014, www.osce.org/odihr/elections/ hungary/121098?download=true; "Val till riksdagen—Röster," 2014, www .val.se/val/val2014/slutresultat/R/rike.

159 **protest of immigration and Islam:** Anthony Faiola and Griff Witte, "Far Right in Europe Sees Opportunity after Wave of Terror in France," *Washington Post,* January 12, 2015, www.washingtonpost.com/world/ europe/far-right-in-europe-sees-opportunity-after-wave-of-terror-in -france/2015/01/12/94cb5fdc-99e3-11e4-86a3-1b56f64925f6_story.html; Linn K. Yttervik and Erlend Ofte Arntsen, "Pegida-demonstrasjon ga rekordoppmøte," *VG,* January 13, 2015, www.vg.no/nyheter/innenriks/pegida -demonstrasjon-ga-rekordoppmoete/a/23373295; "'Anti-Islamisation'

Group Pegida UK Holds Newcastle March," *BBC News*, February 28, 2015, www.bbc.com/news/uk-england-tyne-31657167; "Italy Anti-Immigration Rally Draws Thousands in Rome," *BBC News*, February 28, 2015, www .bbc.com/news/world-europe-31674709.

160 **a profound birth defect in Jeff's baby:** "Historic Alliance Formed by U.S. White Nationalists," National Socialist Movement, April 26, 2016, www .nsm88.org/press/NSM_PressRelease_HistoricAllianceformedbyUSWhite Nationalists_april_2016_.htm.

160 **imaginary weapon of mass destruction:** Nate Thayer, "How a Dis- graced KKK Leader Became a Key FBI Operative in a Bizarre Radioac- tive Ray Gun Case," *Vice*, August 21, 2015, www.vice.com/en_us/article/ kkk-leader-fbi-ray-gun-821.

162 **Mexican immigrants of being rapists:** Staff, "Full Text: Donald Trump Announces a Presidential Bid," *Washington Post*," June 16, 2015, www .washingtonpost.com/news/post-politics/wp/2015/06/16/full-text-donald -trump-announces-a-presidential-bid/?utm_term=.518fbdf5d619.

163 **mantra conceived by David Lane:** Caroline Simon, "5 Times Donald Trump Has Engaged with Alt-Right Racists on Twitter," *Business Insider*, July 9, 2016, www.businessinsider.com/donald-trump-alt-right-2016-7.

163 **right reaches of the political spectrum:** Sarah Posner, "How Don- ald Trump's New Campaign Chief Created an Online Haven for White Nationalists," *Mother Jones*, August 22, 2016, www.motherjones.com /politics/2016/08/stephen-bannon-donald-trump-alt-right-breitbart -news.

165 **misery and used heroin needles.":** Kevin D. Williamson, "Chaos in the Family, Chaos in the State: The White Working Class's Dysfunction," *Na- tional Review*, March 17, 2016, www.nationalreview.com/article/432876 /donald-trump-white-working-class-dysfunction-real-opportunity -needed-not-trump.

170 **took off with her and her kids:** Liz Lohuis, "Candidate for Congress May Be Connected to Missing Children Case," 4WSMV.com, July 18, 2016, www.wsmv.com/story/32474330/candidate-for-congress-may-be -connected-to-missing-children-case.

171 **New Orleans' Survey Research Center:** "Statewide Survey of Louisi- ana Likely Voters on David Duke," University of New Orleans' Survey Research Center (SRC), conducted July 27–28, 2016, www.uno.edu/cola/ political-science/documents/duke-poll.pdf.

CHAPTER 9. HAMMERSKINS

177 **than wanting to "shoot the nigger.":** *Brosky v. State*, 915 S.W.2d 120 (1996), www.leagle.com/decision/19961035915SW2d120_11016.xml/BROSKY %20v.%20STATE.

177 **to death in Birmingham, Alabama:** *Oddo v. State*, 675 So. 2d 58 (1995), http://law.justia.com/cases/alabama/court-of-appeals-criminal/1995/cr -94-1013-0.html.

177 **the unruly skinheads to their causes:** Michael Reynolds, "Hammerskin Nation Emerges from Small Dallas Group," Southern Poverty Law Center,

December 15, 1999, www.splcenter.org/fighting-hate/intelligence-report/ 1999/hammerskin-nation-emerges-small-dallas-group.

184 **hairstyles for closely shaved heads:** Timothy S. Brown, "Subcultures, Pop Music and Politics: Skinheads and 'Nazi Rock' in England and Germany," *Journal of Social History* 38, no. 1 (2004): 157–178.

185 **poor, white areas of south Chicago:** Christian Picciolini, *Romantic Violence: Memoirs of an American Skinhead* (Chicago: Goldmill Group, 2015).

185 **a swastika in Strickland's blood:** Matt O'Connor, "Skinhead Gets 11 Years in Beating," *Chicago Tribune*, June 22, 1989, http://articles.chicagotribune .com/1989-06-22/news/8902110551_1_neo-nazi-skinheads-sentenced.

186 **America found themselves unemployed:** Lois M. Plunkert, "The 1980's: A Decade of Job Growth and Industry Shifts," *Monthly Labor Review* 113, no. 9 (September 1990): 3–16.

186 **heavily armed compound in Idaho:** Wayne King, "Links of Anti-Semitic Band Provoke 6-State Parley," *New York Times*, December 27, 1984, www .nytimes.com/1984/12/27/us/links-of-anti-semitic-band-provoke-6-state -parley.html?pagewanted=all.

186 **had created a deep sense of loss:** Zeskind, *Blood and Politics*, xvii.

187 **only six affiliated with the Hammerskins:** David Holthouse, "Motley Crews: With Decline of Hammerskins, Independent Skinhead Groups Grow," Southern Poverty Law Center, October 19, 2006, www.splcenter .org/fighting-hate/intelligence-report/2006/motley-crews-decline -hammerskins-independent-skinhead-groups-grow.

187 **to recruit new skinheads for the cause:** Keegan Hankes, "Music, Money & Hate," Southern Poverty Law Center, November 20, 2014, www.spl center.org/fighting-hate/intelligence-report/2014/music-money-hate-0.

188 **ban white power music from their servers:** Marc Hogan, "Is White Power Music Finally Getting Booted from the Internet?," *Pitchfork*, August 17, 2017, http://pitchfork.com/thepitch/is-white-power-music-finally -getting-booted-from-the-internet.

189 **been reduced to the "Hammerskin Hamlet.":** Holthouse, "Motley Crews."

191 **putting a bullet in his own head:** Erica Goods and Serge F. Kovaleski, "Wisconsin Killer Fed and Was Fueled by Hate-Driven Music," *New York Times*, August 6, 2012, www.nytimes.com/2012/08/07/us/army-veteran -identified-as-suspect-in-wisconsin-shooting.html.

CHAPTER 10. HARRISBURG

204 **pseudo-science to their anti-Semitism:** "About the Holocaust Denial on Trial Project," Holocaust Denial on Trial, www.hdot.org/about.

210 **race anyway—came fully armed:** Madison Pauly, "A New Wave of Left-Wing Militants Is Ready to Rumble in Portland—and Beyond," *Mother Jones*, May–June 2017, www.motherjones.com/politics/2017/06/ antifa-movement-anti-trump-politics-nazi.

215 **elaborate direction and fabricated scenes:** Nate Thayer, "KKK Leaders Allege Producers Paid Them to Fake Scenes in Canceled A&E Documentary," *Variety*, December 30, 2016, http://variety.com/2016/tv/news/

kkk-leaders-allege-producers-paid-them-to-fake-scenes-in-canceled-ae
-documentary-exclusive-1201950078.

218 **now Donald Trump's campaign chief:** Posner, "How Donald Trump's
New Campaign Chief Created an Online Haven for White Nationalists."

CHAPTER 11. THE SUITS

225 **against a wall to see what would stick:** Glenn Kessler, "Trump's Outrageous Claim That 'Thousands' of New Jersey Muslims Celebrated the
9/11 Attacks," *Washington Post*, November 22, 2015, www.washingtonpost
.com/news/fact-checker/wp/2015/11/22/donald-trumps-outrageous-claim
-that-thousands-of-new-jersey-muslims-celebrated-the-911-attacks;
Philip Rucker, "Trump Says Fox's Megyn Kelly Had 'Blood Coming Out of
Her Wherever,'" *Washington Post*, August 8, 2015, www.washingtonpost
.com/news/post-politics/wp/2015/08/07/trump-says-foxs-megyn-kelly
-had-blood-coming-out-of-her-wherever; "The 155 Craziest Things Trump
Said This Election," *Politico*, November 5, 2016, www.politico.com/magazine
/story/2016/11/the-155-craziest-things-trump-said-this-cycle-214420.

225 **and other things that concern them:** www.radixjournal.com/books
the-chosen-people-a-study-of-jewish-intelligence-and-achievement
(*now defunct*); Charles Lyon, "The Intolerant Politics of Reality," James
Edwards, January 31, 2017, www.thepoliticalcesspool.org/jamesedwards/
the-intolerant-politics-of-reality; F. Roger Devlin, "'Cultural Enrichment'
and Sexual Competition," *Before It's News*, December 20, 2016, http://
beforeitsnews.com/opinion-conservative/2016/12/cultural-enrichment
-and-sexual-competition-3226748.html; www.radixjournal.com/altright
-archive/altright-archive/main/the-magazine/superpowers (*now defunct*).

226 **a 'fashy' (as in fascism) haircut.":** Josh Harkinson, "Meet the White
Nationalist Trying to Ride the Trump Train to Lasting Power," *Mother
Jones*, October 27, 2016, www.motherjones.com/politics/2016/10/richard
-spencer-trump-alt-right-white-nationalist.

230 **weapon against the legacy of Jim Crow:** Valerie Strauss, "Why We
Still Need Affirmative Action for African Americans in College Admis-
sions," *Washington Post*, July 3, 2014, www.washingtonpost.com/news
/answer-sheet/wp/2014/07/03/why-we-still-need-affirmative-action-for
-african-americans-in-college-admissions.

231 **clamp down on freedom of speech:** "The Shuttening: Social Media Companies Form Cartel to Censor 'Extremism'" (originally on Daily Stormer),
VNN Forum, December 6, 2016, https://vnnforum.com/showthread.php
?t=486123.

231 **spread of extremism and fake news:** "Google Search Changes Tackle
Fake News and Hate Speech," *BBC News*, April 25, 2017, www.bbc.com/
news/technology-39707642.

231 **address hate speech on their sites:** Julia Fioretti, "EU States Approve Plans
to Make Social Media Firms Tackle Hate Speech," Reuters, May 23, 2017,
www.reuters.com/article/us-eu-hatespeech-socialmedia-idUSKBN18J25C.

234 **between the alt-right and the "alt-lite.":** Gideon Resnick, "Nazis vs.
Trumpkins: The Prom Tearing Apart the Alt-Right," *Daily Beast*, December

27, 2016, www.thedailybeast.com/nazis-vs-trumpkins-the-prom-tearing -apart-the-alt-right?via=twitter_page.

234 **movement began to hit a critical mass:** Hunter Wallace, "Alt-Right vs. Alt-Lite," *Occidental Dissent*, November 23, 2016, www.occidentaldissent .com/2016/11/23/alt-right-vs-alt-lite.

243 **a lot more abstract than "Nigger, nigger.":** Rick Perlstein, "Exclusive: Lee Atwater's Infamous 1981 Interview on the Southern Strategy," *The Nation*, November 13, 2012, www.thenation.com/article/exclusive-lee -atwaters-infamous-1981-interview-southern-strategy.

CHAPTER 12. THE COLLEGE BOYS

247 **tripled from 34 in 2015 to 101 in 2016:** "Hate Groups Increase for Second Consecutive Year as Trump Electrifies Radical Right," Southern Poverty Law Center, February 15, 2017, www.splcenter.org/news/2017/02/15/ hate-groups-increase-second-consecutive-year-trump-electrifies-radical -right.

247 **hate crimes in general were up 6 percent:** Eric Lichtblau, "U.S. Hate Crimes Surge 6%, Fueled by Attacks on Muslims," *New York Times*, November 14, 2016, www.nytimes.com/2016/11/15/us/politics/fbi-hate -crimes-muslims.html.

247 **self-deputizing in the name of Trump:** Adam Lusher, "Donald Trump Supporters Tell Immigrants 'The Wolves Are Coming, You Are the Hunted' as Race Hate Fears Rise," *Independent*, November 9, 2016, www .independent.co.uk/news/world/americas/us-elections/donald-trump -wins-racist-racism-race-hate-immigrants-nigel-farage-ukip-brexit -post-referendum-a7407951.html.

249 **combatants armed with 'safety gear.'":** "Defend Auburn, Alabama Against the White Power Invasion April 18th!," ItsGoingDown, April 16, 2017, https://itsgoingdown.org/defend-auburn-alabama-white-power -invasion-april-18th.

251 **$30,000 to $50,000 per year:** "Auburn University," CollegeData, www .collegedata.com/cs/data/college/college_pg03_tmpl.jhtml?schoolId=488.

253 **"officially OFF the Trump train.":** Paul Joseph Watson (@PrisonPlanet) tweet, April 6, 2017, 10:19 p.m., Twitter, https://twitter.com/PrisonPlanet/ status/850171163527581697.

259 **current Americans to past generations:** Jessica Boddy, "The Forces Driving Middle-Aged White People's 'Deaths of Despair,'" *Morning Edition*, NPR, March 23, 2017, www.npr.org/sections/health-shots/2017/03/23/521083335 /the-forces-driving-middle-aged-white-peoples-deaths-of-despair.

260 **positive impact on the US GDP.":** James McBride and Mohammed Aly Sergie, "Nafta's Economic Impact," Council on Foreign Affairs, January 24, 2017, www.cfr.org/backgrounder/naftas-economic-impact.

260 **women in high-paying jobs has declined:** Anna Brown and Sara Atske, "Blacks Have Made Gains in U.S. Political Leadership, but Gaps Remain," Pew Research Center, June 28, 2016, www.pewresearch.org/fact -tank/2016/06/28/blacks-have-made-gains-in-u-s-political-leadership

-but-gaps-remain; Susan Ricker, "11 Findings About Diversity in America's Workforce," CareerBuilder, March 26, 2015, www.careerbuilder.com/advice/11-findings-about-diversity-in-americas-workforce.

CHAPTER 13. HAIL HEIMBACH

267 **as many as possible from coming:** James Bruggers, "Pikeville Braces for White-Power Rally; University Tells Students to Leave for the Weekend," *Courier Journal*, April 28, 2017, www.courier-journal.com/story/news/politics/2017/04/28/pikeville-braces-white-power-rally-university-tells-students-leave-weekend/307468001.

267 **businesses promised to stay closed:** James Bruggers, "Residents Told to Avoid Ky. Town over White Nationalist, Counter Rallies," *USA Today*, April 29, 2017, www.usatoday.com/story/news/nation-now/2017/04/29/residents-told-avoid-ky-town-over-white-nationalist-counter-rallies/101067612/#.

267 **I wholeheartedly oppose its mission.":** "Sen. McConnell Releases Statement About Traditionalist Worker Party Conference," Lex18.com, February 10, 2017, www.lex18.com/story/34480381/sen-mcconnell-releases-statement-about-traditionalist-worker-party-conference.

267 **had carried the county by 80 percent:** Bureau of Labor Statistics, Pike County, KY, April 2017, https://data.bls.gov/map/MapToolServlet; "2016 Kentucky Presidential Election Results," *Politico*, December 13, 2016, www.politico.com/2016-election/results/map/president/kentucky.

270 **one** *Daily Stormer* **commenter said:** Hunter Wallace, "Antifas Coming to Pikeville, KY on April 29," *Occidental Dissent*, April 25, 2017.

270 **work out Soooooooo well," said another:** "Antifa Plans to Disrupt Events in Pikeville, KY Next Weekend," Western Rifle Shooters Association, April 23, 2017, https://westernrifleshooters.wordpress.com/2017/04/23/antifa-plans-to-disrupt-events-in-pikeville-ky-next-weekend.

275 **I am pro abortion, not pro choice.":** Greg Johnson, "Abortion & White Nationalism," Counter-Currents Publishing, www.counter-currents.com/2016/04/abortion-and-white-nationalism/in.

275 **wishes to return to white society.":** Ibid.

278 **should feel free to bring them:** "Support the Anti-Nazi Mobilization in Pikeville, KY April 28–29th," ItsGoingDown, April 13, 2017, https://itsgoingdown.org/join-and-support-the-mobilization-in-pikeville-kentucky.

POSTSCRIPT. THE HARD RIGHT

291 **such scrutiny and outrage in its infancy:** Christ Kahn, "A Majority of Americans Want to Preserve Confederate Monuments: Reuters/Ipsos Poll," Reuters, August 21, 2017, www.reuters.com/article/us-usa-protests-poll-idUSKCN1B12EG.

294 **Latinos vastly outnumber whites:** Suzanne Macartney, Alemayehu Bishaw, and Kayla Fontenot, "Poverty Rates for Selected Detailed Race

and Hispanic Groups by State and Place: 2007–2011," American Community Survey Briefs, February 2013, www.census.gov/prod/2013pubs/acsbr11-17.pdf; www.irp.wisc.edu/faqs/faq3.htm.

294 **stereotypes and marginalize them.":** Hunter Wallace, "Why Nationalism 1.0 Failed," *Occidental Dissent*, July 18, 2017, www.occidentaldissent.com/2017/07/18/why-white-nationalism-1-0-failed.

295 **people willing to stand with them:** Omar Etman, "Thousands Counter-Protest 'Free Speech' Rally in Boston," *PBS NewsHour*, August 19, 2017, www.pbs.org/newshour/rundown/thousands-counter-protest-free-speech-rally-boston.

295 **participate in"—seemed laughably naïve:** Wallace, "Why Nationalism 1.0 Failed."

INDEX

ABOUT THE AUTHOR

© Peter van Agtmael

Vegas Tenold has covered the far right in America for years as well as human rights in Russia, conflict in central Africa and the Middle East, and national security in the US. A graduate of Columbia University's School of Journalism, his work has appeared in publications including the *New York Times*, *Rolling Stone*, *New Republic*, and *Al Jazeera America*. He was born and raised in Norway and now lives in Brooklyn.

The Nation Institute

NATION
BOOKS

Founded in 2000, **Nation Books** has become a leading voice in American independent publishing. The imprint's mission is to tell stories that inform and empower just as they inspire or entertain readers. We publish award-winning and bestselling journalists, thought leaders, whistleblowers, and truthtellers, and we are also committed to seeking out a new generation of emerging writers, particularly voices from underrepresented communities and writers from diverse backgrounds. As a publisher with a focused list, we work closely with all our authors to ensure that their books have broad and lasting impact. With each of our books we aim to constructively affect and amplify cultural and political discourse and to engender positive social change.

Nation Books is a project of The Nation Institute, a nonprofit media center established to extend the reach of democratic ideals and strengthen the independent press. The Nation Institute is home to a dynamic range of programs: the award-winning Investigative Fund, which supports groundbreaking investigative journalism; the widely read and syndicated website TomDispatch; journalism fellowships that support and cultivate over twenty-five emerging and high-profile reporters each year; and the Victor S. Navasky Internship Program.

For more information on Nation Books and The Nation Institute, please visit:

www.nationbooks.org
www.nationinstitute.org
www.facebook.com/nationbooks.ny
Twitter: @nationbooks